LANGUAGE: CONCEPTS AND PROCESSES

Prentice-Hall Speech Communication Series

Larry L. Barker
Robert J. Kibler
Consulting Editors

LANGUAGE: CONCEPTS AND PROCESSES

Joseph A. DeVito

*Queens College
of the City University of New York*

PRENTICE-HALL, INC., Englewood Cliffs, New Jersey

Library of Congress Cataloging in Publication Data

DeVito, Joseph A   comp.
  Language: concepts and processes.

  Bibliography: p.
  1. Language and languages—Addresses, essays,
lectures. 2. Communication—Addresses, essays,
lectures. I. Title.
P121.D43   401   72-14102
ISBN 0-13-522912-X
ISBN 0-13-522904-9 (pbk.)

To Maggie & Pop

Printed in the United States of America

10 9 8 7 6 5 4 3 2 1

Prentice-Hall International, Inc. London
Prentice-Hall of Australia, Pty. Ltd. Sydney
Prentice-Hall of Canada, Ltd. Toronto
Prentice-Hall of India Private Limited New Delhi
Prentice-Hall of Japan, Inc. Tokyo

Contents

Preface   *ix*

Acknowledgments   *xii*

LANGUAGE: FORMS AND FUNCTIONS

The Sounding Reed   *3*
  Michael Girsdansky

The Study of Language and Human Communication   *7*
  William G. Moulton

The Origin of Speech   *24*
  Charles F. Hockett

The Uses of Language   *39*
  Bertrand Russell

Sublanguages   *46*
  Paul Goodman

The Sounds of Silence   *56*
  Edward and Mildred Hall

The New Languages   *69*
  Edmund Carpenter

The Language of Responsibility   *85*
  Wendell Johnson

LANGUAGE AND THOUGHT

Language and the Mind   95
  Noam Chomsky

Learning the Language   110
  Ursula Bellugi

Languages and Logic   121
  Benjamin Lee Whorf

Some Limitations of Language   133
  Harry L. Weinberg

The Language of Self-Deception   145
  Ashley Montagu

The Language of Prejudice   157
  Eldon L. Seamans

The English Language Is My Enemy   164
  Ossie Davis

One Small Step for Genkind   171
  Casey Miller and Kate Swift

The Principles of Newspeak   183
  George Orwell

LANGUAGE AND COMMUNICATION

Logos:
Man's Translation of Himself into Language   197
  Gerard Egan

The Semantics of War   209
  Hans Koning

The Semantics of the Generation Gap   212
  Robert A. Hipkiss

Rock-Tongue   221
  Michael L. Hecht

New Language   229
  William Hedgepeth

The Language of Social Control   235
  S. I. Hayakawa

Rhetorical Qualities of Words *247*
> *Richard E. Hughes and P. Albert Duhamel*

Statements *265*
> *Louis B. Salomon*

When to 'Keep Still' *280*
> *Irving J. Lee*

For Further Reading *291*

Index to Concepts and Processes *299*

Index of Names *305*

Preface

The study of language is in large part the study of man. As such it has rightly commanded the interest and attention of persons from numerous and seemingly unrelated specialties. Researchers in biology, communication, education, psychology, sociology, rhetoric, and various other fields have contributed enormously to our insights into language. However, the resultant research has been so specialized that a beginner is almost sure to be lost in a literature of strange words, complex theories, and tons of data. There is, therefore, a need to have assembled in one place articles dealing with language from various different perspectives which can be understood by the nonspecialist. The objective of this collection, then, is twofold: to introduce the beginning student to the study of language from these different points of view and to provide a basis for more advanced study.

Language: Concepts and Processes was designed particularly for introductory and intermediate junior and senior college courses in Communication, Education, English, Linguistics, and Speech. These readings provide the necessary foundation upon which such courses are now being constructed. Consequently, these selections are applicable equally to all forms and dimensions of language and to both theory-oriented and performance-oriented courses.

This collection may be used in either of two general ways. As a supplementary text it may be used in conjunction with any of the standard textbooks in these fields. Since each article can be understood as a separate unit, the selections may be rearranged to suit any number of different purposes and may be easily coordinated with different texts to serve the needs of particular courses.

Since these articles span a broad range of language study, the collection may also be used as the principle text and can be supplemented with any number of available paperbacks and/or lectures.

There are so many excellent articles on language that the task of selecting a small number for inclusion in a volume such as this would have been impossible without certain guidelines. These guidelines should be stated explicitly since taken together they form the rationale and point of view of the book.

First, I selected only those articles which are applicable to language in all its forms, whether written or oral, whether informative or persuasive, whether interpersonal or mass communication, etc.

Second, all articles are introductory in the sense that they do not require any previous background of specific knowledge to be understood and appreciated. I, therefore, avoided articles addressed solely to professionals of one or another academic discipline. On the other hand, there is no article included here which will not prove thought-provoking and challenging.

Third, I attempted to have represented here authors of varied and diverse backgrounds and interests; included here are anthropologists, communicologists, educators, linguists, psychologists, semanticists, sociologists, and even novelists. The value of this diversity of authorship, I think, is that the universality of language and its central position in human behavior becomes clearer when it is seen from different and even opposing points of view.

Fourth, I included only those articles which I was sure would maintain the interest of the nonspecialist. Fortunately, this created little difficulty since so many language researchers are not only insightful theorists but clear and interesting writers as well.

The readings are organized into three major sections. Part I, "Language: Forms and Functions," deals with different approaches to the study of language and man, the language-user. Put differently, these articles focus on the questions: What is language? and, What does it mean to be a language user?

Part II, "Language and Thought," covers the psychological dimensions of language: that is, the relationship between language on the one hand and various psychological processes on the other. The selections here deal with such questions as the connection between language and mental processes, how the child acquires language, how we can deceive ourselves through language, and how language may influence our perceptions, our thoughts, and our behaviors.

Part III, "Language and Communication," deals with the role of language in creating understanding and in dispelling misunderstanding and presents us with some insightful guides to achieving these goals. These selections focus on the function of language symbols in intrapersonal, interpersonal, small group, and public communication.

Following the articles is a brief annotated bibliography of books on language which should provide some guides to your further study. Additional references may be found in all of the works listed here.

Acknowledgments

With any task of this kind much is owed to many.

I especially want to express my appreciation to my students and colleagues at Queens College for their willingness to share with me their insights into language. From them I have learned much.

To the people at Prentice-Hall, especially to consultants Larry Barker and Robert Kibler, both of Florida State University, to Arthur Rittenberg, editor, and to Herbert Nolan, production editor, I am particularly grateful for their reinforcing and helpful comments.

To Boo for inspiration throughout I am most thankful.

Lastly, I want to thank the authors and copyright holders for granting me permission to reprint the articles contained here.

J. A. D.

LANGUAGE:
FORMS AND FUNCTIONS

*For Man's first uncertain words brought
a new thing into the world: awareness. . . By means of Language, Man
pulled himself up by his bootstraps
long before he had boots.*

The Sounding Reed

MICHAEL GIRSDANSKY

In this brief but eloquent essay Michael Girsdansky
clarifies the role of speech and language in making man,
Man. Community and kinship; awareness; conscious love
and hope, hate and fear; knowledge of death are some of
the consequences born of language. Speech and language
is, as Girsdansky puts it, "Man's greatest invention:
brighter than fire, and stronger than spears."

"Man is the weakest reed in the universe—but he is a thinking reed," said French philosopher Blaise Pascal. And he is a sounding reed as well. The breath of spirit blows across him; its sound is voice, and its shape is language.

Modulation of this vibrating column of air, trembling in the throat's moist tube of flesh, is Man's greatest invention: brighter than fire, and stronger than spears. For language, in the lost days of its beginnings, gave warmth and some answer to fear and loneliness. Even after the first fires had rattled into embers, there was the soft and halting sound of voices, and the caves and shabby encampments became for the first time something more than frightened huddling-places.

More than the gift of company, speech gave Man community, too. Weak as individuals, men learned to draw a new strength from the nerve and muscle of language: no saber-tooth or mastodon could stand for long against the *collective* might of those new and strange creatures whose purpose was bound together by the barks and yips their mouths could make.

That delicate thread of shaken air has been Man's badge—and burden—ever since. Even today, men who share a common tongue know themselves as somehow kin; though it is perhaps false knowledge, the feeling is still sincere. Confronted by the babblers of a foreign speech, the tribal man beneath the skin of each of us still bristles with suspicion, or snickers uneasily at an implication of the faintly outlandish or ridiculous. Why not? This is the long-lived remnant of an earlier day, in which the name of the home tribe meant "The Human Beings," or "The Speakers." Those Others—the aliens—were just as often "The Un-Men," "The Stutterers," or "The Mutes."

At least once in every man's lifetime, there comes the feeling that "none of this is real": the solidity of brick, the conventional cut of tie and trouser-cuff, the subject of conversation at the moment, even the

From the book, The Adventure of Language *by Michael Girs-dansky, pp. iii–iv. © 1963 by Prentice-Hall, Inc. Reprinted with permission.*

shape of hill and river; all of these at one time or another seem to grow for a moment or two pale and distant. There have been many explanations of this feeling, but perhaps one which is as close to truth as any other is that, in such instance, we half see our surroundings as lesser creatures do—directly, without the tinted glasses of humanity. At such times language strikes us as irrelevant.

Suddenly, one of the props is knocked out from beneath the long taken-for-granted world of words and human understandings. The universe of words—a universe so much our second nature that we seldom think of it—melts away. It is then that we may feel how truly artificial, how man-made, are the sounds and rules of grammar which float like a thin film over that other and far older world of the hard, the tangible, the *real*.

And here then is Man, lost in the midst of that hard reality, presumptuously pasting his labels to the sequoia and the star, insisting that the universe be cut and shaped to the specifications of individual logics and the categories of particular modes of speech. There are many who would term this insufferable arrogance and call for great rehumility on the part of That Prideful Animal.

I have come to see this presumptuousness in a different light. Though there may be some great part of folly in Man's pride, I think of it as a folly to be respected. The idea of a forked bit of tissue balancing precariously upright while it judges—and christens—the universe is enough to stagger anyone with its incongruity. If this be arrogance, it is an arrogance worthy of awed respect.

For Man's first uncertain words brought a new thing into the world: awareness. With the creation of these patterned sounds, repeatable at will, the gigantic universe around became less important in one sense. No longer was it necessary for a given aspect of reality to be actually present; *now it could be talked about*, resurrected from absence and made vocally real. By means of Language, Man pulled himself up by his bootstraps long before he had boots.

And this new awareness of Man set him once and for all outside the framework of the "natural world"—a world which, before him, had not even known it was. Space and time, change and stasis, nearness and distance, were no longer qualities of a purely indifferent world, or scampering reflexes working blindly within the lower nerve-center of mute breasts. They were reborn as *symbols*, patterns of electric charge dancing through the inconceivably complex network of Man's brain.

But something more than these neutral concepts came into the world together with speech: love and hope—love and hope which recognized themselves. And other, less pleasant, things, for there is always a price to be paid. Conscious hate and fear were born, too—and knowledge of death. Cast out from the Eden of unawareness, men knew Good and Evil. With the possibility of greatness came the unique opportunity to be corrupt, and only Man writes—or makes—tragedies. Wisdom and foresight can be bitter, for "of all creatures, only Man knows that he must die."

Yet, if to be human is to know pain and sorrow beyond that of other, simpler creatures, nonetheless Man has his lonely joys—and a chance at nobility. William Faulkner, in his speech accepting the Nobel Prize for Literature, voiced a concern lest, in the last days of a dying earth, when stars are growing dark and cold, and the very fabric of nature itself begins to ravel at the seams, the last sound of all will be that of the human voice, talking . . . talking . . .

Man is the weakest reed in the universe, but he is a thinking reed. And he is a voiced reed, that creature who is human.

*Though all of these senses are used
in one way or another for purposes
of communication, human beings in
the course of their evolution have
developed one particular type of
communication to such a high degree
that it far surpasses all others in
its flexibility, expressiveness, creativity,
efficiency, and sheer elegance.*

The Study of Language
and Human Communication

WILLIAM G. MOULTON

Any work on language, however conceived or defined, must begin with a description of what language is and what part it plays in human communication. In this thorough but introductory essay William G. Moulton provides an excellent preface for the study of language, covering such areas as nonverbal communication, the uniqueness of language, and the structures of verbal language. This article, then, should provide two basic types of information. First, it provides a clear introduction to the forms and structures of language. Second, it raises a number of significant questions regarding language in relation to human communication and communicators.

LANGUAGE AND HUMAN COMMUNICATION

Communication and Human Beings

Human beings communicate constantly and in a vast variety of ways. It is next to impossible for two or more human beings to be together without communicating in one way or another—most obviously through language, but just as often in other, less obvious ways. Even when we are alone, we continue to make use of communication: perhaps we read a book or a newspaper (communication!), or listen to the radio or watch television (still more communication!), or even in rare moments engage in that silent self-communication that we call "thinking." A significant proportion of our population is professionally engaged in the various communication industries: radio, television, theater, moving pictures, publishing, and advertising, as well as that greatest "communication industry" of them all—our educational institutions.

Much of this communication is voluntary and purposeful. The teacher in front of the classroom purposely uses both audio aids (mostly language) and visual aids (perhaps only the humble blackboard) to communicate the lesson of the day. And the pupil who comes to school tries to communicate with other pupils through his or her manner of dress, his haircut, her hairdo, and numerous sorts of social behavior. Much of this communication is also involuntary and inadvertent. The job applicant who uses unaccepted forms of language in either grammar or pronunciation may inadvertently disqualify himself for the job that he is seeking; and the dinner guest who eats with his knife or wipes his mouth

From Linguistics in School Programs, *the Sixty-Ninth Yearbook of the National Society for the Study of Education, Part II, ed. Albert H. Marckwardt (Chicago: The National Society for the Study of Education, 1970), pp. 5–35. Reprinted with permission of The National Society for the Study of Education.*

on his sleeve may inadvertently mark himself as one to whom no future invitations will be extended.

Let us define human communication as the transmission of information from one person to another. Such a definition immediately gives the three elements which must be present: first, there must be a *sender*; second, there must be a *receiver*; and third, there must some sort of *medium of transmission*. As their medium of transmission, human beings have available to them the familiar five senses—those of taste, smell, touch, sight, and hearing—either singly or in various combinations. Though all of these senses are used in one way or another for purposes of communication, human beings in the course of their evolution have developed one particular type of communication to such a high degree that it far surpasses all others in its flexibility, expressiveness, creativity, efficiency, and sheer elegance. This type, of course, is human language, which uses sound as its medium of transmission. Its use by human beings is so all-pervasive, and the role that it plays in human society is so essential, that it justifies us in distinguishing man from all other living beings by describing him as the "talking animal."

It is interesting to speculate about why human beings should have developed as their primary means of communication a system that uses sound as its medium of transmission rather than one of the other four senses. Why, for example, did they not use the sense of touch? Or, since it is especially acute in human beings, the sense of sight? The choice of sound is all the more remarkable because of the rather surprising source from which it is universally produced in human languages, namely, the respiratory tract—that area of the human body that extends from the diaphragm and the lungs out through the larynx, the pharynx, the mouth, and the nose. This area contains the so-called "organs of speech." Yet their use in producing the sounds of speech is surely a secondary development in terms of human evolution; they function primarily as the organs of breathing and, in part, of eating.

Though we can only speculate, it seems likely that sound produced by the respiratory tract came universally to be used as the medium for communication via language because it possesses a double versatility. First, the use of sound does not require the receiver of our message to be right next to us (as is the case with touch) or in our direct line of vision (as is the case with sight); he can just as well be beside us, behind us, or some distance away; and we can communicate with him in any of these positions even in the dark. Second, the use of the respiratory tract to produce sound does not require us to use our hands to communicate messages (as would most likely be the case if we used touch or sight); and this means that we can transmit messages via sound at the same time that we are doing just about anything else. The only drawback is that, as we transmit messages via sound, we must occasionally pause for breath; and some human beings seem almost able to overcome even this limitation.

Nonverbal Communication

This book is concerned primarily with the use of language as a means of transmitting information, that is to say, with what we customarily call "verbal communication." In order to put this topic in proper perspective, however, it is helpful to consider at least briefly some of the ways we transmit information *without* using language—to discuss various types of "nonverbal communication." This is all the more important because we are often unaware of some of these many other kinds of communication.

Do we ever use the sense of taste to transmit information? We surely do—though only to a very limited extent. The host who serves a well-chosen wine, and the hostess who serves a well-cooked meal, are surely communicating to their dinner guests. To prove the point, we need only consider what the reaction of the guests will be (what the "information" communicated to the guests will be) if the wine is cheap and tasteless and the meal is hastily and carelessly prepared.

Do we ever use the sense of smell to communicate information? Again, we surely do, though it is difficult to discuss the matter because our society places a strong taboo on most discussions of smells. Body smells, in particular, are negatively valued in our society; and the intensity of their negative "communication" can be judged by the fact that it supports a considerable part of the cosmetics industry. Curiously, a well-cooked head of cabbage may possess considerable positive "taste" value; but its "smell" value is highly negative—and again has led to a flourishing industry devoted to its suppression. Perfumes and flower smells, on the other hand, are positively valued; they also have produced flourishing industries.

Though we unquestionably use the senses of taste and smell in order to communicate (though not always intentionally), we do so only to a very limited degree. Far more extensive is the use that we make of the sense of touch. Parents fondle children (and psychologists tell us that this subtle communication is highly important in rearing children); lovers hold hands; campaigning politicians kiss babies; strangers, upon being introduced, shake hands; the more extrovert among us slap old friends on the back; and when we try to comfort someone in grief or pain, we stroke his hand or smooth his brow. In these and many other cases we use the sense of touch as an effective medium for communication, though in no case is its use developed to the point where we can say that it truly constitutes a "system" of communication.

Still more extensive is our use of sight as a medium for communication. Here, however, we must be careful to distinguish clearly between visual symbols which signal meaning directly, and those which signal it only indirectly, through the intermediary of language. We can illustrate these two very different types of visual symbols by considering two common sorts of road signs:

Though the meanings of both signs are ultimately the same, they signal this same meaning in quite different ways. Sign (1) does so directly, without the intermediary of language; hence it can be read equally well by speakers of all languages. Sign (2), on the other hand, signals its meaning only indirectly: the four letters of LEFT stand for the sounds of the spoken English word *left*; and it is only this spoken word which stands for the meaning of the sign. Signs of this type can of course be read only by people who happen to know English, and know how to read it.

"Indirect" visual symbols, which go from sight to meaning only through the intermediary of language, will be considered elsewhere in this book. We wish to consider here only those visual symbols that go directly from sight to meaning. There are many examples: traffic lights, railroad signals, barber poles, smoke signals, and the like. In a few cases the use of visual symbols is perhaps elaborate enough to warrant our calling it a genuine "system." Examples are: Indian sign languages, the system of gestures used in some societies (though hardly in our own), the pennants used by yachtsmen, and European road signs. Note that all of these systems are quite independent of spoken language. They must again be carefully distinguished from such language-dependent systems as the hand-signals of the deaf, the semaphore signals used by Boy Scouts, and the blinking-light signals used for communication from ship to ship at sea. These latter types of signals symbolize letters of the alphabet; combinations of letters, in turn, symbolize the spoken words of language; and it is only these latter that contain the intended "meanings" of messages communicated in this way.

As a final type of visual signal, we need to consider briefly the communicative value of body movements—the study of which has recently come to be called *kinesics*. Some of these movements accompany language, and though they are not a part of language, we use them constantly and to a surprising extent. In order to appreciate the great role that they play as an accompaniment to language, it is helpful and amusing to try the following experiment: turn off the sound track on a television set and watch the constant body movements of the speakers as they talk. They scowl, smile, roll their eyes, shift their weight, gesture with their hands, tilt their heads—and almost *never* stand stock still. Or, as another experiment, watch a couple at a nearby table in a restaurant. The communicative effect of their body movements is so strong that we can often see quite clearly whether they are happy, sad, in love, having a fight, or perhaps concocting some dire plot.

Body movements can be equally communicative even when they do not accompany language. A job applicant waiting for his interview may look around the room, scratch the back of his head, adjust his necktie (for the hundredth time), flick a bit of lint off his jacket, rub his hands together, and the like. And when his turn finally comes, the body movements of his interviewer may communicate very powerfully how well things are—or are not—going. At first the interviewer's body movements will probably be conscious and intentional: he may smile and motion the applicant to a chair. But soon unconscious body movements begin to convey their powerful messages—and woe to the applicant who cannot read them properly. If, after some minutes, the interviewer begins to cross and recross his legs, shift his weight in his chair, "fiddle" with his pencil, move a paper clip on his desk, or repeatedly rub his hand across his mouth, a wise applicant will know that his time is up and that he must leave.

The Uniqueness of Language

In the preceding discussion we pointed out that human beings have developed one type of communication which far surpasses all others, namely, language. Yet we also noted that human beings communicate—often very effectively and subtly—in many other ways. We now need to ask: What justifies us in saying that language "far surpasses" all other types of communication? What, in short, is unique about language?

The answer is easily given: Language permits us, quite literally, to transmit an infinite number of messages. In order to appreciate this unique quality of language, we need only compare it with some of the other communicative devices we use. A barber pole transmits only one message, something like: "This is a place where a man can get a shave and a haircut." A traffic light transmits only three messages: green for "go," amber for "caution," red for "stop." European road signs transmit a score or two of messages dealing with the control of traffic, but they cannot be used for discussing politics. Indian sign language can be used for discussing politics, but not for explaining how an internal combustion engine works. And so on. Only language can be used for all the kinds of messages human beings have occasion to communicate: telling someone where he can get his hair cut, discussing politics, explaining the workings of an internal combustion engine, describing the structure of the atom, and so on and on, quite literally without end.

Some notion of the extraordinary creativity and productivity of language can be given by the following simple yet somehow surprising observation: most of the sentences that (via language) we say and hear are sentences that we have never said or heard before. There are exceptions, of course—sentences like *What time is it?*, *I love you*, and *Please pass the butter*. Yet these are truly exceptions. Most of the sentences that we hear in daily conversation, or that occur in this book, are quite literally sentences that we have never heard or said (or seen or written) before—and probably never will again.

Many of the uses that we make of language strike us as valuable and important—for example: a classroom discussion of the Constitution of the United States, a trial in court, a plea for assistance. Others strike us as unimportant, even trivial—for example, the babbling of a group of teen-agers in a drugstore. The really classic example of trivial use of language comes not from teen-agers, however, but from adults: it is the American cocktail party. The ideal, perhaps, is to produce messages that are interesting and witty; but the most important thing is just to *use* language—to keep talking, with little regard to the content of the messages communicated. The guest who remains silent is regarded as "queer"; and the guest who really tries to communicate a serious message is considered a "bore."

In all of these uses of language—from the sublime to the ridiculous—there is one common denominator. The essential function of language is that of taking an idea (whether profound or trivial) that exists inside the head of the speaker, shaping it so that it can be transmitted as a message, then actually transmitting the message—and hoping that approximately the same idea will somehow miraculously reappear inside the head of the listener. The wonder of it all is not that the system does not work perfectly, but that it works as well as it does.

How are human beings able to use language in this remarkable way? One answer—and, in a very real sense, it is the only honest answer—is to say: As speakers of a language, we all carry around inside our heads a knowledge of this language; and it is this knowledge that enables us to accomplish this remarkable feat. Ideally, we should now try to get inside our heads and examine this knowledge of language directly. But of course we cannot do this. The best we can do is to try to guess from the outside what seems to be going on inside our heads.

We often think of language as consisting essentially of two ingredients: *sound* on the one hand, and *meaning* on the other. Yet sound and meaning are really not language itself, but only its two external manifestations. Suppose, for example, that we are watching two people speak a language we do not know. We can hear all of the sound, and in lucky cases we can even make shrewd guesses as to the meaning. Yet knowing that a given babble of sound will signal a given meaning is not what we would call "knowing" a bit of that language. We must know not only *that* sound signals meaning, but more particularly *how* it signals meaning; that is to say, we must understand the *correlation* between sound and meaning. This correlation between sound and meaning is the essence of language; and since it takes place inside our heads, none of it is directly observable. Nevertheless, by examining the external aspects of this correlation in any given language, we can deduce many details of its internal workings. It is to this topic that we shall now turn.

LANGUAGE AS STRUCTURE

The Two External Ends of Language

We can best think of language as an abstract structure that is connected with concrete reality at two external ends. At one end it is connected with sound—all the noises the speakers of a language make when they talk. At the other end it is connected with human experience—all the things the speakers of a language talk about when they use language. And language itself, as we have just said, is the *correlation* between these two external ends.

The truly remarkable fact about language is, now, the following: *Outside* of language, in the areas of sound and experience, there is no clear structure. We cannot say that the sound of a spoken sentence consists, in any objective sense, of a certain number of pieces in a certain arrangement; and we cannot say that human experience consists, in any objective sense, of a certain number of pieces in a certain arrangement. (It is true that scientists have been able to analyze tangible matter into a certain number of "pieces" in certain "arrangements." But they keep discovering new pieces and arrangements; and, in any case, tangible matter is only a very small part of human experience.) *Inside* of language, on the other hand (insofar as we understand the "inside of language"), everything is neatly structured and consists of units of specific sorts in arrangements of specific sorts. Let us consider how this system seems to work. We shall begin with the end of language where it is connected with sound, since this is the end that we understand the best.

Language and Sound

The sound that reaches our ears when someone speaks to us does not have any clear and consistent structure. Instead of consisting of a specific number of "pieces" of sound in a specific order, as we normally think of it, it is a continuum—an uninterrupted stream of sound. This is precisely the impression we get when we listen to a language we do not know, and acoustic phoneticians have expensive instruments which demonstrate that this impression is entirely correct. Viewed objectively, spoken language is a continuum of sound. As we *understand* spoken language, however, it *does* consist of a specific number of "pieces" in a specific order. Our spoken English word *at* consists of two such pieces, *cat* consists of three, *flat* of four, *blast* of five, and so on. As these examples show, our whole writing system—with all its imperfections and inconsistencies—is based precisely on this principle: we understand spoken language as consisting of "sounds" strung along in a row.

Since these "sounds" do not exist as such in the external, physically observable world, the only place they can exist is inside our heads, as part of our knowledge of our language. It might therefore be useful to call them "internal sounds"; instead of this, the linguist uses the technical term *phonemes*. The essential point to understand about phonemes is this: every bit of spoken language we hear must be interpreted as consisting of a sequence of phonemes, in a particular order. If we cannot make this conversion of a stream of (external) sound into a sequence of (internal) phonemes, then we cannot understand what has been said to us. Suppose, for example, that a friend introduces someone to us by saying: "This is Mr. Gri--on," pronouncing in the middle of the name a consonant sound that we do not hear properly. What can the name be? English offers us precisely twenty-one possibilities, since it has precisely twenty-one consonant phonemes that can occur in this position: *Grippon, Gribbon, Griffon, Grivon, Grimmon*, etc., through all twenty-one possible choices.

We can think of a language as a device which, at the end where it is connected with audible sound, consists of a sieve with a specific number of holes in it, representing the number of phonemes inside the language. In order to enter language and be "understood," the stream of speech outside of language must be filtered through this sieve. Outside of language, speech consists of a stream of sound; inside of language, it consists of a precise sequence of phonemes. We may therefore say that, in this sense, language gives "structure" to sound—a structure that it does not possess in any objectively observable way. And the same stream of sound may be structured differently by different languages.

Language also "structures" sound in another way. We can illustrate this by listing the twenty-four consonant phonemes that occur in all standard varieties of English:

p	t	č	k		*p*ail	*t*ail	*ch*ain	cane
b	d	ǰ	g		*b*ail	*d*ale	*j*ail	*g*ale
f	θ	s	š		*f*ail	*th*in	*s*ail	*sh*ale
v	ð	z	ž		*v*eil	*th*en	*z*eal	a*z*ure
m		n	ŋ		*m*ail	*n*ail		ri*ng*
	l	r				*l*ane	*r*ain	
w		h	y		*w*ail	*h*ail		*Y*ale

Figure 1. The letters to the left represent phonemic symbols; the choice of such symbols is unimportant, though we try to keep as close as possible to the regular letters of the alphabet. The examples to the right are given in regular spelling; italicized letters illustrate typical spellings of the phonemes in question.

These twenty-four consonant phonemes of English do not represent a random selection from among all the various types of consonant sounds that the vocal organs are capable of producing. Instead, they represent an economical system composed of a small number of distinctive phonetic features. Though we cannot go into all details here, we can at least mention the following. The set /p t č k f θ s š/ have the feature *voiceless* (pronounced without simultaneous vibration of the vocal cords); this distinguishes them from the set /b d ǰ g v ð z ž/, which are *voiced* (pronounced with simultaneous vibration of the vocal cords). Further, the set /p t č k b d ǰ g/ are *stops* (pronounced by stopping the breath stream momentarily at some point in the mouth); this distinguishes them from the set /t θ s š v ð z ž/, which are *fricatives* (pronounced by forcing the breath stream through a narrow opening so as to produce friction). All sixteen of these consonants are also *oral* (pronounced without a flow of air through the nose); this distinguishes them from the set /m n ŋ /, which are *nasal* (pronounced with a flow of air through the nose).

All languages also "structure" sound in still another way: in the sequences of phonemes that are permitted in the language. For example, the first twenty-one English consonants can occur after short stressed /i/ and before an unstressed vowel, as in the name *Gri--on*; but the last three consonants (/w, h, y/) cannot occur in this position. Of the twenty-four consonants, twenty-two may occur at the beginning of a word before a vowel; but two of them (/ž/ and /ŋ/) may not. As many as three consonants may occur at the beginning of a word. If so, the first must be /s/; the second must be one of the set /p t k/ (cf. *spring, stroll, scream*); and the third must be one of the set /r l y w/ (cf. *strip, split, skew, squeeze*). These are very strict rules, they cannot be violated and still produce genuine English.

Language and Experience

We have just seen how, at one end of language, the infinite number of sounds that the vocal organs can produce are structured, within language, into a small set of abstract phonological units called phonemes. When we now turn to the other end of language, where it is connected with human experience, we find that the infinite number of things human beings talk about are again structured, within language, into a set of abstract units—semantic units, this time. There are, however, two great differences. First, the number of semantic units at this end of language is far, far greater than the number of phonemes. Second, this end of language is much less well understood.

Perhaps the easiest way of understanding how language gives structure to experience is to consider how the same general area of experience can be structured in different languages. There is an area of experience which we in English symbolize by means of the single word *know*; we use it both for persons ("I *know* him") and for facts ("I *know* where he lives"). French, on the other hand, treats these uses as distinctly different "meanings" and has two quite different words for them: *connaître* for persons ("Je le *connais*") but *savoir* for facts ("Je *sais* où il habite"). Here two words in another language correspond to one word in English. An example of the opposite sort is provided by the Russian word *ruká*, which refers to that part of the human body which extends from the shoulder through the fingertips. In English we structure this into two "meanings" through our words *arm* and *hand*. There is no single word for *ruká* in English any more than there is a single word for *know* in French.

Because we are so used to the way in which our own language structures experience, we are often inclined to think of this as the only "natural" way of handling things. Yet a little thought will reveal innumerable examples within our own language to show that its handling of meaning is not "natural" at all, but highly arbitrary—even whimsical. One example is provided by the words *watch* and *clock*. It would seem "natural" to have a single word to refer to all devices that tell us what time it is; yet we in English insist on dividing such objects into two semantic classes, depending on whether or not they are customarily portable. If such a device is customarily portable, it is a *watch*; if it is *not* customarily portable, it is a *clock*. Or consider the words *bush* and *shrub*. These are clearly two different semantic units in English; yet if someone pointed to two objects in our garden and asked us to tell him which was a *bush* and which was a *shrub*, most of us would be unable to do so.

In showing how languages give structure to sound, we assume that it is possible to devise a universal phonetic grid on which all the speech sounds of all languages can be more or less accurately plotted. We can then determine which areas of this grid are used to reflect, in audible sound, the various phonemes of a particular language; and this, in turn, allows us to describe the phonetic structure of the system of phonemes in the language, in terms of distinctive phonetic features. In showing how languages give structure to experience, we would like to use a similar method. We would like to devise a universal semantic grid on which all the meanings of all languages could be more or less accurately plotted; and we would then like to determine which areas of this grid are used to reflect, in meaning, the various semantic units of a particular language. If we could do this, we could then describe the semantic structure of the system of semantic units in the language, in terms of distinctive semantic features.

Though this might be an ideal way of handling meaning, it is far beyond our capabilities at present—and probably will always remain so. Constructing a "universal semantic grid" would be a task of staggering complexity, and we have no hope of ever being able to accomplish it. The best we can do is to try to describe tiny areas of this total theoretical grid. One such area which has been investigated in many languages is that represented by kinship terms. Interestingly enough, it serves as a classic example of the very different ways in which languages handle one and the same area of experience. In English we find it "natural" that we have a term *brother* to denote a male child of the same parents as ourselves; yet many languages have no word for this, but only for *older brother* or *younger brother*. We also find it "natural" that kinship terms should reflect the difference between male and female: *brother* vs. *sister*, *father* vs. *mother*, *uncle* vs. *aunt*, etc.; yet we in English fail to make this distinction in the case of "child of sibling of our parent" and have only the single word *cousin*. Dutch makes this sex distinction in its words *neef* "male cousin" and *nicht* "female cousin"; but it fails to make the generational distinction that we find so "natural," since *neef* also means "nephew" and *nicht* also means "niece."

Semantics—the study of the way in which each language structures the world of human experience—is an enormously complicated field, about which we know far too little. The one point that we wish to make clear here is: the world of human experience has no clear structure as such; but it receives structure as it is filtered through into language, and each language gives it its own peculiar structure.

Language and Syntax

The essence of language, we have suggested, is the correlation between sound on the one hand and meaning (or experience) on the other. We have now seen how sound filters through into language so as to give a set of meaningless abstract units (phonemes), and how experience filters through into language so as to give a set of meaningful abstract units (semantic units). The correlation between these two types of units takes place in that part of language called *syntax*; and the units within this part of language are customarily called *morphemes* (from Greek *morphé* "form").

The relation between morphemes and phonemes is relatively clear: by and large, a given morpheme is converted into a sequence of phonemes. Thus the English morpheme *if* is converted into two phonemes: /if/; *push* is converted into three phonemes: /puš/; *chest* into four phonemes: /čest/; *thrift* into five: /θrift/; *splint* into six: /splint/; and so on. Sometimes there are complications. The English morpheme "Past Tense" is converted sometimes into /—t/, as in *kept*; sometimes into /—d/, as in *played*; sometimes into /—ed/, as in *waited*; and sometimes it is fused with the verb stem, as in *took* (past tense of *take*), *wound* (past tense of *wind*), etc. Nevertheless, the principle is clear: morphemes are converted into "strings" of phonemes (one phoneme, or sequences of more than one phoneme).

The relation between morphemes and semantic units is less clear, because our understanding of semantics is so rudimentary. By and large, one morpheme corresponds to one semantic unit: cf. *faith, faith-ful, un-faith-ful, un-faith-ful-ness*. Sometimes, however, a single morpheme seems to correspond to more than one semantic unit. This is presumably the case with such morphemes as *eleven* and *twelve*, which seem to be made up of the semantic units "10 + 1," "10 + 2." (But a one-to-one correspondence between semantic units and morphemes presumably exists in *thir-teen, four-teen*, etc.) Sometimes, on the other hand, more than one morpheme seems to correspond to a single semantic unit. This is presumably the case with *get up*, which clearly consists of two morphemes but seems to be only a single semantic unit; and also with *receive*, which consists morphemically of the prefix *re—* plus the stem *—ceive*, though presumably it is again only a single semantic unit.

The function of syntax is that of arranging morphemes in such a way as to produce meaningful sentences. Because of its central position within language, we assume that syntax shows two different types of structure, corresponding to the structure that language gives to sound on the one hand, and to the structure that it gives to meaning on the other. Because sound is *linear* (through the dimension of time), we assume that the *surface structure* of syntax is also linear: it must consist of strings of morphemes, just as phonology consists of strings of phonemes. We can illustrate this with the sentence *The man wound up the clock*:

Surface Structure:	*the man wind Past up the clock*
Phonemic Structure:	/ðe mæn waund ʌp ðə klak/
Sound Structure:	[a continuous stream of sound]

Meaning, on the other hand, does *not* seem to be linear in structure. We do not understand the sentence *The man wound up the clock* as consisting simply of the meaning of *the*, plus the meaning of *man*, plus the meaning of *wind*, plus the meaning of *Past Tense*, etc. Instead, we understand meanings to be arranged in a *hierarchical* structure that we can diagram for this sentence (omitting *Past Tense* for simplicity) as follows:

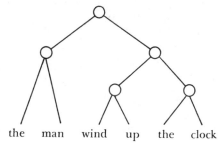

That is to say, we understand *the* and *man* as belonging meaningfully together in the construction *the man; wind* and *up* as belonging meaningfully together in the construction *wind up*; and *the* and *clock* as belonging meaningfully together in the construction *the clock*. Furthermore, we understand the construction *the man* as the "subject" of this sentence, and the construction *wind up the clock* as the "predicate" of this sentence. And we understand the subject *the man* as being in construction with the predicate *wind up the clock* so as to form (with the addition of *Past Tense*) the sentence *The man wound up the clock*.

This hierarchical arrangement of morphemes is the part of syntax called *deep structure*. Whereas surface structure represents the way we *say* a sentence, deep structure represents the way we *understand* it. In between the deep structure and the surface structure we can assume a set of syntactic *transformations* which map the one type of structure into the other.

The assumption that syntax consists of deep structure and surface structure, connected by transformations, allows us to account for a great many facts of language that would otherwise be puzzling. Consider the following pair of sentences:

(1) The man wound up the clock.

(2) The man wound the clock up.

We would like to be able to say that in one sense these two sentences are "the same," but that in another sense they are "different." We can now do so by saying that they have the same deep structure (representing the single way we understand them); that they have different surface structures (representing the two different ways we say them); and that different transformations from deep structure to surface structure account for these differences. Consider now the following two sentences:

(3) Did the man wind up the clock?

(4) Did the man wind the clock up?

We would again like to say that, in some sense, these two sentences are at least very similar to sentences (1) and (2). We can now do so by assuming that all four sentences have the same basic deep structure, but that (1) and (2) contain a morpheme *Statement* whereas (3) and (4) contain a morpheme *Question*. Transformations delete these two morphemes in going from deep structure to surface structure, but their effect is still present in the very different word order of the surface structures. Consider finally the following two sentences:

(5) The clock was wound up by the man.

(6) Was the clock wound up by the man?

Again we would like to say that in some sense these two sentences are "the same" as all the others. We can do so by assuming that the first four sentences contain, in their deep structures, the morpheme *Active*, whereas these last two contain the morpheme *Passive*. Transformations again delete these morphemes as such in going from deep structure to surface structure, but their effect is still present in the very different word order of the surface structures (as well as in the presence of the word *was*, in the fact that *wound* is now past participle rather than past tense, and in the presence of the word *by*).

The Infinite Productivity of Language

In discussing the uniqueness of language, as opposed to other forms of human communication, we noted that language is infinitely productive: that it permits us, quite literally, to transmit an infinite number of messages. In concluding this section, "Language as Structure," we must mention briefly the two design features that make this infinite productivity possible. Both features are disarmingly simple: they involve what is known in mathematics as *recursion*. First, two or more sentences may simply be joined together in the deep structure; this is syntactic *coordination*. Second, one sentence may be embedded inside another sentence in the deep structure; this is syntactic *subordination*.

Coordination can be illustrated by the following sentences:

(1) John told Bill, and Bill told Jim, and Jim told Joe, . . .

(2) Henry bought a hat, a tie, some handkerchiefs, . . .

In (1), the sentence structures *John told Bill, Bill told Jim, Jim told Joe* have been conjoined by means of the word *and* so as to give a single sentence; such conjoining can obviously go on indefinitely. In (2), the sentence structures *Henry bought a hat, Henry bought a tie, Henry bought some handkerchiefs* have been conjoined by means of the word *and*, first giving *Henry bought a hat and Henry bought a tie and Henry bought*; transformations now delete all but the first occurrence of *and*. As written above, we have omitted this last *and* to indicate that here also conjoining can go on indefinitely.

Subordination can be illustrated with the following famous example:

This is the cat	(1) This is the cat.
that killed the rat	(2) The cat killed the rat.
that ate the malt	(3) The rat ate the malt.
that lay in the house	(4) The malt lay in the house.
that Jack built.	(5) Jack built the house.

Here sentence (5) has been embedded within sentence (4); the resulting sentence has been embedded within sentence (3); the resulting sentence has been embedded within sentence (2); and the resulting sentence has been embedded within sentence (1). A whole cycle of transformations has thus produced the single sentence to the left. Recursion of this sort can of course also go on indefinitely.

Another, more intricate example of embedding is illustrated by the following sentence:

The man was troubled by	(1) Something troubled the man + Passive.
his son's	(2) The man had a son.
being accused of	(3) Someone accused the son of something + Passive
stealing.	(4) The son stole something.

A whole cycle of transformations has again converted the sentence structures labeled (1), (2), (3), (4) into the single sentence to the left.

Coordination and subordination are very powerful devices for combining two or more sentence structures into a single sentence. They have a triple effect: (*a*) there is in any language an infinite number of sentences; (*b*) there is no such thing in any language as a "longest sentence"; and (*c*) it is now easy to understand how it is possible that most of the sentences we say and hear are sentences we have never said or heard before.

"There need be no apology for reopening the issue of the origins of human speech."

The Origin of Speech

CHARLES F. HOCKETT

Here Hockett offers 13 "design-features" of human language, features which, taken together, might define human language and distinguish it from animal communications systems as well as from human systems other than language. These design features are then examined in terms of various animal communication systems in an attempt to specify the evolutionary development of human language.

In a later article Hockett has proposed three additional design-features: prevarication (messages may be false or meaningless in the logical sense), reflexiveness (language may be used to communicate about language), and learnability (a speaker of one language can learn another language). ("The Problem of Universals in Language," in *Universals of Language*, ed., Joseph H. Greenberg. Cambridge, Mass.: M.I.T. Press, 1963, pp. 1–22.)

About 50 years ago the Linguistic Society of Paris established a standing rule barring from its sessions papers on the origin of language. This action was a symptom of the times. Speculation about the origin of language had been common throughout the 19th century, but had reached no conclusive results. The whole enterprise in consequence had come to be frowned upon—as futile or crackpot—in respectable linguistic and philological circles. Yet amidst the speculations there were two well-reasoned empirical plans that deserve mention even though their results were negative.

A century ago there were still many corners of the world that had not been visited by European travelers. It was reasonable for the European scholar to suspect that beyond the farthest frontiers there might lurk half-men or manapes who would be "living fossils" attesting to earlier stages of human evolution. The speech (or quasi-speech) of these men (or quasi-men) might then similarly attest to earlier stages in the evolution of language. The search was vain. Nowhere in the world has there been discovered a language that can validly and meaningfully be called "primitive." Edward Sapir wrote in 1921: "There is no more striking general fact about language than its universality. One may argue as to whether a particular tribe engages in activities that are worthy of the name of religion or of art, but we know of no people that is not possessed of a fully developed language. The lowliest South African Bushman speaks in the forms of a rich symbolic system that is in essence perfectly comparable to the speech of the cultivated Frenchman."

The other empirical hope in the 19th century rested on the comparative method of historical linguistics, the discovery of which was one of the triumphs of the period. Between two languages the resemblances are sometimes so extensive and orderly that they cannot be attributed to chance or to parallel development. The alternative explanation is that the two are divergent descendants of a single earlier language. English,

Charles F. Hockett, "The Origin of Speech," Scientific American, *203 (September 1960), 89–96. Reprinted by permission of* Scientific American, *Inc.*

Dutch, German and the Scandinavian languages are related in just this way. The comparative method makes it possible to examine such a group of related languages and to construct, often in surprising detail, a portrayal of the common ancestor, in this case the proto-Germanic language. Direct documentary evidence of proto-Germanic does not exist, yet understanding of its workings exceeds that of many languages spoken today.

There was at first some hope that the comparative method might help determine the origin of language. This hope was rational in a day when it was thought that language might be only a few thousands or tens of thousands of years old, and when it was repeatedly being demonstrated that languages that had been thought to be unrelated were in fact related. By applying the comparative method to all the languages of the world, some earliest reconstructable horizon would be reached. This might not date back so early as the origin of language, but it might bear certain earmarks of primitiveness, and thus it would enable investigators to extrapolate toward the origin. This hope also proved vain. The earliest reconstructable stage for any language family shows all the complexities and flexibilities of the languages of today.

These points had become clear a half-century ago, by the time of the Paris ruling. Scholars cannot really approve of such a prohibition. But in this instance it had the useful result of channeling the energies of investigators toward the gathering of more and better information about languages as they are today. The subsequent progress in understanding the workings of language has been truly remarkable. Various related fields have also made vast strides in the last half-century: zoologists know more about the evolutionary process, anthropologists know more about the nature of culture, and so on. In the light of these developments there need be no apology for reopening the issue of the origins of human speech.

Although the comparative method of linguistics, as has been shown, throws no light on the origin of language, the investigation may be furthered by a comparative method modeled on that of the zoologist. The frame of reference must be such that all languages look alike when viewed through it, but such that within it human language as a whole can be compared with the communicative systems of other animals, especially the other hominoids, man's closest living relatives, the gibbons and great apes. The useful items for this sort of comparison cannot be things such as the word for "sky"; languages have such words, but gibbon calls do not involve words at all. Nor can they be even the signal for "danger," which gibbons do have. Rather, they must be the basic features of design that can be present or absent in any communicative system, whether it be a communicative system of humans, of animals or of machines.

With this sort of comparative method it may be possible to reconstruct the communicative habits of the remote ancestors of the hominoid line, which may be called the protohominoids. The task, then, is to work out the sequence by which that ancestral system became language as the hominids—the man-apes and ancient men—became man.

A set of 13 design-features is presented in the illustration shown on page 30. There is solid empirical justification for the belief that all the languages of the world share every one of them. At first sight some appear so trivial that no one looking just at language would bother to note them. They become worthy of mention only when it is realized that certain animal systems—and certain human systems other than language —lack them.

The first design-feature—the "vocal-auditory channel"—is perhaps the most obvious. There are systems of communication that use other channels; for example, gesture, the dancing of bees or the courtship ritual of the stickleback. The vocal-auditory channel has the advantage—at least for primates—that it leaves much of the body free for other activities that can be carried on at the same time.

The next two design-features—"rapid fading" and "broadcast transmission and directional reception," stemming from the physics of sound —are almost unavoidable consequences of the first. A linguistic signal can be heard by any auditory system within earshot, and the source can normally be localized by binaural direction-finding. The rapid fading of such a signal means that it does not linger for reception at the hearer's convenience. Animal tracks and spoors, on the other hand, persist for a while; so of course do written records, a product of man's extremely recent cultural evolution.

The significance of "interchangeability" and "total feedback" for language becomes clear upon comparison with other systems. In general a speaker of a language can reproduce any linguistic message he can understand, whereas the characteristic courtship motions of the male and female stickleback are different, and neither can act out those appropriate to the other. For that matter in the communication of a human mother and infant neither is apt to transmit the characteristic signals or to manifest the typical responses of the other. Again, the speaker of a language hears, by total feedback, everything of linguistic relevance in what he himself says. In contrast, the male stickleback does not see the colors of his own eye and belly that are crucial in stimulating the female. Feedback is important, since it makes possible the so-called internalization of communicative behavior that constitutes at least a major portion of "thinking."

The sixth design-feature, "specialization," refers to the fact that the bodily effort and spreading sound waves of speech serve no function except as signals. A dog, panting with his tongue hanging out, is performing a biologically essential activity, since this is how dogs cool themselves off and maintain the proper body temperature. The panting dog incidentally produces sound, and thereby may inform other dogs (or humans) as to where he is and how he feels. But this transmission of information is strictly a side effect. Nor does the dog's panting exhibit the design-feature of "semanticity." It is not a signal meaning that the dog is hot; it is part of being hot. In language, however, a message triggers the particular result it does because there are relatively fixed associations between elements in messages (e.g., words) and recurrent features or situations of the world around us. For example, the English word "salt" means salt, not sugar or pepper. The calls of gibbons also possess semanticity. The gibbon has a danger call, for example, and it does not in principle matter that the meaning of the call is a great deal broader and more vague than, say, the cry of "Fire!"

In a semantic communicative system the ties between meaningful message-elements and their meanings can be arbitrary or nonarbitrary. In language the ties are arbitrary. The word "salt" is not salty nor granular; "dog" is not "canine"; "whale" is a small word for a large object; "microorganism" is the reverse. A picture, on the other hand, looks like what it is a picture of. A bee dances faster if the source of nectar she is reporting is closer, and slower if it is farther away. The design feature of "arbitrariness" has the disadvantage of being arbitrary, but the great advantage that there is no limit to what can be communicated about.

Human vocal organs can produce a huge variety of sound. But in any one language only a relatively small set of ranges of sound is used, and the differences between these ranges are functionally absolute. The English words "pin" and "bin" are different to the ear only at one point. If a speaker produces a syllable that deviates from the normal pronunciation of "pin" in the direction of that of "bin," he is not producing still a third word, but just saying "pin" (or perhaps "bin") in a noisy way. The hearer compensates if he can, on the basis of context, or else fails to understand. This feature of "discreteness" in the elementary signaling units of a language contrasts with the use of sound effects by way of vocal gesture. There is an effectively continuous scale of degrees to which one may raise his voice as in anger, or lower it to signal confidentiality. Bee-dancing also is continuous rather than discrete.

Man is apparently almost unique in being able to talk about things that are remote in space or time (or both) from where the talking goes on. This feature—"displacement"—seems to be definitely lacking in the vocal signaling of man's closest relatives, though it does occur in bee-dancing.

One of the most important design-features of language is "productivity"; that is, the capacity to say things that have never been said or heard before and yet to be understood by other speakers of the language. If a gibbon makes any vocal sound at all, it is one or another of a small finite repertory of familiar calls. The gibbon call system can be characterized as closed. Language is open, or "productive," in the sense that one can coin new utterances by putting together pieces familiar from old utterances, assembling them by patterns of arrangement also familiar in old utterances.

Human genes carry the capacity to acquire a language, and probably also a strong drive toward such acquisition, but the detailed conventions of any one language are transmitted extragenetically by learning and teaching. To what extent such "traditional transmission" plays a part in gibbon calls or for other mammalian systems of vocal signals is not known, though in some instances the uniformity of the sounds made by a species, wherever the species is found over the world is so great that genetics must be responsible.

The meaningful elements in any language—"words" in everyday parlance, "morphemes" to the linguist—constitute an enormous stock. Yet they are represented by small arrangements of a relatively very small stock of distinguishable sounds which are in themselves wholly meaningless. This "duality of patterning" is illustrated by the English words "tack," "cat" and "act." They are totally distinct as to meaning, and yet are composed of just three basic meaningless sounds in different permutations. Few animal communicative systems share this design-feature of language—none among the other hominoids, and perhaps none at all.

It should be noted that some of these 13 design-features are not independent. In particular, a system cannot be either arbitrary or nonarbitrary unless it is semantic, and it cannot have duality of patterning unless it is semantic. It should also be noted that the listing does not attempt to include all the features that might be discovered in the communicative behavior of this or that species, but only those that are clearly important for language.

It is probably safe to assume that nine of the 13 features were already present in the vocal-auditory communication of the protohominoids—just the nine that are securely attested for the gibbons and humans of today. That is, there were a dozen or so distinct calls, each the appropriate vocal response (or vocal part of the whole response) to a recurrent and biologically important type of situation: the discovery of food, the detection of a predator, sexual interest, need for maternal care, and so on. The problem of the origin of human speech, then, is that of trying to determine how such a system could have developed the four additional properties of displacement, productivity and full-blown traditional transmission. Of course the full story involves a great deal more than communicative behavior alone. The development must be visual-

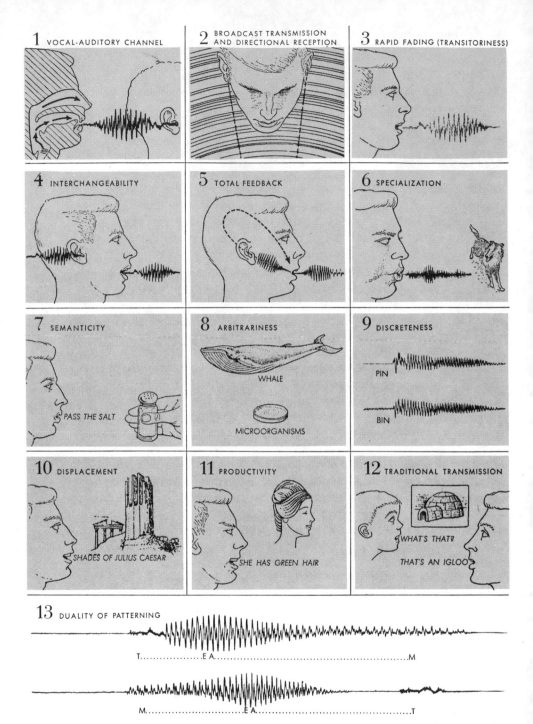

Figure 1. Thirteen design features of animal communication, discussed in detail in this reading, are symbolized in Figure 1. The patterns of the words "pin," "bin," "team," and "meat" were recorded at Bell Telephone Laboratories.

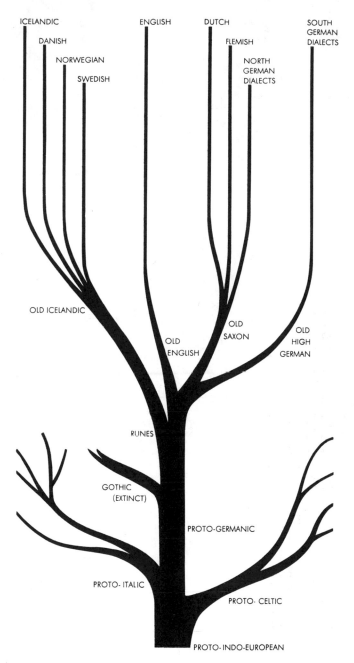

Figure 2. Origin of modern Germanic languages, as indicated by this "family tree," was proto-Germanic, spoken some 2,700 years ago. Comparison of present-day languages has provided detailed knowledge of proto-Germanic, although no direct documentary evidence for the language exists. It grew, in turn, from the proto-Indo-European of 5000 B.C. Historical studies cannot, however, trace origins of language back much further in time.

31

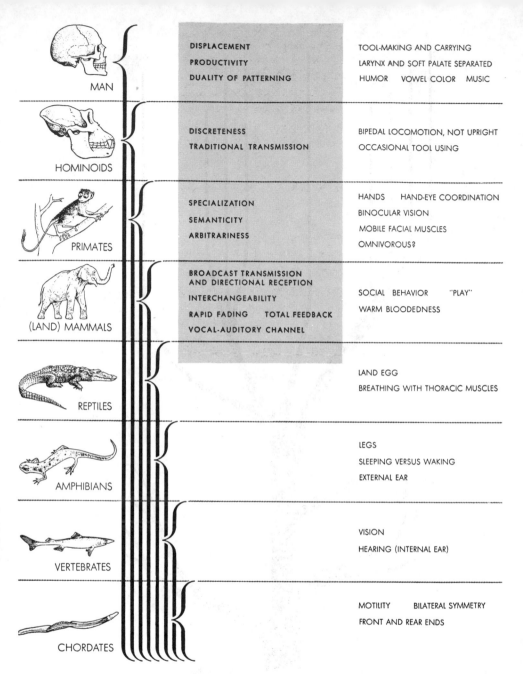

MAN

DISPLACEMENT
PRODUCTIVITY
DUALITY OF PATTERNING

TOOL-MAKING AND CARRYING
LARYNX AND SOFT PALATE SEPARATED
HUMOR   VOWEL COLOR   MUSIC

HOMINOIDS

DISCRETENESS
TRADITIONAL TRANSMISSION

BIPEDAL LOCOMOTION, NOT UPRIGHT
OCCASIONAL TOOL USING

PRIMATES

SPECIALIZATION
SEMANTICITY
ARBITRARINESS

HANDS   HAND-EYE COORDINATION
BINOCULAR VISION
MOBILE FACIAL MUSCLES
OMNIVOROUS?

(LAND) MAMMALS

BROADCAST TRANSMISSION
AND DIRECTIONAL RECEPTION
INTERCHANGEABILITY
RAPID FADING   TOTAL FEEDBACK
VOCAL-AUDITORY CHANNEL

SOCIAL   BEHAVIOR   "PLAY"
WARM BLOODEDNESS

REPTILES

LAND EGG
BREATHING WITH THORACIC MUSCLES

AMPHIBIANS

LEGS
SLEEPING VERSUS WAKING
EXTERNAL EAR

VERTEBRATES

VISION
HEARING (INTERNAL EAR)

CHORDATES

MOTILITY   BILATERAL SYMMETRY
FRONT AND REAR ENDS

Figure 3. Evolution of language and some related characteristics are suggested by this classification of chordates. The lowest form of animal in each classification exhibits the features listed at the right of the class. Brackets indicate that each group possesses or has evolved beyond the characteristics exhibited by all the groups below. The 13 design-features of language appear in the colored rectangle. Some but by no means all of the characteristics associated with communication are presented in the column at right.

	A SOME GRYLLIDAE AND TETTIGONIDAE	B BEE DANCING	C STICKLEBACK COURTSHIP	D WESTERN MEADOWLARK SONG	E GIBBON CALLS	F PARALINGUISTIC PHENOMENA	G LANGUAGE	H INSTRUMENTAL MUSIC
1 THE VOCAL-AUDITORY CHANNEL	AUDITORY NOT VOCAL	NO	NO	YES	YES	YES	YES	AUDITORY NOT VOCAL
2 BROADCAST TRANSMISSION AND DIRECTIONAL RECEPTION	YES	YES	YES	YES	YES	YES	YES	YES
3 RAPID FADING (TRANSITORINESS)	YES, REPEATED	?	?	YES	YES, REPEATED	YES	YES	YES
4 INTERCHANGEABILITY	LIMITED	LIMITED	NO	?	YES	LARGELY YES	YES	?
5 TOTAL FEEDBACK	YES	?	NO	YES	YES	YES	YES	YES
6 SPECIALIZATION	YES?	?	IN PART	YES?	YES	YES?	YES	YES
7 SEMANTICITY	NO?	YES	NO	IN PART?	YES?	YES?	YES	NO (IN GENERAL)
8 ARBITRARINESS	?	NO	?	IF SEMANTIC, YES	YES	IN PART	YES	?
9 DISCRETENESS	YES?	NO	?	?	YES	LARGELY NO	YES	IN PART
10 DISPLACEMENT		YES, ALWAYS		?	NO	IN PART	YES, OFTEN	
11 PRODUCTIVITY	NO	YES	NO	?	NO	YES	YES	YES
12 TRADITIONAL TRANSMISSION	NO?	PROBABLY NOT	NO?	?	?	YES	YES	YES
13 DUALITY OF PATTERNING	?(TRIVIAL)	NO		?	NO	NO	YES	

Figure 4. Eight systems of communication possess in varying degrees the 13 design-features of language. Column A refers to members of the Crisket family. Column H concerns only Western music since the time of Bach. A question mark means that it is doubtful or not known if the system has the particular feature. A blank space indicates that feature cannot be determined because another feature is lacking or is indefinite.

ized as occurring in the context of the evolution of the primate horde into the primitive society of food-gatherers and hunters, an integral part, but a part, of the total evolution of behavior.

It is possible to imagine a closed system developing some degree of productivity, even in the absence of the other three features. Human speech exhibits a phenomenon that could have this effect, the phenomenon of "blending." Sometimes a speaker will hesitate between two words or phrases, both reasonably appropriate for the situation in which he is speaking, and actually say something that is neither wholly one nor wholly the other, but a combination of parts of each. Hesitating between "Don't shout so loud" and "Don't yell so loud," he might come out with "Don't shell so loud." Blending is almost always involved in slips of the tongue, but it may also be the regular mechanism by which a speaker of a language says something that he has not said before. Anything a speaker says must be either an exact repetition of an utterance he has heard before, or else some blended product of two or more such familiar utterances. Thus even such a smooth and normal sentence as "I tried to get there, but the car broke down" might be produced as a blend, say, of "I tried to get there but couldn't" and "While I was driving down Main Street the car broke down."

Children acquiring the language of their community pass through a stage that is closed in just the way gibbon calls are. A child may have a repertory of several dozen sentences, each of which, in adult terms, has an internal structure, and yet for the child each may be an indivisible whole. He may also learn new whole utterances from surrounding adults. The child takes the crucial step, however, when he first says something that he has not learned from others. The only way in which the child can possibly do this is by blending two of the whole utterances that he already knows.

In the case of the closed call-system of the gibbons or the protohominoids, there is no source for the addition of new unitary calls to the repertory except perhaps by occasional imitation of the calls and cries of other species. Even this would not render the system productive, but would merely enlarge it. But blending might occur. Let AB represent the food call and CD the danger call, each a fairly complex phonetic pattern. Suppose a protohominoid encountered food and caught sight of a predator at the same time. If the two stimuli were balanced just right, he might emit the calls ABCD or CDAB in quick sequence, or might even produce AD or CB. Any of these would be a blend. AD, for example, would mean "both food and danger." By virtue of this, AB and CD would acquire new meanings, respectively "food without danger" and "danger without food." And all three of these calls—AB, CD and AD— would now be composite rather than unitary, built out of smaller elements with their own individual meanings: A would mean "food"; B, "no danger"; C, "no food"; and D, "danger."

But this is only part of the story. The generation of a blend can have no effect unless it is understood. Human beings are so good at understanding blends that it is hard to tell a blend from a rote repetition, except in the case of slips of the tongue and some of the earliest and most tentative blends used by children. Such powers of understanding cannot be ascribed to man's prehuman ancestors. It must be supposed, therefore, that occasional blends occurred over many tens of thousands of years (perhaps, indeed, they still may occur from time to time among gibbons or the great apes), with rarely any appropriate communicative impact on hearers, before the understanding of blends became speedy enough to reinforce their production. However, once that did happen, the earlier closed system had become open and productive.

It is also possible to see how faint traces of displacement might develop in a call system even in the absence of productivity, duality and thoroughgoing traditional transmission. Suppose an early hominid, a man-ape say, caught sight of a predator without himself being seen. Suppose that for whatever reason—perhaps through fear—he sneaked silently back toward others of his band and only a bit later gave forth the danger call. This might give the whole band a better chance to escape the predator, thus bestowing at least slight survival value on whatever factor was responsible for the delay.

Something akin to communicative displacement is involved in lugging a stick or a stone around—it is like talking today about what one should do tomorrow. Of course it is not to be supposed that the first tool-carrying was purposeful, any more than that the first displaced communication was a discussion of plans. Caught in a *cul-de-sac* by a predator, however, the early hominid might strike out in terror with his stick or stone and by chance disable or drive off his enemy. In other words, the first tool-carrying had a consequence but not a purpose. Because the outcome was fortunate, it tended to reinforce whatever factor, genetic or traditional, prompted the behavior and made the outcome possible. In the end such events do lead to purposive behavior.

Although elements of displacement might arise in this fashion, on the whole it seems likely that some degree of productivity preceded any great proliferation of communicative displacement as well as any significant capacity for traditional transmission. A productive system requires the young to catch on to the ways in which whole signals are built out of smaller meaningful elements, some of which may never occur as whole signals in isolation. The young can do this only in the way that human children learn their language: by learning some utterances as whole units, in due time testing various blends based on that repertory, and finally adjusting their patterns of blending until the bulk of what they say matches what adults would say and is therefore understood. Part of this learning process is bound to take place away from the precise situations for which the responses are basically appropriate, and this means the promotion of displacement. Learning and teaching, moreover, call on any capacity for traditional transmission that the band may have. Insofar as the communicative system itself has survival value, all this bestows survival value also on the capacity for traditional transmission and for displacement. But these in turn increase the survival value of the communicative system. A child can be taught how to avoid certain dangers before he actually encounters them.

These developments are also necessarily related to the appearance of large and convoluted brains, which are better storage units for the conventions of a complex communicative system and for other traditionally transmitted skills and practices. Hence the adaptative value of the behavior serves to select genetically for the change in structure. A lengthened period of childhood helplessness is also a longer period of plasticity for learning. There is therefore selection for prolonged childhood and, with it, later maturity and longer life. With more for the young to learn, and with male as well as female tasks to be taught, fathers become more domesticated. The increase of displacement promotes retention and foresight; a male can protect his mate and guard her jealously from other males even when he does not at the moment hunger for her.

There is excellent reason to believe that duality of patterning was the last property to be developed, because one can find little if any reason why a communicative system should have this property unless it is highly complicated. If a vocal-auditory system comes to have a larger and larger number of distinct meaningful elements, those elements inevitably come to be more and more similar to one another in sound. There is a practical limit, for any species or any machine, to the number of distinct stimuli that can be discriminated, especially when the discriminations typically have to be made in noisy conditions. Suppose that Samuel F. B. Morse, in devising his telegraph code, had proposed a signal .1 second long for "A," .2 second long for "B," and so on up to 2.6 seconds for "Z." Operators would have enormous difficulty learning and using any such system. What Morse actually did was to incorporate the principle of duality of patterning. The telegraph operator has to learn to discriminate, in the first instance, only two lengths of pulse and about three lengths of pause. Each letter is coded into a different arrangement of these elementary meaningless units. The arrangements are easily kept apart because the few meaningless units are plainly distinguishable.

The analogy explains why it was advantageous for the forerunner of language, as it was becoming increasingly complex, to acquire duality of

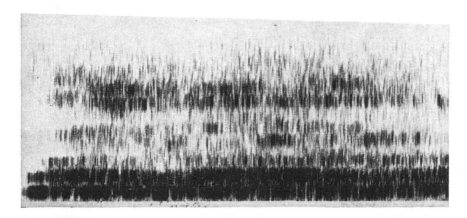

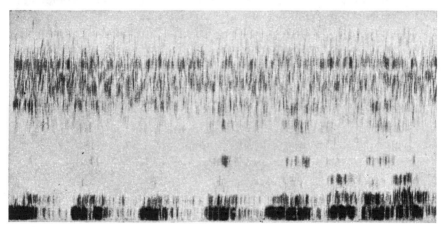

Figure 5. Subhuman primate calls are represented here by sound spectograms of the roar (*top*) and bark (*bottom*) of the howler monkey. Frequencies are shown vertically; time, horizontally. Roaring, the most prominent howler vocalization, regulates interactions and movements of groups of monkeys, and has both defensive and offensive functions. Barking has similar meanings but occurs when the monkeys are not quite so excited. Spectograms were produced at Bell Telephone Laboratories from recordings made by Charles Southwick of the University of Southern Ohio during an expedition to Barro Colorado Island in the Canal Zone. The expedition was directed by C. R. Carpenter of Pennsylvania State University.

patterning. However it occurred, this was a major breakthrough; without it language could not possibly have achieved the efficiency and flexibility it has.

One of the basic principles of evolutionary theory holds that the initial survival value of any innovation is conservative in that it makes possible the maintenance of a largely traditional way of life in the face of changed circumstances. There was nothing in the makeup of the protohominoids that destined their descendants to become human. Some of them, indeed, did not. They made their way to ecological niches where food was plentiful and predators sufficiently avoidable, and where the development of primitive varieties of language and culture would have bestowed no advantage. They survive still, with various sorts of specialization, as the gibbons and the great apes.

Man's own remote ancestors, then, must have come to live in circumstances where a slightly more flexible system of communication, the incipient carrying and shaping of tools, and a slight increase in the capacity for traditional transmission made just the difference between surviving—largely, be it noted, by the good old protohominoid way of life—and dying out. There are various possibilities. If predators become more numerous and dangerous, any nonce use of a tool as a weapon, any cooperative mode of escape or attack might restore the balance. If food became scarcer, any technique for cracking harder nuts, for foraging over a wider territory, for sharing food so gathered or storing it when it was plentiful might promote survival of the band. Only after a very long period of such small adjustments to tiny changes of living conditions could the factors involved—incipient language, incipient tool-carrying and toolmaking, incipient culture—have started leading the way to a new pattern of life, of the kind called human.

Language serves not only to express thoughts, but to make possible thoughts which could not exist without it.

The Uses of Language

BERTRAND RUSSELL

To express emotions, to influence the behavior of others, to communicate information, to command, to question, to enable us to entertain certain thoughts are some of the uses of language which Bertrand Russell here discusses. Language, as Russell so clearly demonstrates, is an extremely useful tool. But, it is also an extremely dangerous one in its suggestion that there is a definiteness, a discreteness, and a quasipermanence in objects which they do not in reality possess.

Language, like other things of mysterious importance, such as breath, blood, sex, and lightning, has been viewed superstitiously ever since men were capable of recording their thoughts. Savages fear to disclose their true name to an enemy, lest he should work evil magic by means of it. Origen assures us that pagan sorcerers could achieve more by using the sacred name Jehovah than by means of the names Zeus, Osiris, or Brahma. Familiarity makes us blind to the linguistic emphasis in the Commandment: "Thou shalt not take the *name* of the Lord in vain." The habit of viewing language superstitiously is not yet extinct. "In the beginning was the Word," says our version of St. John's Gospel, and in reading some logical positivists I am tempted to think that their view is represented by this mistranslated text.

Philosophers, being bookish and theoretical folk, have been interested in language chiefly as a means of making statements and conveying information, but this is only one of its purposes, and perhaps not the most primitive. What is the purpose of language to a sergeant major? On the one hand there is the language of words of command, designed to cause identical simultaneous bodily movements in a number of hearers; on the other hand there is bad language, designed to cause humility in those in whom the expected bodily movements have not been caused. In neither case are words used, except incidentally, to state facts or convey information.

Language can be used to express emotions, or to influence the behavior of others. Each of these functions can be performed, though with less adequacy, by pre-linguistic methods. Animals emit shrieks of pain, and infants, before they can speak, can express rage, discomfort, desire, delight, and a whole gamut of feelings by cries and gurgles of different kinds. A sheep dog emits imperatives to his flock by means hardly distinguishable from those that the shepherd employs toward him. Between

From Human Knowledge: Its Scope and Limits *by Bertrand Russell. New York: Simon and Schuster, 1948, pp. 57–63. Reprinted with permission of Simon & Schuster and George Allen & Unwin Ltd.*

such noises and speech no sharp line can be drawn. When the dentist hurts you, you may emit an involuntary groan; this does not count as speech. But if he says, "Let me know if I hurt you," and you then make the very same sound, it has become speech, and moreover speech of the sort intended to convey information. This example illustrates the fact that, in the matter of language as in other respects, there is a continuous gradation from animal behavior to that of the most precise man of science, and from pre-linguistic noises to the polished diction of the lexicographer.

A sound expressive of emotion I shall call an "interjection." Imperatives and interjections can already be distinguished in the noises emitted by animals. When a hen clucks at her brood of chickens, she is uttering imperatives, but when she squawks in terror she is expressing emotion. But as appears from your groan at the dentist's, an interjection may convey information, and the outside observer cannot tell whether or not it is intended to do so. Gregarious animals emit distinctive noises when they find food, and other members of the herd are attracted when they hear these noises, but we cannot know whether the noises merely express pleasure or are also intended to state "food here."

Whenever an animal is so constructed that a certain kind of circumstance causes a certain kind of emotion, and a certain kind of emotion causes a certain kind of noise, the noise conveys to a suitable observer two pieces of information, first, that the animal has a certain kind of feeling, and second, that a certain kind of circumstance is present. The sound that the animal emits is public, and the circumstance may be public—e.g., the presence of a shoal of fish if the animal is a sea gull. The animal's cry may act directly on the other members of its species, and *we* shall then say that they "understand" its cry. But this is to suppose a "mental" intermediary between the hearing of the cry and the bodily reaction to the sound, and there is no real reason to suppose any such intermediary except when the response is delayed. Much of the importance of language is connected with delayed responses, but I will not yet deal with this topic.

Language has two primary purposes, expression and communication. In its most primitive forms it differs little from some other forms of behavior. A man may express sorrow by sighing, or by saying, "Alas!" or "Woe is me!" He may communicate by pointing or by saying, "Look." Expression and communication are not necessarily separated; if you say, "Look" because you see a ghost, you may say it in a tone that expresses horror. This applies not only to elementary forms of language; in poetry, and especially in songs, emotion and information are conveyed by the same means. Music may be considered as a form of language in which emotion is divorced from information, while the telephone book gives information without emotion. But in ordinary speech both elements are usually present.

Communication does not consist only of giving information; commands and questions must be included. Sometimes the two are scarcely separable; if you are walking with a child and you say, "There's a puddle there," the command "Don't step in it" is implicit. Giving information may be due solely to the fact that the information interests you, or may be designed to influence behavior. If you have just seen a street accident, you will wish to tell your friends about it because your mind is full of it; but if you tell a child that six times seven is forty-two you do so merely in the hope of influencing his (verbal) behavior.

Language has two interconnected merits: first, that it is social, and second, that it supplies public expression for "thoughts" which would otherwise remain private. Without language, or some pre-linguistic analogue, our knowledge of the environment is confined to what our own senses have shown us, together with such inferences as our congenital constitution may prompt; but by the help of speech we are able to know what others can relate, and to relate what is no longer sensibly present but only remembered. When we see or hear something which a companion is not seeing or hearing, we can often make him aware of it by the one word "look" or "listen," or even by gestures. But if half an hour ago we saw a fox, it is not possible to make another person aware of this fact without language. This depends upon the fact that the word "fox" applies equally to a fox seen or a fox remembered, so that our memories, which in themselves are private, are represented to others by uttered sounds, which are public. Without language, only that part of our life which consists of public sensations would be communicable, and that only to those so situated as to be able to share the sensations in question.

It will be seen that the utility of language depends upon the distinction between public and private experiences, which is important in considering the empirical basis of physics. This distinction, in turn, depends partly on physiology, partly on the persistence of sound waves and light quanta, which makes possible the two forms of language, speech and writing. Thus language depends upon physics, and could not exist without the approximately separable causal chains which, as we shall see, make physical knowledge possible; and since the publicity of sensible objects is only approximate, language applying to them, considered socially, must have a certain lack of precision. I need hardly say that I am *not* asserting that the existence of language requires a *knowledge* of physics. What I am saying is that language would be impossible if the physical world did not in fact have certain characteristics, and that the *theory* of language is at certain points dependent upon a knowledge of the physical world. Language is a means of externalizing and publicizing our own experiences. A dog cannot relate his autobiography; however eloquently he may bark, he cannot tell you that his parents were honest though poor. A man can do this, and he does it by correlating "thoughts" with public sensations.

Language serves not only to express thoughts, but to make possible thoughts which could not exist without it. It is sometimes maintained that there can be no thought without language, but to this view I cannot assent: I hold that there can be thought, and even true and false belief, without language. But however that may, it cannot be denied that all fairly elaborate thoughts require words. I can know, in a sense, that I have five fingers without knowing the word "five," but I cannot know that the population of London is about eight millions unless I have acquired the language of arithmetic, nor can I have any thought at all closely corresponding to what is asserted in the sentence: "The ratio of the circumference of a circle to the diameter is approximately 3.14159." Language, once evolved, acquires a kind of autonomy: we can know, especially in mathematics, that a sentence asserts something true, although what it asserts is too complex to be apprehended even by the best minds. Let us consider for a moment what happens psychologically in such cases.

In mathematics, we start from rather simple sentences which we believe ourselves capable of understanding, and proceed, by rules of inference which we also believe ourselves to understand, to build up more and more complicated symbolic statements, which, if our initial assumptions are true, must be true whatever they may mean. As a rule it is unnecessary to know what they "mean," if their "meaning" is taken to be a thought which might occur in the mind of a superhuman mathematical genius. But there is another kind of "meaning," which gives occasion for pragmatism and instrumentalism. According to those who adopt this view of "meaning," what a complicated mathematical sentence does is to give a rule for practical procedure in certain kinds of cases. Take, for instance, the above statement about the ratio of the circumference of a circle to the diameter. Suppose you are a brewer, and you desire hoops of a given diameter for your beer barrels, then the sentence gives you a rule by which you can find out how much material you will need. This rule may consist of a fresh sentence for each decimal point, and there is therefore no need ever to grasp its significance as a whole. The autonomy of language enables you to forgo this tedious process of interpretation except at crucial moments.

There are two other uses of language that are of great importance: it enables us to conduct our transactions with the outer world by means of symbols that have (1) a certain degree of permanence in time, (2) a considerable degree of discreteness in space. Each of these merits is more marked in writing than in speech, but is by no means wholly absent in speech. Suppose you have a friend called Mr. Jones. As a physical object his boundaries are somewhat vague, both because he is continually losing and acquiring electrons and because an electron, being a distribution of energy, does not cease abruptly at a certain distance from its center. The surface of Mr. Jones, therefore, has a certain ghostly, impalpable quality which you do not like to associate with your solid-seeming friend. It is not necessary to go into the niceties of theoretical physics in order to show that Mr. Jones is sadly indeterminate. When he is cutting his toe nails, there is a finite time, though a short one, during which it is doubtful whether the parings are still part of him or not. When he eats a mutton chop, at what moment does it become part of him? When he breathes out carbon dioxide, is the carbon part of him until it passes his nostrils? Even if we answer in the affirmative, there is a finite time during which it is questionable whether certain molecules have or have not passed beyond his nostrils. In these and other ways, it is doubtful what is part of Mr. Jones and what is not. So much for spatial vagueness.

There is the same problem as regards time. To the question "What are you looking at?" you may answer, "Mr. Jones," although at one time you see him full-face, at another in profile, and at another from behind, and although at one time he may be running a race and at another time dozing in an armchair. There is another question, namely "What are you thinking of?," to which you may also answer, "Mr. Jones," though what is actually in your mind may be very different on different occasions: it may be Mr. Jones as a baby, or Mr. Jones being cross because his breakfast is late, or Mr. Jones receiving the news that he is to be knighted. What you are experiencing is very different on these various occasions, but for many practical purposes it is convenient to regard them as all having a common object, which we suppose to be the meaning of the name "Mr. Jones." This name, especially when printed, though it cannot wholly escape the indefiniteness and transience of all physical objects, has much less of both than Mr. Jones has. Two instances of the printed words "Mr. Jones" are much more alike than (for instance) the spectacle of Mr. Jones running and the memory of Mr. Jones as a baby. And each instance, if printed, changes much more slowly than Mr. Jones does: it does not eat or breathe or cut its toe nails. The name, accordingly, makes it much easier than it would otherwise be to think of Mr. Jones as a single quasi-permanent entity, which, though untrue, is convenient in daily life.

Language, as appears from the above discussion of Mr. Jones, though a useful and even indispensable tool, is a dangerous one, since it begins by suggesting a definiteness, discreteness, and quasi-permanence in objects which physics seems to show that they do not possess. The philosopher, therefore, is faced with the difficult task of using language to undo the false beliefs that it suggests. Some philosophers, who shrink from the problems and uncertainties and complications involved in such a task, prefer to treat language as autonomous, and try to forget that it is intended to have a relation to fact and to facilitate dealings with the environment. Up to a point, such a treatment has great advantages: logic and mathematics would not have prospered as they have done if logicians and mathematicians had continually remembered that symbols should mean something. "Art for art's sake" is a maxim which has a legitimate sphere in logic as in painting (though in neither case does it give the whole truth). It may be that singing began as an incident in courtship and that its biological purpose was to promote sexual intercourse, but this fact (if it be a fact) will not help a composer to produce good music. Language is useful when you wish to order a meal in a restaurant, but this fact, similarly, is of no importance to the pure mathematician.

The philosopher, however, must pursue truth even at the expense of beauty, and in studying language he must not let himself be seduced by the siren songs of mathematics. Language, in its beginnings, is pedestrian and practical, using rough and ready approximations which have at first no beauty and only a very limited degree of truth. Subsequent refinements have too often had aesthetic rather than scientific motives, but from the inquiry upon which we are about to embark aesthetic motives must, however reluctantly, be relentlessly banished.

*The goal of education must be for
children to regain their free speech
without class limitations.*

Sublanguages

PAUL GOODMAN

The development and function of "sublanguages"—
languages used "to glue together" specific groups—are
analyzed in this essay by psychologist-educator-philosopher
Paul Goodman. A sublanguage, Goodman argues, "defines
and affirms the group's identity and commits the members
to it. There is a willful withdrawal from the common,
creating what amounts to a proper sublanguage as a badge."

Innumerable sentences that are said are mainly social-cement, keeping people together by engaging in the sociable action of speaking and listening, playing with the common code like any other game, and telling enough information to avoid the pain of a blank mind. Or we can put this in a way that is not quite the same: We are communal animals, an important part of our communal nature is speaking, so when we can we speak. To call it cement describes better the talk in a bar, where people might otherwise be lonely. To avoid blankness of mind is the reason for most reading of newspapers, which must be the largest proportion of all reading. But to call it the chatter of a communal species better describes the small talk of chance meetings on the street or across the back fence, drop-in visits, talk around card tables, ordinary (pleasant) family life, ceremonial dinners.

I have no statistics, but my impression is that, on the whole, small talk sticks closer to the constant and supra-individual code than more concerned or intimate talk. It has more standard subject-predicate sentences and probably better pronunciation, if only because to deviate far from the expected would jeopardize harmony and be bad manners. But by the same token, it is necessary to avoid saying much, whether giving information, explaining, debating, or having any instrumental purpose. Consider a pep talk before a ball game or a political rally during a campaign: The purpose is solidarity for action, to win, to get out the vote. It would be disastrous if anybody made sense.

Harold Garfinkel ran a poignant experiment to show the need actively to *prevent* communication in small talk. He had his students go home and insist on the literal meaning, and truth or falsity, of the chatter. Let me give two excerpts:

Hi, Ray, how is your girl friend feeling?—What do you mean how is she feeling, do you mean physical or mental?—I mean how is she

From Speaking and Language: Defence of Poetry, *by Paul Goodman. Copyright © 1971 by Paul Goodman. Reprinted by permission of Random House, Inc.*

47

feeling. What's the matter with *you*?—Nothing. Just explain a little clearer what you want to know.—Skip it. Hey, are you sick?

All these old movies have the same kind of old iron bedstead in them.—What do you mean? Do you mean all old movies, or some of them, or just the ones you have seen?—What's the matter with you? You know what I mean.—I wish you would be more specific.—Drop dead.

1

It is different, however, when this kind of talk is *used* to glue together not people in general, but a specific group, clique, adolescent gang, or thieves' gang. We at once come to a different kind of language, that defines and affirms the group's identity and commits the members to it. There is a willful withdrawal from the common code, creating what amounts to a proper sublanguage as a badge. Let me give an extreme example: Adolescents at the University of Hawaii, which is an uneasy place for many of them, speak perfectly good English while they are on campus, even when they are at the same table in the cafeteria; but off campus they will talk only pidgin, and they have scorn for anybody who treasonably speaks English.

A badge language may or may not communicate more accurately or relevantly. Usually such willed languages are pretty weak. A clique attitude depoverishes experience rather than enriching it by making it deep and intimate. In a circle of junkies the sublangauge seems (to me at least) to be as appallingly limited as their purposes. Thus, there is an essential difference between such an argot and the selective and intimate use of the common code by family, friends, neighbors, and co-workers. Intimate language develops naturally, to be able to say people's real interests better than the common code can; it does not aim to modify the common code, it just does it. An argot affirms itself, consciously or unconsciously, against the common code. Sometimes, for purposes of self-defense, it tries to be commonly incomprehensible, like thieves' language or jive.

Jespersen made the remarkable empirical observation that a child of immigrant parents may learn the new language at home, but he takes on the accent of his (slightly older) peer group on the street—that is, as he psychologically draws away from his parents at age five to six, he models himself on his ideal gang, like putting on a hockey shirt and speech is the badge. Speaking is here again a direct act, naming, self-naming, self-appointing. (Wittgenstein points out that naming is not yet part of the "language game" for a logician.) The same can be seen with adults who are sexually infatuated or infatuated with a political cause and unconsciously mimic a new accent and speech rhythm; but these adult cases are more pathetic, for such a commitment is not likely to last long—if speech is labile, so is character.

Contrariwise, the children of immigrants may, as they grow older, retain or revert to some of the old language—perhaps their parents' foreign accent—as a self-naming defensive maneuver against assimilation. It is a return of the repressed. They may rationalize that the old language has phrases that say what the common language can't say, and which, of course, affirm their feeling of having a special cast of mind. Jews have done a lot of this. Urban blacks claim that their Southern language and country food have soul. The Jews are a striking case in that, as a people in exile, their own common code was already a self-naming amalgam—Yiddish or Ladino—and the revived Israeli Hebrew must itself for a time be a self-conscious language, though no longer a sublanguage.

It is the factor of artificial boundaries, whether willed or resignedly recognized, that makes a sublanguage. A Yiddish or Black English spoken spontaneously, as by a child, is a creole or mixture, but it is a native tongue like any other. But will, pride, suspicion, and fear are a bad way to be in the world linguistically as otherwise.

2

When the rich become squeamish and the poor become a caste, social classes develop sublanguages. So long as decent poverty is possible, poor people may have an exceptionally good intimate language selected from the common code—concrete, realistic, and feelingful—at least as good as any other speech in the society. Wordsworth famously singled out the language of "humble and rustic life" as the source for his poetic diction, because it came from a beautiful scene and natural affections, it was under less restraint and was plainer, it was "far more philosophical . . . because such men hourly communicate with the best objects from which the best part of language is originally derived"; whereas the upper and middle classes and the new industrial proletariat were bitched up in various ways. During the same era Jefferson wanted to rely politically on freeholding yeomen for their independence, morality, and democracy. And a little later, Marx singled out the Elizabethan yeomanry as the best condition so far achieved by humanity.

City poverty, too, has had good language, slangy, polyglot, rapid, and argumentative. The common people of Rome, Paris, and New York have all been written up as vivid talkers. They interrupt you in the middle of a sentence because they know all about it beforehand, and often they do. But here too, in order to choose what suits them out of the common code, people have to be free in their own homes and neighborhoods and have to have access to the rest of society.

The case is very different in depressed rural areas or big city slums, where the poor are powerless, segregated, unable to get into the inflationary general economy, unskilled to cope with a centralized high technology, and many of the city youth are the children of uprooted rural migrants. The common code may then be pretty useless to them as a basis for practical communication. Consider a sad example: Large numbers of Spanish-speaking kids in the New York public schools apparently speak English quite fluently to talk about public nonsense, but they cannot say, "I am hungry," "I have a toothache," "My pal is dying in the basement." They have to say these in Spanish, but then the teacher or cop does not know what they are talking about. In the recent trial of Black Panthers in New Haven, the defense attacked the disproportion of whites on the jury rolls because, as their linguistic experts put it, "blacks had developed a significant and unique nonverbal form of communication" and "whites were apt to miss or misunderstand meanings of the Black English dialect and the voice inflections unique to black communication."

As a native speaker of his own dialect, a poor black child has, of course, as much linguistic power as any other child; he has plenty of Chomsky's innate algebra. To borrow examples from Labov: If he says, "He a'way' look' fo' trouble when he red [past tense of "read"] de news," he obviously uses "look'" as past; and although he says, "It John book," he can say, when necessary, "It *is* John's." In the history of English, indeed, there has been a secular tendency to drop the case endings and soft-pedal the copula, so that this dialect is not even out of the mainstream.

But under conditions of alienation, there develops a self-defensive and self-affirming sublanguage *against* the common code, a language to fit the sub-"culture of poverty," as Oscar Lewis used to call it, which is not an independent culture. Consider when the children go to an official school. They do not really use the dominant code. They are not allowed to use their own dialect, and certainly they are not encouraged to improve it. Then they are made to feel stupid, as if they did not have intellectual powers.[1] Humanly, they have no alternative but to affirm their

---

[1]"Correcting" a child's language, as if he did not have a proper language, is identical with the theory of Head Start that disadvantaged children need special training for their intellectual faculties to prepare them for learning. "But there is nothing wrong with their intellectual faculties; they have learned to speak and can make practical syllogisms very nicely if they need to and are not

language all the more tenaciously. But then they have still less access to the common goods. The situation is explosive.

3

Dialects and creoles are simply languages. Intimate language is superior language; it gives everybody more articulate experience and so enriches the common code too. But class sublanguages thin out every class's experience and language and depoverish the common code.

Basil Bernstein has a profound but confused study of the differences of syntax between lower class and middle class children in London. Let me quote some of his comparisons:

> [Poor children use] short sentences, poor syntax, active voice, repetitive use of conjunctions, no subordination, limited use of adjectives and adverbs, infrequent use of "one" or "it" as subjects, stereotyped idioms. [Middle class children use] accurate order and syntax, complex construction, frequent use of prepositions for logical, temporal, and spatial relation, frequent use of "I," discriminating use of adjectives and adverbs.

These terms, so far, are rather value-laden; yet I think there is truth in them: What they imply is that speech is not so big a deal for the communication of London poor children as for London middle class children. In fact, poor children—not only in London—do an enormous amount of punching, nudging, hand-stroking in lieu of speaking, whereas this almost never occurs in the middle class. And the lower class child will use many more phrases to ask for his speech to be validated, like "you see?" "you know what I mean?" whereas the middle class child takes speech more for granted as asserting what it says.[2]

Bernstein gives a typical comparative sequence of sentences. The lower class mother says, "Sit down.—Why?—Because I say so." The middle class mother says, "Sit down.—Why?—Because you're a big boy, you see how all the other people are doing." And he explains, "By expressing direct authority, the lower class language tends to discourage the experi-

---

thwarted. If black children do not have the patterns to succeed in school, the plausible move is to change the school rather than to badger the children" (*New Reformation*, p. 83).

[2] I do not think that the child's "you know" is the same as the "you know" of embarrassed adolescents. The adolescents are doubtful that they have a world to assert; the child has a world, but he is not sure that speaking is the way of asserting it.

ence of guilt; in middle class language the child's intent becomes important." Also, "the lower class child is not given much instrumental teaching"—at least in words, although he may be shown as much—"whereas the middle class child is continually verbally exposed to connection and sequence, and if one set of reasons is challenged, another set of reasons is elicited." In general,

> Lower working class children have a society limited to a form of spoken language in which complex verbal procedures are made irrelevant by the system of nonverbal closely-shared identifications—plus more naked, less internalized authority. . . . Inherent in the middle class linguistic relationship is a pressure to verbalize feeling in an individual manner. To make explicit subjective intent . . . The lower class child learns a form of language which symbolizes the norms of a local group, rather than the individuated experience of its members.

All this is beautifully analyzed. It is not hard to fill in the economic background of both groups, and he tells us something very important about the psychology of verbalizing. But then, unfortunately, Bernstein concludes that the middle class speech is far superior. I don't think so. *Both* are defensive languages. Each has its virtues, which are not class virtues but human virtues: The poor child's speech has the human virtues of animality, plainness, community, emotional vulnerability, and semantic bluntness (though not frankness—they are frightful little liars); the middle class child's speech has the human virtues of prudence, self-reliance, subtle distinction, the ability to move abroad, and responsibility to the verbal truth (but they are already terrible little hypocrites). In both types, however, we can see developing the outlines of pathological speech. The poor kid has to prove his potency; if his stereotyped sentence is not accepted at face value, he has no back-up, is acutely embarrassed, and bursts into tears; he has to diminish anxiety by impulsive reactions and can become totally confused and lose all prudence; he becomes stupid out of spite. The other kid escapes from physical and emotional contact by verbalizing; he speaks correctly to control his spontaneity; he rationalizes and deceives himself; his consciousness of "I" isolates him and makes him needlessly competitive; he is guilt-ridden.

The poor kid's use of language does not get him enough of the cushioning protection that symbolic action can give; as Kurt Goldstein puts it, he is liable to catastrophic reactions. But the other lives too much by language; he tries to make it do more than it can or should, and so he immobilizes himself and loses vitality. (We shall return to these two types in the next chapter.)

Bernstein says, "Middle class children will have access to both forms of speech, which will be used according to the social context." Yet C. J. Bailey categorically says just the opposite: "It is known that speakers of a prestige idiom have genuine problems in understanding a fairly similar idiom of low prestige, that do not exist on the other side." It is possible that both authors may be superficially correct, but from my limited experience, in street and campus troubles, I think they are both profoundly wrong. Neither group has much access. It is plausible that the lower speakers may hear the upper speakers better because the latter's speech is more articulate and more like the standard speech of, for instance, the mass media. It is plausible that the upper group would find the lower speech simpler and something like their own careless speech.[3] But though the lower speakers hear the others' words, they do not really hear the distinctions, the concessions, the subordinations, and the abstractions; they quickly dismiss it as all bullshit. And the upper speakers are fatally put off by the bluntness and violence, much of which is ritual insult precisely to calm things down; they take the stereotypes too literally; they think that because the language is childish, the reasoning is—but it's not. When the atmosphere heats up, communication breaks down badly.

The goal of education must be for children to regain their free speech without class limitations. (I don't know whether class conflict should be moderated or not, but it should make sense.) There are two possible strategies. The teacher can go along with the child's sub-language as he has it and help him to say and do more with it. This has been the line of a number of teachers in American ghetto schools and of Paolo Freire in Brazil, whether to help poor kids write poetry or to formulate political demands. Or the teacher can try, like Sylvia Ashton-Warner teaching reading to little Maoris, to evoke from the children their own primary words, rising from their fear, hunger, loneliness, and sexuality—in effect, to live through the old traumas in the more favorable circumstances of her school. But note that such efforts are made with lower class children. I have not heard of anything comparable to liberate the speech of middle class children, and if the attempt were made it would be strongly resisted by middle class parents and school authorities.

4

The mighty development of our language from Old English may be instructively regarded as winning its way from being colonized as a sub-language. Twice it was touch and go—during the Danish conquest and

---

[3] In this particular comparison, also, Cockney is possibly unusually more inarticulate, compared to Bailey's American "lower class speech."

especially the Norman conquest. In Walter Scott's classical illustration, the French conqueror said, "beef," "veal," "pork," "mutton," "meat," for the food on the table; the English, who did the farm work, said, "ox," "calf," "swine," "sheep," and "flesh," and these might have become debased words. But luckily the language was creolized instead. Class boundaries were broken and the language was enriched. (In effect, it happened a third time, with the influx of academic Latin during the Renaissance.) "The introduction of French words into English," Baugh points out, "followed the adoption of English by the upper classes"—when the élite gives up its squeamishness, it can do some good as well as harm.

One may meditate also on the *absence* of mixing where it might have been expected, the paucity of Celtic in Old English or of Red Indian words in American English—but they are not so rare as references to Red Indian people in classical American literature.

5

Much of slang is first invented as a neologism of a gang or special group, e.g. "take the rap" or "kibitzer," yet it comes into circulation as slang precisely by breaking out of its subculture. When the boundary is broken, there is a different kind of language, not self-naming and defensive but common and wild. For instance, if a group becomes generally interesting or newsworthy, some terms of its language may become widespread, because they are topical; and they may prove to be colorful, exciting, or to have a valuable new nuance of meaning. Usually they are transient; sometimes they become a permanent part of the common code. As we saw, a Jewish second generation kept many Yiddish words as part of its identity; but since these Jews have been important in entertainment and business, the words have become common slang. Black argot began to become slang through the jazz musicians, but now it has come in strongly through the civil rights and black liberation movements, and the association with blacks by the youth of the white majority.

Slang is not a sub-language. Both sublanguage and slang are a violation of the common code. Like Dada in art, they mean to destroy the convention, either for spite or as an act of liberation. (Spite is the vitality of the powerless.) But whereas the sublanguage is purposeful—to affirm and defend and be a new code—slang tends to be wildly gratuitous, and it sometimes enriches the common code. For a moment, when slang is introduced, it obliterates altogether the distinction between *langue* and *parole*, given code and spontaneous speaking. So Eric Partridge says, "Slang is the only speech in which linguistic process can be observed in unrestrained activity."

Slang creates new language, just like poetry, and it can be regarded as a kind of folk poetry. "It results," says A. C. Baugh, "from an instinctive desire for freshness and novelty of expression." But in one important respect it is not poetry at all, and this tells us something important about poetry. The speaker of slang still retains the feeling of being "wrong," of breaking the law, of being an individual; but the poet, like every fine artist, is himself the lawgiver—he speaks universally, though he has no warrant whatever. (In Rorschach tests it is hard to distinguish artists from psychopathic personalities.)

Various students of slang all bring out the lawlessness and the language-creating. Whitman says, "Slang is the lawless germinal element below all words and sentences and behind all poetry." Ernest Weekley says, "Phonetic laws have no control over argotic formulations." Carnoy: "Slang is a particular vocabulary in which purposeful fantasy plays a predominant role." Séchrist: "Slang pays no mind to the routine activities of life. It is radical, puts off restraint, but stays close to the objective common-sense world of things." And Partridge mentions acutely, "The instinctive desire to speak bad English."

In these descriptions we are hovering around age two. A child is learning to speak. He tries out his own expressions till he finds the ones that work. He is resentful when he is corrected. He gets the corresponding satisfaction of defying the corrector.

None of us will ever become fully knowledgeable of the importance of every nonverbal signal. But as long as each of us realizes the power of these signals, this society's diversity can be a source of great strength rather than a further—and subtly powerful—source of division.

The Sounds of Silence

EDWARD AND MILDRED HALL

Although we probably all communicate more information more frequently with nonverbal than with verbal language we are seldom aware of it. Here Edward and Mildred Hall describe some of the dimensions of these nonverbal languages—the language of gestures, of the eyes, of space, of the body. "Nonverbal communications," note the Halls, "signal to members of your own group what kind of person you are, how you feel about others, whether you're assured or anxious, the degree to which you feel comfortable with the standards of your own culture, as well as deeply significant feelings about the self, including the state of your own psyche."

Bob leaves his apartment at 8:15 A.M. and stops at the corner drugstore for breakfast. Before he can speak, the counterman says, "The usual?" Bob nods yes. While he savors his Danish, a fat man pushes onto the adjoining stool and overflows into his space. Bob scowls and the man pulls himself in as much as he can. Bob has sent two messages without speaking a syllable.

Henry has an appointment to meet Arthur at 11 o'clock; he arrives at 11:30. Their conversation is friendly, but Arthur retains a lingering hostility. Henry has unconsciously communicated that he doesn't think the appointment is very important or that Arthur is a person who needs to be treated with respect.

George is talking to Charley's wife at a party. Their conversation is entirely trivial, yet Charley glares at them suspiciously. Their physical proximity and the movements of their eyes reveal that they are powerfully attracted to each other.

José Ybarra and Sir Edmund Jones are at the same party and it is important for them to establish a cordial relationship for business reasons. Each is trying to be warm and friendly, yet they will part with mutual distrust and their business transaction will probably fall through. José, in Latin fashion, moved closer and closer to Sir Edmund as they spoke, and this movement was miscommunicated as pushiness to Sir Edmund, who kept backing away from this intimacy, and this was miscommunicated to José as coldness. The silent languages of Latin and English cultures are more difficult to learn than their spoken languages.

In each of these cases, we see the subtle power of nonverbal communication. The only language used throughout most of the history of humanity (in evolutionary terms, vocal communication is relatively recent), it is the first form of communication you learn. You use this preverbal language, consciously and unconsciously, every day to tell other people how you feel about yourself and them. This language includes your

Edward and Mildred Hall, "The Sounds of Silence," Playboy, *18 (June 1971), 139–140, 148, 204, 206. Originally appeared in* PLAYBOY *Magazine; copyright © 1971 by Playboy.*

posture, gestures, facial expressions, costume, the way you walk, even your treatment of time and space and material things. All people communicate on several different levels at the same time but are usually aware of only the verbal dialog and don't realize that they respond to nonverbal messages. But when a person says one thing and really believes something else, the discrepancy between the two can usually be sensed. Nonverbal-communication systems are much less subject to the conscious deception that often occurs in verbal systems. When we find ourselves thinking, "I don't know what it is about him, but he doesn't seem sincere," it's usually this lack of congruity between a person's words and his behavior that makes us anxious and uncomfortable.

Few of us realize how much we all depend on body movement in our conversation or are aware of the hidden rules that govern listening behavior. But we know instantly whether or not the person we're talking to is "tuned in" and we're very sensitive to any breach in listening etiquette. In white middle-class American culture, when someone wants to show he is listening to someone else, he looks either at the other person's face or, specifically, at his eyes, shifting his gaze from one eye to the other.

If you observe a person conversing, you'll notice that he indicates he's listening by nodding his head. He also makes little "Hmm" noises. If he agrees with what's being said, he may give a vigorous nod. To show pleasure or affirmation, he smiles; if he has some reservations, he looks skeptical by raising an eyebrow or pulling down the corners of his mouth. If a participant wants to terminate the conversation, he may start shifting his body position, stretching his legs, crossing or uncrossing them, bobbing his foot or diverting his gaze from the speaker. The more he fidgets, the more the speaker becomes aware that he has lost his audience. As a last measure, the listener may look at his watch to indicate the imminent end of the conversation.

Talking and listening are so intricately intertwined that a person cannot do one without the other. Even when one is alone and talking to oneself, there is part of the brain that speaks while another part listens. In all conversations, the listener is positively or negatively reinforcing the speaker all the time. He may even guide the conversation without knowing it, by laughing or frowning or dismissing the argument with a wave of his hand.

The language of the eyes—another age-old way of exchanging feelings —is both subtle and complex. Not only do men and women use their eyes differently but there are class, generation, regional, ethnic and national cultural differences. Americans often complain about the way foreigners stare at people or hold a glance too long. Most Americans look away from someone who is using his eyes in an unfamiliar way because it makes them self-conscious. If a man looks at another man's wife in a certain way, he's asking for trouble, as indicated earlier. But he might not be ill mannered or seeking to challenge the husband. He might be a European in this country who hasn't learned our visual mores. Many American women visiting France or Italy are acutely embarrassed because, for the first time in their lives, men really look at them—their eyes, hair, nose, lips, breasts, hips, legs, thighs, knees, ankles, feet, clothes, hairdo, even their walk. These same women, once they have become used to being looked at, often return to the United States and are overcome with the feeling that "No one ever really looks at me anymore."

Analyzing the mass of data on the eyes, it is possible to sort out at least three ways in which the eyes are used to communicate: dominance *vs.* submission, involvement *vs.* detachment and positive *vs.* negative attitude. In addition, there are three levels of consciousness and control, which can be categorized as follows: (1) conscious use of the eyes to communicate, such as the flirting blink and the intimate nose-wrinkling squint; (2) the very extensive category of unconscious but learned behavior governing where the eyes are directed and when (this unwritten set of rules dictates how and under what circumstances the sexes, as well as people of all status categories, look at each other); and (3) the response of the eye itself, which is completely outside both awareness and control —changes in the cast (the sparkle) of the eye and the pupillary reflex.

The eye is unlike any other organ of the body, for it is an extension of the brain. The unconscious pupillary reflex and the cast of the eye have been known by people of Middle Eastern origin for years—although most are unaware of their knowledge. Depending on the context, Arabs and others look either directly at the eyes or deeply *into* the eyes of their interlocutor. We became aware of this in the Middle East several years ago while looking at jewelry. The merchant suddenly started to push a particular bracelet at a customer and said, "You buy this one." What interested us was that the bracelet was not the one that had been consciously selected by the purchaser. But the merchant, watching the pupils of the eyes, knew what the purchaser really wanted to buy. Whether he specifically knew *how* he knew is debatable.

A psychologist at the University of Chicago, Eckhard Hess, was the first to conduct systematic studies of the pupillary reflex. His wife remarked one evening, while watching him reading in bed, that he must be very interested in the text because his pupils were dilated. Following up on this, Hess slipped some pictures of nudes into a stack of photographs that he gave to his male assistant. Not looking at the photographs but watching his assistant's pupils, Hess was able to tell precisely when the assistant came to the nudes. In further experiments, Hess retouched the eyes in a photograph of a woman. In one print, he made the pupils small, in another, large; nothing else was changed. Subjects who were given the photographs found the woman with the dilated pupils much more attractive. Any man who has had the experience of seeing a woman look at him as her pupils widen with reflex speed knows that she's flashing him a message.

The eye-sparkle phenomenon frequently turns up in our interviews of couples in love. It's apparently one of the first reliable clues in the other person that love is genuine. To date, there is no scientific data to explain eye sparkle; no investigation of the pupil, the cornea or even the white sclera of the eye shows how the sparkle originates. Yet we all know it when we see it.

One common situation for most people involves the use of the eyes in the street and in public. Although eye behavior follows a definite set of rules, the rules vary according to the place, the needs and feelings of the people, and their ethnic background. For urban whites, once they're within definite recognition distance (16–32 feet for people with average eyesight), there is mutual avoidance of eye contact—unless they want something specific: a pickup, a handout or information of some kind. In the West and in small towns generally, however, people are much more likely to look at and greet one another, even if they're strangers.

It's permissible to look at people if they're beyond recognition distance; but once inside this sacred zone, you can only steal a glance at strangers. You *must* greet friends, however; to fail to do so is insulting. Yet, to stare too fixedly even at them is considered rude and hostile. Of course, all of these rules are variable.

A great many blacks, for example, greet each other in public even if they don't know each other. To blacks, most eye behavior of whites has the effect of giving the impression that they aren't there, but this is due to white avoidance of eye contact with *anyone* in the street.

Another very basic difference between people of different ethnic backgrounds is their sense of territoriality and how they handle space. This is the silent communication, or miscommunication, that caused friction between Mr. Ybarra and Sir Edmund Jones in our earlier example. We know from research that everyone has around himself an invisible bubble of space that contrasts and expands depending on several factors: his emotional state, the activity he's performing at the time and his cultural background. This bubble is a kind of mobile territory that he will defend against intrusion. If he is accustomed to close personal distance between himself and others, his bubble will be smaller than that of someone who's accustomed to greater personal distance. People of North European heritage—English, Scandinavian, Swiss and German —tend to avoid contact. Those whose heritage is Italian, French, Spanish, Russian, Latin American or Middle Eastern like close personal contact.

People are very sensitive to any intrusion into their spatial bubble.

If someone stands too close to you, your first instinct is to back up. If that's not possible, you lean away and pull yourself in, tensing your muscles. If the intruder doesn't respond to these body signals, you may then try to protect yourself, using a briefcase, umbrella or raincoat. Women—especially when traveling alone—often plant their pocketbook in such a way that no one can get very close to them. As a last resort, you may move to another spot and position yourself behind a desk or a chair that provides screening. Everyone tries to adjust the space around himself in a way that's comfortable for him; most often, he does this unconsciously.

Emotions also have a direct effect on the size of a person's territory. When you're angry or under stress, your bubble expands and you require more space. New York psychiatrist Augustus Kinzel found a difference in what he calls Body-Buffer Zones between violent and nonviolent prison inmates. Dr. Kinzel conducted experiments in which each prisoner was placed in the center of a small room and then Dr. Kinzel slowly walked toward him. Nonviolent prisoners allowed him to come quite close, while prisoners with a history of violent behavior couldn't tolerate his proximity and reacted with some vehemence.

Apparently, people under stress experience other people as looming larger and closer than they actually are. Studies of schizophrenic patients have indicated that they sometimes have a distorted perception of space, and several psychiatrists have reported patients who experience their body boundaries as filling up an entire room. For these patients, anyone who comes into the room is actually inside their body, and such an intrusion may trigger a violent outburst.

Unfortunately, there is little detailed information about normal people who live in highly congested urban areas. We do know, of course, that the noise, pollution, dirt, crowding and confusion of our cities induce feelings of stress in most of us, and stress leads to a need for greater space. The man who's packed into a subway, jostled in the street, crowded into an elevator and forced to work all day in a bull pen or in a small office without auditory or visual privacy is going to be very stressed at the end of his day. He needs places that provide relief from constant overstimulation of his nervous system. Stress from overcrowding is cumulative and people can tolerate more crowding early in the day than later; note the increased bad temper during the evening rush hour as compared with the morning melee. Certainly one factor in people's desire to commute by car is the need for privacy and relief from crowding (except, often, from other cars); it may be the only time of the day when nobody can intrude.

In crowded public places, we tense our muscles and hold ourselves stiff, and thereby communicate to others our desire not to intrude on their space and, above all, not to touch them. We also avoid eye contact, and the total effect is that of someone who has "tuned out." Walking along the street, our bubble expands slightly as we move in a stream of strangers, taking care not to bump into them. In the office, at meetings, in restaurants, our bubble keeps changing as it adjusts to the activity at hand.

Most white middle-class Americans use four main distances in their business and social relations: intimate, personal, social and public. Each of these distances has a near and a far phase and is accompanied by changes in the volume of the voice. Intimate distance varies from direct physical contact with another person to a distance of six to eighteen inches and is used for our most private activities—caressing another person or making love. At this distance, you are overwhelmed by sensory inputs from the other person—heat from the body, tactile stimulation from the skin, the fragrance of perfume, even the sound of breathing—all of which literally envelop you. Even at the far phase, you're still within easy touching distance. In general, the use of intimate distance in public between adults is frowned on. It's also much too close for strangers, except under conditions of extreme crowding.

In the second zone—personal distance—the close phase is one and a half to two and a half feet; it's at this distance that wives usually stand from their husbands in public. If another woman moves into this zone, the wife will most likely be disturbed. The far phase—two and a half to four feet—is the distance used to "keep someone at arm's length" and is the most common spacing used by people in conversation.

The third zone—social distance—is employed during business transactions or exchanges with a clerk or repairman. People who work together tend to use close social distance—four to seven feet. This is also the distance for conversations at social gatherings. To stand at this distance from someone who is seated has a dominating effect (e.g., teacher to pupil, boss to secretary). The far phase of the third zone—seven to twelve feet—is where people stand when someone says, "Stand back so I can look at you." This distance lends a formal tone to business or social discourse. In an executive office, the desk serves to keep people at this distance.

The fourth zone—public distance—is used by teachers in classrooms or speakers at public gatherings. At its farthest phase—25 feet and beyond—it is used for important public figures. Violations of this distance can lead to serious complications. During his 1970 U.S. visit, the president of France, Georges Pompidou, was harassed by pickets in Chicago, who were permitted to get within touching distance. Since pickets in France are kept behind barricades a block or more away, the president was outraged by this insult to his person, and President Nixon was obliged to communicate his concern as well as offer his personal apologies.

It is interesting to note how American pitchmen and panhandlers exploit the unwritten, unspoken conventions of eye and distance. Both take advantage of the fact that once explicit eye contact is established, it is rude to look away, because to do so means to brusquely dismiss the other person and his needs. Once having caught the eye of his mark, the panhandler then locks on, not letting go until he moves through the public zone, the social zone, the personal zone and, finally, into the intimate sphere, where people are most vulnerable.

Touch also is an important part of the constant stream of communication that takes place between people. A light touch, a firm touch, a blow, a caress are all communications. In an effort to break down barriers among people, there's been a recent upsurge in group-encounter activities, in which strangers are encouraged to touch one another. In special situations such as these, the rules for not touching are broken with group approval and people gradually lose some of their inhibitions.

Although most people don't realize it, space is perceived and distances are set not by vision alone but with all the senses. Auditory space is perceived with the ears, thermal space with the skin, kinesthetic space with the muscles of the body and olfactory space with the nose. And, once again, it's one's culture that determines how his senses are programmed —which sensory information ranks highest and lowest. The important thing to remember is that culture is very persistent. In this country, we've noted the existence of culture patterns that determine distance between people in the third and fourth generations of some families, despite their prolonged contact with people of very different cultural heritages.

Whenever there is great cultural distance between two people, there are bound to be problems arising from differences in behavior and expectations. An example is the American couple who consulted a psychiatrist about their marital problems. The husband was from New England and had been brought up by reserved parents who taught him to control his emotions and to respect the need for privacy. His wife was from an Italian family and had been brought up in close contact with all the members of her large family, who were extremely warm, volatile and demonstrative.

When the husband came home after a hard day at the office, dragging his feet and longing for peace and quiet, his wife would rush to him and smother him. Clasping his hands, rubbing his brow, crooning over his weary head, she never left him alone. But when the wife was upset or anxious about her day, the husband's response was to withdraw completely and leave her alone. No comforting, no affectionate embrace, no attention—just solitude. The woman became convinced her husband didn't love her and, in desperation, she consulted a psychiatrist. Their problem wasn't basically psychological but cultural.

Why has man developed all these different ways of communicating messages without words? One reason is that people don't like to spell out certain kinds of messages. We prefer to find other ways of showing our feelings. This is especially true in relationships as sensitive as courtship. Men don't like to be rejected and most women don't want to turn a man down bluntly. Instead, we work out subtle ways of encouraging or discouraging each other that save face and avoid confrontations.

How a person handles space in dating others is an obvious and very sensitive indicator of how he or she feels about the other person. On a first date, if a woman sits or stands so close to a man that he is acutely conscious of her physical presence—inside the intimate-distance zone— the man usually construes it to mean that she is encouraging him. However, before the man starts moving in on the woman, he should be sure what message she's really sending; otherwise, he risks bruising his ego. What is close to someone of North European background may be neutral or distant to someone of Italian heritage. Also, women sometimes use space as a way of misleading a man and there are few things that put men off more than women who communicate contradictory messages— such as women who cuddle up and then act insulted when a man takes the next step.

How does a woman communicate interest in a man? In addition to such familiar gambits as smiling at him, she may glance shyly at him, blush and then look away. Or she may give him a real come-on look and move in very close when he approaches. She may touch his arm and ask for a light. As she leans forward to light her cigarette, she may brush him lightly, enveloping him in her perfume. She'll probably continue to smile at him and she may use what ethologists call preening gestures— touching the back of her hair, thrusting her breasts forward, tilting her hips as she stands or crossing her legs if she's seated, perhaps even exposing one thigh or putting a hand on her thigh and stroking it. She may also stroke her wrists as she converses or show the palm of her hand as a way of gaining his attention. Her skin may be unusually flushed or quite pale, her eyes brighter, the pupils larger.

If a man sees a woman whom he wants to attract, he tries to present himself by his posture and stance as someone who is self-assured. He moves briskly and confidently. When he catches the eye of the woman, he may hold her glance a little longer than normal. If he gets an encouraging smile, he'll move in close and engage her in small talk. As they converse, his glance shifts over her face and body. He, too, may make preening gestures—straightening his tie, smoothing his hair or shooting his cuffs.

How do people learn body language? The same way they learn spoken language—by observing and imitating people around them as they're growing up. Little girls imitate their mothers or an older female. Little boys imitate their fathers or a respected uncle or a character on television. In this way, they learn the gender signals appropriate for their sex. Regional, class and ethnic patterns of body behavior are also learned in childhood and persist throughout life.

Such patterns of masculine and feminine body behavior vary widely from one culture to another. In America, for example, women stand with their thighs together. Many walk with their pelvis tipped slightly forward and their upper arms close to their body. When they sit, they cross their legs at the knee or, if they are well past middle age, they may cross their ankles. American men hold their arms away from their body, often swinging them as they walk. They stand with their legs apart (an extreme example is the cowboy, with legs apart and thumbs tucked into his belt). When they sit, they put their feet on the floor with legs apart and, in some parts of the country, they cross their legs by putting one ankle on the other knee.

Leg behavior indicates sex, status and personality. It also indicates whether or not one is at ease or is showing respect or disrespect for the other person. Young Latin-American males avoid crossing their legs. In their world of *machismo*, the preferred position for young males when with one another (if there is no older dominant male present to whom they must show respect) is to sit on the base of their spine with their leg muscles relaxed and their feet wide apart. Their respect position is like our military equivalent; spine straight, heels and ankles together—almost identical to that displayed by properly brought up young women in New England in the early part of this century.

American women who sit with their legs spread apart in the presence of males are *not* normally signaling a come-on—they are simply (and often unconsciously) sitting like men. Middle-class women in the presence of other women to whom they are very close may on occasion throw themselves down on a soft chair or sofa and let themselves go. This is a signal that nothing serious will be taken up. Males, on the other hand, lean back and prop their legs up on the nearest object.

The way we walk, similarly, indicates status, respect, mood and ethnic or cultural affiliation. The many variants of the female walk are too well known to go into here, except to say that a man would have to be blind not to be turned on by the way some women walk—a fact that made Mae West rich before scientists ever studied these matters. To white Americans, some French middle-class males walk in a way that is both humorous and suspect. There is a bounce and looseness to the French walk, as though the parts of the body were somehow unrelated. Jacques Tati, the French movie actor, walks this way; so does the great mime, Marcel Marceau.

Blacks and whites in America—with the exception of middle- and upper-middle-class professionals of both groups—move and walk very differently from each other. To the blacks, whites often seem incredibly stiff, almost mechanical in their movements. Black males, on the other hand, have a looseness and coordination that frequently makes whites a little uneasy; it's too different, too integrated, too alive, too male. Norman Mailer has said that squares walk from the shoulders, like bears, but blacks and hippies walk from the hips, like cats.

All over the world, people walk not only in their own characteristic way but have walks that communicate the nature of their involvement with whatever it is they're doing. The purposeful walk of North Europeans is an important component of proper behavior on the job. Any male who has been in the military knows how essential it is to walk properly (which makes for a continuing source of tension between blacks and whites in the Service). The quick shuffle of servants in the Far East in the old days was a show of respect. On the island of Truk, when we last visited, the inhabitants even had a name for the respectful walk that one used when in the presence of a chief or when walking past a chief's house. The term was *sufan*, which meant to be humble and respectful.

The notion that people communicate volumes by their gestures, facial expressions, posture and walk is not new; actors, dancers, writers and psychiatrists have long been aware of it. Only in recent years, however, have scientists begun to make systematic observations of body motions. Ray L. Birdwhistell of the University of Pennsylvania is one of the pioneers in body-motion research and coined the term kinesics to describe this field. He developed an elaborate notation system to record both facial and body movements, using an approach similar to that of the linguist, who studies the basic elements of speech. Birdwhistell and other kinesicists such as Albert Sheflen, Adam Kendon and William Condon take movies of people interacting. They run the film over and over again, often at reduced speed for frame-by-frame analysis, so that they can observe even the slightest body movements not perceptible at normal interaction speeds. These movements are then recorded in notebooks for later analysis.

To appreciate the importance of nonverbal-communication systems, consider the unskilled inner-city black looking for a job. His handling of time and space alone is sufficiently different from the white middle-class pattern to create great misunderstandings on both sides. The black is told to appear for a job interview at a certain time. He arrives late. The white interviewer concludes from his tardy arrival that the black is irresponsible and not really interested in the job. What the interviewer doesn't know is that the black time system (often referred to by blacks as C. P. T.—colored people's time) isn't the same as that of whites. In the words of a black student who had been told to make an appointment to see his professor: "Man, you *must* be putting me on. I never had an appointment in my life."

The black job applicant, having arrived late for his interview, may further antagonize the white interviewer by his posture and his eye behavior. Perhaps he slouches and avoids looking at the interviewer; to him, this is playing it cool. To the interviewer, however, he may well look shifty and sound uninterested. The interviewer has failed to notice the actual signs of interest and eagerness in the black's behavior, such as the subtle shift in the quality of the voice—a gentle and tentative excitement—an almost imperceptible change in the cast of the eyes and a relaxing of the jaw muscles.

Moreover, correct reading of black-white behavior is continually complicated by the fact that both groups are comprised of individuals—some of whom try to accommodate and some of whom make it a point of pride *not* to accommodate. At present, this means that many Americans, when thrown into contact with one another, are in the precarious position of not knowing which pattern applies. Once identified and analyzed, nonverbal-communication systems can be taught, like a foreign language. Without this training, we respond to nonverbal communications in terms of our own culture; we read everyone's behavior as if it were out own, and thus we often misunderstand it.

Several years ago in New York City, there was a program for sending children from predominantly black and Puerto Rican low-income neighborhoods to summer school in a white upper-class neighborhood on the East Side. One morning, a group of young black and Puerto Rican boys raced down the street, shouting and screaming and overturning garbage cans on their way to school. A doorman from an apartment building nearby chased them and cornered one of them inside a building. The boy drew a knife and attacked the doorman. This tragedy would not have occurred if the doorman had been familiar with the behavior of boys from low-income neighborhoods, where such antics are routine and socially acceptable and where pursuit would be expected to invite a violent response.

The language of behavior is extremely complex. Most of us are lucky to have under control one subcultural system—the one that reflects our sex, class, generation and geographic region within the United States. Because of its complexity, efforts to isolate bits of nonverbal communication and generalize from them are in vain; you don't become an instant expert on people's behavior by watching them at cocktail parties. Body language isn't something that's independent of the person, something that can be donned and doffed like a suit of clothes.

Our research and that of our colleagues has shown that, far from being a superficial form of communication that can be consciously manipulated, nonverbal-communication systems are interwoven into the fabric of the personality and, as sociologist Erving Goffman has demonstrated, into society itself. They are the warp and woof of daily interactions with others and they influence how one expresses oneself, how one experiences oneself as a man or a woman.

Nonverbal communications signal to members of your own group what kind of person you are, how you feel about others, how you'll fit into and work in a group, whether you're assured or anxious, the degree to which you feel comfortable with the standards of your own culture, as well as deeply significant feelings about the self, including the state of your own psyche. For most of us, it's difficult to accept the reality of another's behavioral system. And, of course, none of us will ever become fully knowledgeable of the importance of every nonverbal signal. But as long as each of us realizes the power of these signals, this society's diversity can be a source of great strength rather than a further—and subtly powerful—source of division.

English is a mass medium. All languages are mass media. The new mass media—film, radio, TV—are new languages, their grammars as yet unknown. Each codifies reality differently; each conceals a unique metaphysics.

The New Languages

EDMUND CARPENTER

The revolution in communication—occasioned largely by the writings of Marshall McLuhan—has forced us to think in new ways about the media, its structures and its functions. Here Edmund Carpenter discusses these "new languages," the implications they have for education and society in general as well as for the older print medium. As Carpenter puts it, "What is really being asked, of course, is: Can books' monopoly of knowledge survive the challenge of the new languages? The answer is: no. What should be asked is: What can print do better than any other medium and is that worth doing?" This is a question which every educator, every communicator, every one interested in language should ask. The answer may well be surprising.

Brain of the New World,
What a task is thine,
To formulate the modern
. . . to recast poems, churches, art

WHITMAN

English is a mass medium. All languages are mass media. The new mass media—film, radio, TV—are new languages, their grammars as yet unknown. Each codifies reality differently; each conceals a unique metaphysics. Linguists tell us it's possible to say anything in any language if you use enough words or images, but there's rarely time; the natural course is for a culture to exploit its media biases.

Writing, for example, didn't record oral language; it was a new language, which the spoken word came to imitate. Writing encouraged an analytical mode of thinking with emphasis upon lineality. Oral languages tended to be polysynthetic, composed of great, tight conglomerates, like twisted knots, within which images were juxtaposed, inseparably fused; written communications consisted of little words chronologically ordered. Subject became distinct from verb, adjective from noun, thus separating actor from action, essence from form. Where preliterate man imposed form diffidently, temporarily—for such transitory forms lived but temporarily on the top of his tongue, in the living situation—the printed word was inflexible, permanent, in touch with eternity: it embalmed truth for posterity.

This embalming process froze language, eliminated the art of ambiguity, made puns "the lowest form of wit," destroyed word linkages. The word became a static symbol, applicable to and separate from that which it symbolized. It now belonged to the objective world; it could be seen. Now came the distinction between being and meaning, the dispute as to whether the Eucharist *was* or only *signified* the body of the Sacrifice. The word became a neutral symbol, no longer an inextricable part of a creative process.

Gutenberg completed the process. The manuscript page with pictures, colors, correlation between symbol and space, gave way to uniform type, the black-and-white page, read silently, alone. The format of the book favored lineal expression, for the argument ran like a thread from cover

From E. Carpenter and M. McLuhan, eds., Explorations in Communication, *pp. 162–179. Copyright © 1960 by the Beacon Press. Reprinted by permission of Beacon Press.*

to cover: subject to verb to object, sentence to sentence, paragraph to paragraph, chapter to chapter, carefully structured from beginning to end, with value embedded in the climax. This was not true of great poetry and drama, which retained multi-perspective, but it was true of most books, particularly texts, histories, autobiographies, novels. Events were arranged chronologically and hence, it was assumed, causally; relationship, not being, was valued. The author became an *authority*; his data were serious, that is, *serially* organized. Such data, if sequentially ordered and printed, conveyed value and truth; arranged any other way, they were suspect.

The newspaper format brought an end to book culture. It offers short, discrete articles that give important facts first and then taper off to incidental details, which may be, and often are, eliminated by the make-up man. The fact that reporters cannot control the length of their articles means that, in writing them, emphasis can't be placed on structure, at least in the traditional linear sense, with climax or conclusion at the end. Everything has to be captured in the headline; from there it goes down the pyramid to incidentals. In fact there is often more in the headline than in the article; occasionally, no article at all accompanies the banner headline.

The position and size of articles on the front page are determined by interest and importance, not content. Unrelated reports from Moscow, Sarawak, London, and Ittipik are juxtaposed; time and space, as separate concepts, are destroyed and the *here* and *now* presented as a single Gestalt. Subway readers consume everything on the front page, then turn to page 2 to read, in incidental order, continuations. A Toronto banner headline ran: TOWNSEND TO MARRY PRINCESS; directly beneath this was a second headline: *Fabian Says This May Not Be Sex Crime.* This went unnoticed by eyes and minds conditioned to consider each newspaper item in isolation.

Such a format lends itself to simultaneity, not chronology or lineality. Items abstracted from a total situation aren't arranged in casual sequence, but presented holistically, as raw experience. The front page is a cosmic *Finnegans Wake.*

The disorder of the newspaper throws the reader into a producer role. The reader has to process the news himself; he has to co-create, to cooperate in the creation of the work. The newspaper format calls for the direct participation of the consumer.

In magazines, where a writer more frequently controls the length of his article, he can, if he wishes, organize it in traditional style, but the majority don't. An increasingly popular presentation is the printed symposium, which is little more than collected opinions, pro and con. The magazine format as a whole opposes lineality; its pictures lack tenses. In

Life, extremes are juxtaposed: space ships and prehistoric monsters, Flemish monasteries and dope addicts. It creates a sense of urgency and uncertainty: the next page is unpredictable. One encounters rapidly a riot in Teheran, a Hollywood marriage, the wonders of the Eisenhower administration, a two-headed calf, a party on Jones beach, all sandwiched between ads. The eye takes in the page as a whole (readers may pretend this isn't so, but the success of advertising suggests it is), and the page—indeed, the whole magazine—becomes a single Gestalt where association, though not causal, is often lifelike.

The same is true of the other new languages. Both radio and TV offer short, unrelated programs, interrupted between and within by commercials. I say "interrupted," being myself an anachronism of book culture, but my children don't regard them as interruptions, as breaking continuity. Rather, they regard them as part of a whole, and their reaction is neither one of annoyance nor one of indifference. The ideal news broadcast has half a dozen speakers from as many parts of the world on as many subjects. The London correspondent doesn't comment on what the Washington correspondent has just said; he hasn't even heard him.

The child is right in not regarding commercials as interruptions. For the only time anyone smiles on TV is in commercials. The rest of life, in news broadcasts and soap operas, is presented as so horrible that the only way to get through life is to buy this product: then you'll smile. Aesop never wrote a clearer fable. It's heaven and hell brought up to date: Hell in the headline, Heaven in the ad. Without the other, neither has meaning.

There's pattern in these new media—not line, but knot; not lineality or causality or chronology, nothing that leads to a desired climax; but a Gordian knot without antecedents or results, containing within itself carefully selected elements, juxtaposed, inseparably fused; a knot that can't be untied to give the long, thin cord of lineality.

This is especially true of ads that never present an ordered, sequential, rational argument but simply present the product associated with desirable things or attitudes. Thus Coca-Cola is shown held by a beautiful blonde, who sits in a Cadillac, surrounded by bronze, muscular admirers, with the sun shining overhead. By repetition these elements become associated, in our minds, into a pattern of sufficient cohesion so that one element can magically evoke the others. If we think of ads as designed solely to sell products, we miss their main effect: to increase pleasure in the consumption of the product. Coca-Cola is far more than a cooling drink; the consumer participates, vicariously, in a much larger experience. In Africa, in Melanesia, to drink a Coke is to participate in the American way of life.

Of the new languages, TV comes closest to drama and ritual. It combines music and art, language and gesture, rhetoric and color. It favors simultaneity of visual and auditory images. Cameras focus not on speakers but on persons spoken to or about; the audience *hears* the accuser but *watches* the accused. In a single impression it hears the prosecutor, watches the trembling hands of the big-town crook, and sees the look of moral indignation on Senator Tobey's face. This is real drama, in process, with the outcome uncertain. Print can't do this; it has a different bias.

Books and movies only pretend uncertainty, but live TV retains this vital aspect of life. Seen on TV, the fire in the 1952 Democratic Convention threatened briefly to become a conflagration; seen on newsreel, it was history, without potentiality.

The absence of uncertainty is no handicap to other media, if they are properly used, for their biases are different. Thus it's clear from the beginning that Hamlet is a doomed man, but, far from detracting in interest, this heightens the sense of tragedy.

Now, one of the results of the time-space duality that developed in Western culture, principally from the Renaissance on, was a separation within the arts. Music, which created symbols in time, and graphic art, which created symbols in space, became separate pursuits, and men gifted in one rarely pursued the other. Dance and ritual, which inherently combined them, fell in popularity. Only in drama did they remain united.

It is significant that of the four new media, the three most recent are dramatic media, particularly TV, which combines language, music, art, dance. They don't, however, exercise the same freedom with time that the stage dares practice. An intricate plot, employing flash backs, multiple time perspectives and overlays, intelligible on the stage, would mystify on the screen. The audience has no time to think back, to establish relations between early hints and subsequent discoveries. The picture passes before the eyes too quickly; there are no intervals in which to take stock of what has happened and make conjectures of what is going to happen. The observer is in a more passive state, less interested in subtleties. Both TV and film are nearer to narrative and depend much more upon the episodic. An intricate time construction can be done in film, but in fact rarely is. The soliloquies of *Richard III* belong on the stage; the film audience was unprepared for them. On stage Ophelia's death was described by three separate groups: one hears the announcement and watches the reactions simultaneously. On film the camera flatly shows her drowned where "a willow lies aslant a brook."

Media differences such as these mean that it's not simply a question of communicating a single idea in different ways but that a given idea or insight belongs primarily, though not exclusively, to one medium, and can be gained or communicated best through that medium.

Thus the book was ideally suited for discussing evolution and progress. Both belonged, almost exclusively, to book culture. Like a book, the idea of progress was an abstracting, organizing principle for the interpretation and comprehension of the incredibly complicated record of human experience. The sequence of events was believed to have a direction, to follow a given course along an axis of time; it was held that civilization, like the reader's eye (in J. B. Bury's words), "has moved, is moving, and will move in a desirable direction. Knowledge will advance, and with that advance, reason and decency must increasingly prevail among men." Here we see the three main elements of book lineality: the line, the point moving along that line, and its movement toward a desirable goal.

The Western conception of a definite moment in the present, of the present as a definite moment or a definite point, so important in book-dominated languages, is absent, to my knowledge, in oral languages. Absent as well, in oral societies, are such animating and controlling ideas as Western individualism and three-dimensional perspective, both related to this conception of the definite moment, and both nourished, probably bred, by book culture.

Each medium selects its ideas. TV is a tiny box into which people are crowded and must live; film gives us the wide world. With its huge screen, film is perfectly suited for social drama, Civil War panoramas, the sea, land erosion, Cecil B. DeMille spectaculars. In contrast, the TV screen has room for two, at the most three, faces, comfortably. TV is closer to stage, yet different. Paddy Chayefsky writes:

> The theatre audience is far away from the actual action of the drama. They cannot see the silent reactions of the players. They must be told in a loud voice what is going on. The plot movement from one scene to another must be marked, rather than gently shaded as is required in television. In television, however, you can dig into the most humble, ordinary relationships; the relationship of bourgeois children to their mother, of middle-class husband to his wife, of white-collar father to his secretary—in short, the relationships of the people. We relate to each other in an incredibly complicated manner. There is far more exciting drama in the reasons why a man gets married than in why he murders someone. The man who is unhappy in his job, the wife who thinks of a lover, the girl who wants to get into television, your father, your mother, sister, brothers, cousins, friends—all these are better subjects for drama than Iago. What makes a man ambitious? Why does a girl always try to steal her kid sister's boy friends? Why does your uncle attend his annual class reunion faithfully every year? Why do you always find it depressing to visit your father? These are the substances of good television drama; and the deeper you probe into and examine the twisted, semi-formed complexes of emotional entanglements, the more exciting your writing becomes.[1]

[1] *Television Plays*, New York, Simon and Schuster, 1955, pp. 176–78.

This is the primary reason, I believe, why Greek drama is more readily adapted to TV than to film. The boxed-in quality of live TV lends itself to static literary tragedy with greater ease than does the elastic, energetic, expandable movie. Guthrie's recent movie of *Oedipus* favored the panoramic shot rather than the selective eye. It consisted of a succession of tableaux, a series of elaborate, unnatural poses. The effect was of congested groups of people moving in tight formation as though they had trained for it by living for days together in a self-service elevator. With the lines, "I grieve for the City, and for myself and you . . . and walk through endless ways of thought," the inexorable tragedy moved to its horrible "come to realize" climax as though everyone were stepping on everyone else's feet.

The tight, necessary conventions of live TV were more sympathetic to Sophocles in the Aluminum Hour's *Antigone*. Restrictions of space are imposed on TV as on the Greek stage by the size and inflexibility of the studio. Squeezed by physical limitations, the producer was forced to expand the viewer's imagination with ingenious devices.

When T. S. Eliot adapted *Murder in the Cathedral* for film, he noted a difference in realism between cinema and stage:

> Cinema, even where fantasy is introduced, is much more realistic than the stage. Especially in an historical picture, the setting, the costume, and the way of life represented have to be accurate. Even a minor anachronism is intolerable. On the stage much more can be overlooked or forgiven; and indeed, an excessive care for accuracy of historical detail can become burdensome and distracting. In watching a stage performance, the member of the audience is in direct contact with the actor playing a part. In looking at a film, we are much more passive; as audience, we contribute less. We are seized with the illusion that we are observing an actual event, or at least a series of photographs of the actual event; and nothing must be allowed to break this illusion. Hence the precise attention to detail.[2]

If two men are on a stage in a theatre, the dramatist is obliged to motivate their presence; he has to account for their existing on the stage at all. Whereas if a camera is following a figure down a street or is turned to any object whatever, there is no need for a reason to be provided. Its grammar contains that power of statement of motivation, no matter what it looks at.

In the theatre, the spectator sees the enacted scene as a whole in space, always seeing the whole of the space. The stage may present only one corner of a large hall, but that corner is always totally visible all

[2]George Hoellering and T. S. Eliot, *Film of Murder in the Cathedral.* New York, Harcourt, Brace & Co., 1952, p. vi; London, Faber & Faber, 1952.

through the scene. And the spectator always sees that scene from a fixed, unchanging distance and from an angle of vision that doesn't change. Perspective may change from scene to scene, but within one scene it remains constant. Distance never varies.

But in film and TV, distance and angle constantly shift. The same scene is shown in multiple perspective and focus. The viewer sees it from here, there, then over here; finally he is drawn inexorably into it, becomes part of it. He ceases to be a spectator. Balázs writes:

> Although we sit in our seats, we do not see Romeo and Juliet from there. We look up into Juliet's balcony with Romeo's eyes and look down on Romeo with Juliet's. Our eye and with it our consciousness is identified with the characters in the film, we look at the world out of their eyes and have no angle of vision of our own. We walk amid crowds, ride, fly or fall with the hero and if one character looks into the other's eyes, he looks into our eyes from the screen, for, our eyes are in the camera and become identical with the gaze of the characters. They see with our eyes. Herein lies the psychological act of identification. Nothing like this "identification" has ever occurred as the effect of any other system of art and it is here that the film manifests its absolute artistic novelty.
>
> . . . Not only can we see, in the isolated "shots" of a scene, the very atoms of life and their innermost secrets revealed at close quarters, but we can do so without any of the intimate secrecy being lost, as always happens in the exposure of a stage performance or of a painting. The new theme which the new means of expression of film art revealed was not a hurricane at sea or the eruption of a volcano: it was perhaps a solitary tear slowly welling up in the corner of a human eye.
>
> . . . Not to speak does not mean that one has nothing to say. Those who do not speak may be brimming over with emotions which can be expressed only in forms and pictures, in gesture and play of feature. The man of visual culture uses these not as substitutes for words, as a deaf-mute uses his fingers.[3]

The gestures of visual man are not intended to convey concepts that can be expressed in words, but inner experiences, nonrational emotions, which would still remain unexpressed when everything that can be told has been told. Such emotions lie in the deepest levels. They cannot be approached by words that are mere reflections of concepts, any more than musical experiences can be expressed in rational concepts. Facial expression is a human experience rendered immediately visible without

[3]Béla Balázs, *Theory of Film*, New York, Roy Publishers, 1953, pp. 48, 31, 40; London, Denis Dobson, 1952.

the intermediary of word. It is Turgenev's "living truth of the human face."

Printing rendered illegible the faces of men. So much could be read from paper that the method of conveying meaning by facial expression fell into desuetude. The press grew to be the main bridge over which the more remote interhuman spiritual exchanges took place; the immediate, the personal, the inner, died. There was no longer need for the subtler means of expression provided by the body. The face became immobile; the inner life, still. Wells that dry up are wells from which no water is dipped.

Just as radio helped bring back inflection in speech, so film and TV are aiding us in the recovery of gesture and facial awareness—a rich, colorful language, conveying moods and emotions, happenings and characters, even thoughts, none of which could be properly packaged in words. If film had remained silent for another decade, how much faster this change might have been!

Feeding the product of one medium through another medium creates a new product. When Hollywood buys a novel, it buys a title and the publicity associated with it: nothing more. Nor should it.

Each of the four versions of the *Caine Mutiny*—book, play, movie, TV had a different hero: Willie Keith, the lawyer Greenwald, the United States Navy, and Captain Queeg, respectively. Media and audience biases were clear. Thus the book told, in lengthy detail, of the growth and making of Ensign William Keith, American man, while the movie camera with its colorful shots of ships and sea, unconsciously favored the Navy as hero, a bias supported by the fact the Navy cooperated with the movie makers. Because of stage limitations, the play was confined, except for the last scene, to the courtroom, and favored the defense counsel as hero. The TV show, aimed at a mass audience, emphasized patriotism, authority, allegiance. More important, the cast was reduced to the principals and the plot to its principles; the real moral problem—the refusal of subordinates to assist an incompetent, unpopular superior—was clear, whereas in the book it was lost under detail, in the film under scenery. Finally, the New York play, with its audience slanted toward Expense Account patronage—Mr. Sampson, Western Sales Manager for the Cavity Drill Company—became a morality play with Willie Keith, innocent American youth, torn between two influences: Keefer, clever author but moral cripple, and Greenwald, equally brilliant but reliable, a businessman's intellectual. Greenwald saves Willie's soul.

The film *Moby Dick* was in many ways an improvement on the book, primarily because of its explicitness. For *Moby Dick* is one of those admittedly great classics, like *Robinson Crusoe* or Kafka's *Trial*, whose plot and situation, as distilled apart from the book by time and familiarity, are actually much more imposing than the written book itself. It's the drama of Ahab's defiance rather than Melville's uncharted leviathan meanderings that is the greatness of *Moby Dick*. On film, instead of laborious tacks through leagues of discursive interruptions, the most vivid descriptions of whales and whaling become part of the action. On film, the viewer was constantly aboard ship: each scene an instantaneous shot of whaling life, an effect achieved in the book only by illusion, by constant, detailed reference. From start to finish, all the action of the film served to develop what was most central to the theme—a man's magnificent and blasphemous pride in attempting to destroy the brutal, unreasoning force that maims him and turns man-made order into chaos. Unlike the book, the film gave a spare, hard, compelling dramatization, free of self-conscious symbolism.

Current confusion over the respective roles of the new media comes largely from a misconception of their function. They are art-forms, not substitutes for human contact. Insofar as they attempt to usurp speech and personal, living relations, they harm. This, of course, has long been one of the problems of book culture, at least during the time of its monopoly of Western middle-class thought. But this was never a legitimate function of books, nor of any other medium. Whenever a medium goes claim jumping, trying to work areas where it is ill-suited, conflicts occur with other media, or, more accurately, between the vested interests controlling each. But, when media simply exploit their own formats, they become complementary and cross-fertile.

Some people who have no one around talk to cats, and you can hear their voices in the next room, and they sound silly, because the cat won't answer, but that suffices to maintain the illusion that their world is made up of living people, while it is not. Mechanized mass media reverse this: now mechanical cats talk to humans. There's no genuine feedback.

This charge is often leveled by academicians at the new media, but it holds equally for print. The open-mouthed, glaze-eyed TV spectator is merely the successor of the passive, silent, lonely reader whose head moved back and forth like a shuttlecock.

When we read, another person thinks for us: we merely repeat his mental process. The greater part of the work of thought is done for us. This is why it relieves us to take up a book after being occupied by our own thoughts. In reading, the mind is only the playground for another's ideas. People who spend most of their lives in reading often lose the capacity for thinking, just as those who always ride forget how to walk. Some people read themselves stupid. Chaplin did a wonderful take-off of this in *City Lights*, when he stood up on a chair to eat the endless confetti that he mistook for spaghetti.

Eliot remarks: "It is often those writers whom we are lucky enough to know whose books we can ignore; and the better we know them personally, the less need we may feel to read what they write."

Frank O'Connor highlights a basic distinction between oral and written traditions: " 'By the hokies, there was a man in this place one time by name of Ned Sullivan, and he had a queer thing happen to him late one night and he coming up the Valley Road from Durlas.' This is how a folk story begins, or should begin. . . . Yet that is how no printed short story should begin, because such a story seems tame when you remove it from its warm nest by the cottage fire, from the sense of an audience with its interjections, and the feeling of terror at what may lurk in the darkness outside."

Face-to-face discourse is not as selective, abstract, nor explicit as any mechanical medium; it probably comes closer to communicating an unabridged situation than any of them, and, insofar as it exploits the give-take of dynamic relationship, it's clearly the most indispensably human one.

Of course, there can be personal involvement in the other media. When Richardson's *Pamela* was serialized in 1741, it aroused such interest that in one English town, upon receipt of the last installment, the church bell announced that virtue had been rewarded. Radio stations have reported receiving quantities of baby clothes and bassinets when, in a soap opera, a heroine had a baby. One of the commonest phrases used by devoted listeners to daytime serials is that they "visited with" Aunt Jenny or Big Sister. BBC and *News Chronicle* report cases of women viewers who kneel before TV sets to kiss male announcers good night.

Each medium, if its bias is properly exploited, reveals and communicates a unique aspect of reality, of truth. Each offers a different perspective, a way of seeing an otherwise hidden dimension of reality. It's not a question of one reality being true, the others distortions. One allows us to see from here, another from there, a third from still another perspective; taken together they give us a more complete whole, a greater truth. New essentials are brought to the fore, including those made invisible by the "blinders" of old languages.

This is why the preservation of book culture is as important as the development of TV. This is why new languages, instead of destroying old ones, serve as a stimulant to them. Only monopoly is destroyed. When actor-collector Edward G. Robinson was battling actor-collector Vincent Price on art on TV's *$64,000 Challenge*, he was asked how the quiz had affected his life; he answered petulantly, "Instead of looking at the pictures in my art books, I now have to read them." Print, along with all old languages, including speech, has profited enormously from the development of the new media. "The more the arts develop," writes

E. M. Forster, "the more they depend on each other for definition. We will borrow from painting first and call it pattern. Later we will borrow from music and call it rhythm."

The appearance of a new medium often frees older media for creative effort. They no longer have to serve the interests of power and profit. Elia Kazan, discussing the American theatre, says:

> Take 1900–1920. The theatre flourished all over the country. It had no competition. The box office boomed. The top original fare it had to offer was *The Girl of the Golden West*. Its bow to culture was fusty productions of Shakespeare. . . . Came the moving pictures. The theatre had to be better or go under. It got better. It got so spectacularly better so fast that in 1920–1930 you wouldn't have recognized it. Perhaps it was an accident that Eugene O'Neill appeared at that moment—but it was no accident that in that moment of strange competition, the theatre had room for him. Because it was disrupted and hard pressed, it made room for his experiments, his unheard-of subjects, his passion, his power. There was room for him to grow to his full stature. And there was freedom for the talents that came after his.[4]

Yet a new language is rarely welcomed by the old. The oral tradition distrusted writing, manuscript culture was contemptuous of printing, book culture hated the press, that "slag-heap of hellish passions," as one 19th century scholar called it. A father, protesting to a Boston newspaper about crime and scandal, said he would rather see his children "in their graves while pure in innocence, than dwelling with pleasure upon these reports, which have grown so bold."

What really disturbed book-oriented people wasn't the sensationalism of the newspaper, but its nonlineal format, its nonlineal codifications of experience. The motto of conservative academicians became: *Hold that line!*

A new language lets us see with the fresh, sharp eyes of the child; it offers the pure joy of discovery. I was recently told a story about a Polish couple who, though long resident in Toronto, retained many of the customs of their homeland. Their son despaired of ever getting his father to buy a suit cut in style or getting his mother to take an interest in Canadian life. Then he bought them a TV set, and in a matter of months a major change took place. One evening the mother remarked that "Edith Piaf is the latest thing on Broadway," and the father appeared in "the kind of suit executives wear on TV." For years the father had passed this same suit in store windows and seen it both in advertise-

---

[4]"Writers and Motion Pictures," *The Atlantic Monthly*, 199, 1957, p. 69.

ments and on living men, but not until he saw it on TV did it become meaningful. This same statement goes for all media: each offers a unique presentation of reality, which when new has a freshness and clarity that is extraordinarily powerful.

This is especially true of TV. We say, "We have a radio" but "We have television"— as if something had happened to us. It's no longer "The skin you love to touch" but "The Nylon that loves to touch you." We don't watch TV; it watches us: it guides us. Magazines and newspapers no longer convey "information" but offer ways of seeing things. They have abandoned realism as too easy: they substitute themselves for realism. *Life* is totally advertisements: its articles package and sell emotions and ideas just as its paid ads sell commodities.

Several years ago, a group of us at the University of Toronto undertook the following experiment: 136 students were divided, on the basis of their over-all academic standing of the previous year, into four equal groups who either (1) heard and saw a lecture delivered in a TV studio, (2) heard and saw this same lecture on a TV screen, (3) heard it over the radio, or (4) read it in manuscript. Thus there were, in the CBS studios, four controlled groups who simultaneously received a single lecture and then immediately wrote an identical examination to test both understanding and retention of content. Later the experiment was repeated, using three similar groups; this time the same lecture was (1) delivered in a classroom, (2) presented as a film (using the kinescope) in a small theatre, and (3) again read in print. The actual mechanics of the experiment were relatively simple, but the problem of writing the script for the lecture led to a consideration of the resources and limitations of the dramatic forms involved.

It immediately became apparent that no matter how the script was written and the show produced, it would be slanted in various ways for and against each of the media involved; no show could be produced that did not contain these biases, and the only real common denominator was the simultaneity of presentation. For each communication channel codifies reality differently and thus influences, to a surprising degree, the content of the message communicated. A medium is not simply an envelope that carries any letter; it is itself a major part of that message. We therefore decided not to exploit the full resources of any one medium, but to try to chart a middle-of-the-road course between all of them.

The lecture that was finally produced dealt with linguistic codifications of reality and metaphysical concepts underlying grammatical systems. It was chosen because it concerned a field in which few students could be expected to have prior knowledge; moreover, it offered opportunities for the use of gesture. The cameras moved throughout the lecture, and took close-ups where relevant. No other visual aids were used, nor were shots taken of the audience while the lecture was in progress. Instead, the cameras simply focused on the speaker for 27 minutes.

The first difference we found between a classroom and a TV lecture was the brevity of the latter. The classroom lecture, if not ideally, at least in practice, sets a slower pace. It's verbose, repetitive. It allows for greater elaboration and permits the lecturer to take up several *related* points. TV, however, is stripped right down; there's less time for qualifications or alternative interpretations and only time enough for *one* point. (Into 27 minutes we put the meat of a two-hour classroom lecture.) The ideal TV speaker states his point and then brings out different facets of it by a variety of illustrations. But the classroom lecturer is less subtle and, to the agony of the better students, repeats and repeats his identical points in the hope, perhaps, that ultimately no student will miss them, or perhaps simply because he is dull. Teachers have had captive audiences for so long that few are equipped to compete for attention via the new media.

The next major difference noted was the abstracting role of each medium, beginning with print. Edmund M. Morgan, Harvard Law Professor, writes:

> One who forms his opinion from the reading of any record alone is prone to err, because the printed page fails to produce the impression or convey the idea which the spoken word produced or conveyed. The writer has read charges to the jury which he had previously heard delivered, and has been amazed to see an oral deliverance which indicated a strong bias appear on the printed page as an ideally impartial exposition. He has seen an appellate court solemnly declare the testimony of a witness to be especially clear and convincing which the trial judge had orally characterized as the most abject perjury.[5]

Selectivity of print and radio are perhaps obvious enough, but we are less conscious of it in TV, partly because we have already been conditioned to it by the shorthand of film. Balázs writes:

> A man hurries to a railway station to take leave of his beloved. We see him on the platform. We cannot see the train, but the questing eyes of the man show us that his beloved is already seated in the train. We see only a close-up of the man's face, we see it twitch as if startled and then strips of light and shadow, light and shadow flit across it in quickening rhythm. Then tears gather in the eyes and that ends the scene. We are expected to know what hap-

[5]G. Louis Joughin and Edmund M. Morgan, *The Legacy of Sacco and Vanzetti*, New York, Harcourt, Brace & Co., 1948, p. 34.

pened and today we do know, but when I first saw this film in Berlin, I did not at once understand the end of this scene. Soon, however, everyone knew what had happened: the train had started and it was the lamps in its compartment which had thrown their light on the man's face as they glided past ever faster and faster.[6]

As in a movie theatre, only the screen is illuminated, and, on it, only points of immediate relevance are portrayed; everything else is eliminated. This explicitness makes TV not only personal but forceful. That's why stage hands in a TV studio watch the show over floor monitors, rather than watch the actual performance before their eyes.

The script of the lecture, timed for radio, proved too long for TV. Visual aids and gestures on TV not only allow the elimination of certain words, but require a unique script. The ideal radio delivery stresses pitch and intonation to make up for the absence of the visual. That flat, broken speech in "sidewalk interviews" is the speech of a person untrained in radio delivery.

The results of the examination showed that TV had won, followed by lecture, film, radio, and finally print. Eight months later the test was readministered to the bulk of the students who had taken it the first time. Again it was found that there were significant differences between the groups exposed to different media, and these differences were the same as those on the first test, save for the studio group, an uncertain group because of the chaos of the lecture conditions, which had moved from last to second place. Finally, two years later, the experiment was repeated, with major modifications, using students at Ryerson Institute. Marshall McLuhan reports:

> In this repeat performance, pains were taken to allow each medium full play of its possibilities with reference to the subject, just as in the earlier experiment each medium was neutralized as much as possible. Only the mimeograph form remained the same in each experiment. Here we added a printed form in which an imaginative typographical layout was followed. The lecturer used the blackboard and permitted discussion. Radio and TV employed dramatization, sound effects and graphics. In the examination, radio easily topped TV. Yet, as in the first experiment, both radio and TV manifested a decisive advantage over the lecture and written forms. As a conveyor both of ideas and information, TV was, in this second experiment, apparently enfeebled by the deployment of its dramatic resources, whereas radio benefited from such lavishness. "Technology is explicitness," writes Lyman Bryson. Are both radio

[6]Béla Balázs, *op. cit.*, pp. 35–36.

and TV more explicit than writing or lecture? Would a greater explicitness, if inherent in these media, account for the ease with
which they top other modes of performance?[7]

Announcement of the results of the first experiment evoked considerable interest. Advertising agencies circulated the results with the comment that here, at last, was scientific proof of the superiority of TV. This
was unfortunate and missed the main point, for the results didn't indicate the superiority of one medium over others. They merely directed
attention toward differences between them, differences so great as to be
of kind rather than degree. Some CBC officials were furious, not because
TV won, but because print lost.

The problem has been falsely seen as democracy *vs.* the mass media.
But the mass media *are* democracy. The book itself was the first mechanical mass medium. What is really being asked, of course, is: can books'
monopoly of knowledge survive the challenge of the new languages? The
answer is: no. What should be asked is: what can print do better than
any other medium and is that worth doing?

[7]From a personal communication to the author.

The most important thing to understand, I think, is that there is a fundamental limitation to our ability to understand.

The Language of Responsibility

WENDELL JOHNSON

In this highly personal yet broadly applicable account Wendell Johnson reflects on his own experience as one of the "handicapped" and draws on this insight to develop guidelines for "the language of responsibility." "This approach to problems," says Johnson, "amounts to a basic or general 'method of understanding.' It is nothing more nor less than a pattern of mature behavior that can be cultivated by anyone. It is more suitable in some situations than in others, but it is practically never wholly inappropriate or ineffective." I think Johnson is right and that what he says contains more truth and wisdom than a dozen scholarly papers replete with footnotes and lengthy bibliographies.

Since the night I stood here thirty years ago to receive my own Doctoral degree I have enjoyed a wonderful privilege. Along with millions of other people throughout the world, I shall always be deeply grateful to the University of Iowa for pioneering the scientific study of stuttering and other speech disorders. I came to Iowa as a stuttering Kansas farm boy as soon as my family heard of the research program that was being started here, and I arrived in 1926 just in time to serve as a subject in the first experiments to be undertaken in the new speech pathology laboratory. That turned out to be the beginning of a long apprenticeship as a "professional white rat," which led to my becoming a specialist in my own distress—and for me a happier choice of life work I cannot imagine.

I find it hard to believe that there could be anything more fascinating than the problem called stuttering. Caught up within it are practically all of the elements of life, swirled into an intriguing snarl as challenging as a tangled fish line: Working with this and related problems—or, rather, with persons involved in these problems—I have made some observations about people that I would like to share with you during the next few moments that we are to spend together.

What has impressed me most about people, as I have been privileged to know them, is their longing to be understood—and to be understanding. Almost everyone seems to mean well, nearly always. Stuttering to people for half a century has left me with the deep conviction that they are terribly kind. When they do not appear to mean well, to be kind and understanding, they have themselves, it seems to me, an aching need to be understood—and most especially they need the maturity and serenity that would enable them to be understanding of themselves.

Now, what I sense in working with people in the speech clinic is that as they "get better," as they learn and improve and show more understanding of themselves and of others, they seem to develop a more and more substantial sense of responsibility. One of my old teachers, the

From Wendell Johnson, "The Language of Responsibility," University of Iowa Extension Bulletin *(November 1, 1961).*

psychiatrist Dr. John Dorsey, once put it this way: he said that as a person grows up he progresses through three stages. First he says, "Please help me." Then he says, "I can take care of myself." Finally he says, "Please let me help you."

There is something, I think, extremely fundamental about the relationship between one's sense of responsibility and one's capacity for being understanding—and, especially, for feeling understood. This relationship has to do in a peculiarly crucial way, I feel, with what might be thought of as "the language of responsibility."

So—what does it mean to understand someone, and to be understood by some other person? You talk with your children. What does it mean to say that you understand what your child says to you, or that he understands what you say to him, or that there is understanding between the two of you? Working in a clinic trying to help people, I have had building up in me over the years a stronger and stronger feeling that we need much more understanding in the world. I've known ever so many mothers and fathers who feel, in some instances quite desperately, that they don't understand their children. Husbands and wives, children and parents, students and teachers often seem to be reaching toward each other across a great gulf. We don't understand the Russians, and they don't understand us. The rich people don't understand the poor people, and vice versa. "Labor" doesn't understand "Management" and something seems to have come between the scientists and the people who are not sure just what the scientists are up to. Well—why don't we understand each other more fully than we do?

One reason, of course, is that no two of us are exactly the same. For many years I have been trying to help students who want to go into speech pathology understand persons who have disorders of speech. To me there is a baffling fascination in trying to tell the students who speak normally how to be understanding of the stutterers in the speech clinic. I'm terribly impressed with how hard they try, and I am just as much impressed by the difficulty they seem to have in achieving what they can feel within themselves to be a good understanding of what it must be like to be a stutterer. And then I think of the kinds of persons I don't understand very well myself. Among them, of course, are the very students I have just been talking about. They speak normally, you see, and I must confess that although I feel I know what it is like to be a person who speaks "pretty much all right," because I think I speak quite fluently myself now most of the time, I simply do not know what it would be like to talk with absolutely no concern whatever about being able to get started and keep going. It is just as hard for a stutterer to understand what it is like to be a normal speaker as it is for a normal speaker to understand that a stutterer doesn't understand that.

I am sure each one of you can match this sort of experience in trying to get another person's point of view. Many a grandfather, who loves to tend his garden and walk now and then to the pond to fish or to the feed store to pass the time of day with his old cronies, shakes his head in bafflement when his grandson insists that he has to have a car—to drive to college and to Ft. Lauderdale, and to Los Angeles to visit his roommate, and a block to the drive-in to get a hamburger. Even I can remember when horses were, at least in our little Kansas valley, the most common means of transportation, and so I find it difficult to catch on to what my twelve-year-old friends are telling me these days about the urgency of traveling faster than the speed of sound.

Wrapped up in these words I've been saying is a kernel of conviction: The most important thing to understand, I think, is that there is a fundamental limitation to our ability to understand. The kindest people, the ones who are nicest to be around, are those who don't presume to understand completely our most intimate and personal feelings. In their lack of presumptuousness we sense the basic respect they feel for us. We all know how easy it is to get too wordy in trying to console a friend in sadness. Silence often says so much more than words ever could at such times, and what our silence acknowledges is in part, of course, the other person's inescapable aloneness.

The understanding we cannot give others we can hardly expect of them. I remember sitting one day in a hotel lobby somewhere with Earl Schenck Miers, one of the many great human beings I have come to know in the course of my work with so-called handicapped persons. He is a tall shaggy-headed fellow with steady brown eyes and unsteady movements, who accommodates himself with patience and dignity to the incoordinations of cerebral palsy. He is also a very fine editor and the author of several excellent books. We were talking with a man who was sitting in a wheelchair between us, a man whose legs had been amputated. With his head bobbing about a bit from the cerebral palsy, Earl Miers looked earnestly at the man in the wheelchair and said, "You know, you can't expect people to know just what to do when they first see you." And after a little while he went on to say, "What those of us," and he smiled, "those of us who are called handicapped have to learn to do is to put people at ease when we meet them. It is *our* responsibility to try to understand *them* as best we can."

Earl Miers was speaking to every one of us, not just those who are called, often rather unreflectively, "the handicapped." We can't realistically expect to be understood very completely by others who can't know from personal experience what it's like to be like we are. That's asking too much of people, and so it can only lead to disappointment.

Many of the people I see and come to know in the clinic have never come to terms with this limitation. They have never accepted themselves, because they have never accepted their own inescapable aloneness. Even when others understand them as well as they could be expected to, they still feel that they are not understood. They are tortured by what they can never say and by wanting to hear what no one else can ever say to them. There is a silent level of understanding or awareness. This is what you "feel in your bones." It is the knowing that is ache and throb and tingle. It is what you are left with after you've told someone else all you can about what you feel or know. And if you expect others to understand this, then you can only feel that you are not understood by them, and the reason is very simple: they cannot feel in your bones. And you cannot feel in theirs. There is a loneliness that is known by everyone. To understand this is, by so much, to know serenity.

To understand this is to be accepting of the irrevocable changes that come with growing up and with growing older—especially the changes in your children as they grow up, and in your parents as they grow older. We can in no way be more wise, it seems to me, than in our appreciation of the differences between youth and age. They may never be wholly understood, but they can be profoundly appreciated. You have come, by a ziggity zaggity path, to where you are tonight from the time when you almost always needed your parents, or someone else, to help you, and for your parents this is Commencement too, because more than ever before they face the need to understand that, with all your gratitude, you want now to take care of yourselves. But change, which is nearly all we can be sure of in this life, is hardly ever very neat, of course, and, for all our rituals and rites, most transitions take a long time, if indeed they are ever completed. So, while we are mostly wanting to take care of ourselves we do need help sometimes, and one of the most wonderful lessons we have to learn is that there are times when others help us most by letting us help them—and when we help others by letting them help us.

One of the very most important observations that I have been privileged to make of people is that they differ tremendously in "helpability." It seems to me that one of the most distinguishing marks of the mature person is that he seeks the criticism and the help he needs, and he appreciates them and uses them well. To be helped you must be helpable. To be taught you must be teachable. We help our children most of all, it seems to me, by teaching them to be helpable—and we do this best, as we do most teaching best, by personal example. You are most helpable, teachable, when you learn to listen well and face reality and talk clearly and responsibly about facts at hand. This means, too, of course, that you are most helpful to others when you listen well to them, in ways that encourage them to talk more earnestly about themselves and about other people and their relationships with them, and more realistically about the situations with which they are concerned.

When you listen to understand you listen without preconceptions. You listen without irritation or anger. You listen without strong prejudice. You keep your own need to be understood from coming between you and the other person you are trying to understand. You listen not to refute and not to persuade, but only to hear the speaker out, to understand just as well as you possibly can what he is trying to say. This sort of listening is extremely rare, of course. I believe deeply that the world would be better if there were more of it. The work I do in the clinic has left me, as I have said, with the profound conviction that we need much more understanding in the world, and I do not know of any more direct way to better understanding than that of better listening. The art of listening is the better part of the art of helping people in the sort of clinic with which I am familiar, and I know of no reason to doubt that it is the better part of helping people anywhere.

Incidentally, for a long while I have suspected that the best diets are to be found in hospitals and are eaten by the sick, the best teaching methods are to be found in special schools for the mentally retarded, and the best philosophies of living and principles of personal relationships are to be found in clinics for the distressed and maladjusted and in hospitals for the mentally ill. I think it is high time that these diets and teaching methods and these philosophies and principles of sane and effective living were made available to everybody. With all the good things to be had these days in hospitals, clinics, and rehabilitation centers, it is coming to be a positive disadvantage not to be sick, handicapped, or maladjusted. To be normal, to have nothing wrong with you, is to be neglected!

Seriously, we do have much to learn from what have come to be called the helping professions about being helpful to our children and to our parents, to those who work for us and those for whom we work, to those who are with us and those who are against us. By the helping professions I mean, besides my own field of speech pathology and audiology, the professions of medicine, clinical psychology and social work, nursing and rehabilitation, teaching and law, and all other counseling and professional services. In these helping professions—as, indeed, in the sciences also—it is so well known that it is taken for granted and seldom said that it is essential to examine the facts thoroughly, report them accurately, and to base recommendations and courses of action upon the findings objectively evaluated. That is essentially how you help people who come seeking help for problems of body or soul that they find distressful, and when you have reached the stage of maturity at which you not only want to take care of yourself but to help others, too, that is how you can be helpful to other people, whoever they may be and wherever you may find them. That is also how anyone else can best help you and how you can take care of yourself.

This approach to problems, which is so thoroughly taken for granted by most research scientists and clinical counselors, amounts to a basic or general "method of understanding." It is nothing more nor less than a pattern of mature behavior than can be cultivated by anyone. It is more suitable in some situations than in others, but it is practically never wholly inappropriate or ineffective. I observe it in the clinic as the way in which people behave more and more as they progress in dealing with their problems. And perhaps because I work in a clinic where speech and language problems are a major concern, I am particularly sensitive to the importance of the kind of language that goes with this "method of understanding."

People in distress or confusion have difficulty as a rule making clear to others, and to themselves as well, what their problems are. In part, this is because they use a vague language, speaking in generalities and, often for reasons that are deeply revealing, leaving out important details. Also, they have an essentially irresponsible way of mixing fact and opinion, of confusing "is" with "looks like," of talking about what might happen as though it most certainly would happen, or had already come to pass. Their statements tend to be too pat, to be about a world that is black and white, with none of the grays of which the wise and mature are so keenly aware. They do not always talk as though they recognize the necessity—or enjoy the discipline—of basing conclusions on good evidence. They are inclined to issue—and to accept—the verbal equivalents of bad checks. They do not understand themselves or their problems very well partly, at least, because they do not try very hard to find out what the crucial facts are. They do not talk clearly about the facts they do observe. They do not make good use of the information they have in trying to understand their problems and in figuring out what, if anything, to do about them.

As people become more mature they use language more and more responsibly to report accurately what they learn when they listen well and in all other ways observe carefully the facts that are of interest and concern to them. They demonstrate the language of responsibility in describing clearly and in detail what they themselves do and what others do that needs to be understood. They speak the language of who, when, where, what and then what, and of the various possible whys, the language of honest and full report and of disciplined explanation—of thoughtful understanding.

With the serenity that comes with self-acceptance, and the maturity reflected in the language of responsibility, you can feel prepared to meet the problems that lie ahead with a heartening capacity for understanding. You are able, then, to seek and make good use of the help you may need, but mostly you will be able to take care of yourself, when you are not helping others—to be more understanding and to feel understood.

You go, I realize all too well, into a future that promises to become increasingly bewildering because of the mounting problems of urbanization, automation, population, crime, delinquency, nationalism, war and destruction, nuclear energy, radioactive fallout, outer space, and all the other items in our expanding lexicon of tension and distress. You go, inevitably, to wrestle the problems of the world as well as your own perplexities. Which of these you will find the more enormous is not to be easily predicted. Your own personal problems will, I am quite sure, matter more to you from day to day and from moment to moment, and that is why I have talked with you as I have. And I have talked with you as I have because I agree with Confucius in the conviction that in order to govern the State wisely you must know first how to govern the family, and in order to do well by your family you must first be understanding of yourself.

LANGUAGE
AND THOUGHT

I see little reason to doubt that what is true of language is true of other forms of human knowledge as well.

Language and the Mind

NOAM CHOMSKY

Noam Chomsky's generative-transformational grammar has revolutionized the study of language. No one attempting to study language can ignore these insights. In this paper Chomsky explores in some depth the relationship between the nature of the human mind and language. In so doing Chomsky raises some provocative questions concerning perception, beliefs, memory, the acquisition of knowledge generally and of linguistic knowledge specifically, and also clarifies the nature of language as viewed in generative-transformational linguistics. This viewpoint seems to have been embraced by most researchers in communication, education, linguistics, psychology, sociology, and other fields and is used as a theoretical foundation for further language exploration and study.

How does the mind work? To answer this question we must look at some of the work performed by the mind. One of its main functions is the acquisition of knowledge. The two major factors in acquisition of knowledge, perception and learning, have been the subject of study and speculation for centuries. It would not, I think, be misleading to characterize the major positions that have developed as outgrowths of classical rationalism and empiricism. The rationalist theories are marked by the importance they assign to *intrinsic* structures in mental operations—to central processes and organizing principles in perception, and to innate ideas and principles in learning. The empiricist approach, in contrast, has stressed the role of experience and control by environmental factors.

The classical empiricist view is that sensory images are transmitted to the brain as impressions. They remain as ideas that will be associated in various ways, depending on the fortuitous character of experience. In this view a language is merely a collection of words, phrases, and sentences, a habit system, acquired accidentally and extrinsically. In the formulation of Williard Quine, knowledge of a language (and, in fact, knowledge in general) can be represented as "a fabric of sentences variously associated to one another and to nonverbal stimuli by the mechanism of conditioned response." Acquisition of knowledge is only a matter of the gradual construction of this fabric. When sensory experience is interpreted, the already established network may be activated in some fashion. In its essentials, this view has been predominant in modern behavioral science, and it has been accepted with little question by many philosophers as well.

The classical rationalist view is quite different. In this view the mind contains a system of "common notions" that enable it to interpret the scattered and incoherent data of sense in terms of objects and their relations, cause and effect, whole and part, symmetry, gestalt properties, functions, and so on. Sensation, providing only fleeting and meaningless images, is degenerate and particular. Knowledge, much of it beyond im-

Reprinted from Psychology Today *Magazine (February 1968),* 48, 50–51, 66–68. *Copyright © Communications/Research/Machines, Inc.*

mediate awareness, is rich in structure, involves universals, and is highly organized. The innate general principles that underlie and organize this knowledge, according to Leibniz, "enter into our thoughts, of which they form the soul and the connection . . . although we do not at all think of them."

This "active" rationalist view of the acquisition of knowledge persisted through the romantic period in its essentials. With respect to language, it achieves its most illuminating expression in the profound investigations of Wilhelm von Humboldt. His theory of speech perception supposes a generative system of rules that underlies speech production as well as its interpretation. The system is generative in that it makes infinite use of finite means. He regards a language as a structure of forms and concepts based on a system of rules that determine their interrelations, arrangement, and organization. But these finite materials can be combined to make a never-ending product.

In the rationalist and romantic tradition of linguistic theory, the normal use of language is regarded as characteristically innovative. We construct sentences that are entirely new to us. There is no substantive notion of "analogy" or "generalization" that accounts for this creative aspect of language use. It is equally erroneous to describe language as a "habit structure" or as a network of associated responses. The innovative element in normal use of language quickly exceeds the bounds of such marginal principles as analogy or generalization (under any substantive interpretation of these notions). It is important to emphasize this fact because the insight has been lost under the impact of the behaviorist assumptions that have dominated speculation and research in the twentieth century.

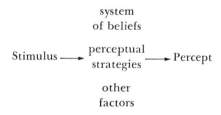

Figure 1. Model for perception. Each physical stimulus, after interpretation by the mental processes, will result in a percept.

In Humboldt's view, acquisition of language is largely a matter of maturation of an innate language capacity. The maturation is guided by internal factors, by an innate "form of language" that is sharpened, differentiated, and given its specific realization through experience. Language is thus a kind of latent structure in the human mind, developed and fixed by exposure to specific linguistic experience. Humboldt believes that all languages will be found to be very similar in their grammatical form, similar not on the surface but in their deeper inner structures. The innate organizing principles severely limit the class of possible languages, and these principles determine the properties of the language that is learned in the normal way.

The active and passive views of perception and learning have elaborated with varying degrees of clarity since the seventeenth century. These views can be confronted with empirical evidence in a variety of ways. Some recent work in psychology and neurophysiology is highly suggestive in this regard. There is evidence for the existence of central processes in perception, specifically for control over the functioning of sensory neurons by the brain-stem reticular system. Behavioral counterparts of this central control have been under investigation for several years. Furthermore, there is evidence for innate organization of the perceptual system of a highly specific sort at every level of biological organization. Studies of the visual system of the frog, the discovery of specialized cells responding to angle and motion in the lower cortical centers of cats and rabbits, and the somewhat comparable investigations of the auditory system of frogs—all are relevant to the classical questions of intrinsic structure mentioned earlier. These studies suggest that there are highly organized, innately determined perceptual systems that are adapted closely to the animal's "life space" and that provide the basis for what we might call "acquisition of knowledge." Also relevant are certain behavioral studies of human infants, for example those showing the preference for faces over other complex stimuli.

These and other studies make it reasonable to inquire into the possibility that complex intellectual structures are determined narrowly by innate mental organization. What is perceived may be determined by mental processes of considerable depth. As far as language learning is concerned, it seems to me that a rather convincing argument can be made for the view that certain principles intrinsic to the mind provide invariant structures that are a precondition for linguistic experience. In the course of this article I would like to sketch some of the ways such conclusions might be clarified and firmly established.

There are several ways linguistic evidence can be used to reveal properties of human perception and learning. In this section we consider one research strategy that might take us nearer to this goal.

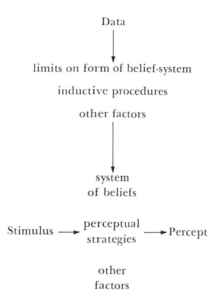

Figure 2. Model for learning. One's system of beliefs, a part of the perception model, is acquired from data as shown above.

Let us say that in interpreting a certain physical stimulus a person constructs a "percept." This percept represents some of his conclusions (in general, unconscious) about the stimulus. To the extent that we can characterize such percepts, we can go on to investigate the mechanisms that relate stimulus and percept. Imagine a model of perception that takes stimuli as inputs and arrives at percepts as "outputs." The model might contain a system of beliefs, strategies for interpreting stimuli, and other factors, such as the organization of memory. We would then have a perceptual model that might be represented graphically (see Figure 1, page 97).

Consider next the system of beliefs that is a component of the perceptual model. How was this acquired? To study this problem, we must investigate a second model, which takes certain data as input and gives as "output" (again, internally represented) the system of beliefs operating in the perceptual model. This second model, a model of learning, would have its own intrinsic structure, as did the first. This structure might consist of conditions on the nature of the system of beliefs that can be acquired, of innate inductive strategies, and again, of other factors such as the organization of memory (see Figure 2, above).

Under further conditions, which are interesting but not relevant here, we can take these perceptual and learning models as theories of the acquisition of knowledge, rather than of belief. How then would the models apply to language? The input stimulus to the perceptual model is a speech signal, and the percept is a representation of the utterance that the hearer takes the signal to be and of the interpretation he assigns to it. We can think of the percept as the structural description of a linguistic expression which contains certain phonetic, semantic, and syntactic information. Most interesting is the syntactic information, which best can be discussed by examining a few typical cases. The three sentences in the example seem to be the same syntactic structure (see Figure 3, page 101). Each contains the subject *I*, and the predicate of each consists of a verb (*told, expected, persuaded*), a noun phrase (*John*), and an embedded predicate phrase (*to leave*). This similarity is only superficial, however—a similarity in what we may call the "surface structure" of these sentences, which differ in important ways when we consider them with somewhat greater care.

The differences can be seen when the sentences are paraphrased or subjected to certain grammatical operations, such as the conversion from active to passive forms. For example, in normal conversation the sentence "I told John to leave" can be roughly paraphrased as "What I told John was to leave." But the other two sentences cannot be paraphrased as "What I persuaded John was to leave" or "What I expected John was to leave." Sentence 2 can be paraphrased as: "It was expected by me that John would leave." But the other two sentences cannot undergo a corresponding formal operation, yielding: "It was persuaded by me that John would leave" or "It was told by me that John should leave."

Sentences 2 and 3 differ more subtly. In Sentence 3 *John* is the direct object of *persuade*, but in Sentence 2 *John* is not the direct object of *expect*. We can show this by using these verbs in slightly more complex sentences: "I persuaded the doctor to examine John" and "I expected the doctor to examine John." If we replace the embedded proposition *the doctor to examine John* with its passive form *John to be examined by the doctor*, the change to the passive does not, in itself, change the meaning. We can accept as paraphrases "I expected the doctor to examine John" and " I expected John to be examined by the doctor." But we cannot accept as paraphrases "I persuaded the doctor to examine John" and "I persuaded John to be examined by the doctor."

The parts of these sentences differ in their grammatical functions. In "I persuaded John to leave" *John* is both the object of *persuade* and the subject of *leave*. These facts must be represented in the percept since they are known, intuitively, to the hearer of the speech signal. No special

(1)   I told John to leave
(2)   I expected John to leave
(3)   I persuaded John to leave

FIRST PARAPHRASE:

(1a)   What I told John was to leave (ACCEPTABLE)
(2a)   What I expected John was to leave (UNACCEPTABLE)
(3a)   What I persuaded John was to leave (UNACCEPTABLE)

SECOND PARAPHRASE:

(1b)   It was told by me that John would leave (UNACCEPTABLE)
(2b)   It was expected by me that John would leave (ACCEPTABLE)
(3b)   It was persuaded by me that John would leave (UNACCEPTABLE)
(4)   I expected the doctor to examine John
(5)   I persuaded the doctor to examine John

PASSIVE REPLACEMENT AS PARAPHRASE:

(4a)   I expected John to be examined by the doctor (MEANING RETAINED)
(5a)   I persuaded John to be examined by the doctor (MEANING CHANGED)

Figure 3. Superficial similarity. When the sentences above are paraphrased or are converted from active to passive forms, differences in their deep structure appear.

training or instruction is necessary to enable the native speaker to understand these examples, to know which are "wrong" and which "right," although they may all be quite new to him. They are interpreted by the native speaker instantaneously and uniformly, in accordance with structural principles that are known tacitly, intuitively, and unconsciously.

These examples illustrate two significant points. First, the surface structure of a sentence, its organization into various phrases, may not reveal or immediately reflect its deep syntactic structure. The deep structure is not represented directly in the form of the speech signal; it is abstract. Second, the rules that determine deep and surface structure and their interrelation in particular cases must themselves be highly abstract. They are surely remote from consciousness, and in all likelihood they cannot be brought to consciousness.

A study of such examples, examples characteristic of all human languages that have been carefully studied, constitutes the first stage of the linguistic investigation outlined above, namely the study of the percept. The percept contains phonetic and semantic information related through the medium of syntactic structure. There are two aspects to this syntactic structure. It consists of a surface directly related to the phonetic form, and a deep structure that underlies the semantic interpretation. The deep structure is represented in the mind and rarely is indicated directly in the physical signal.

A language, then, involves a set of semantic-phonetic percepts, of sound-meaning correlations, the correlations being determined by the kind of intervening syntactic structure just illustrated. The English language correlates sound and meaning in one way, Japanese in another, and so on. But the general properties of percepts, their forms and mechanisms, are remarkably similar for all languages that have been carefully studied.

Returning to our models of perception and learning, we can now take up the problem of formulating the system of beliefs that is a central component in perceptual processes. In the case of language, the "system of beliefs" would now be called the "generative grammar," the system of rules that specifies the sound-meaning correlation and generates the class of structural descriptions (percepts) that constitute the language in question. The generative grammar, then, represents the speaker-hearer's knowledge of his language. We can use the term *grammar of a language* ambiguously, as referring not only to the speaker's internalized, subconscious knowledge but to the professional linguist's representation of this internalized and intuitive system of rules as well.

How is this generative grammar acquired? Or, using our learning model, what is the internal structure of the device that could develop a generative grammar?

We can think of every normal human's internalized grammar as, in effect, a theory of his language. This theory provides a sound-meaning correlation for an infinite number of sentences. It provides an infinite set of structural descriptions; each contains a surface structure that determines phonetic form and a deep structure that determines semantic content.

In formal terms, then, we can describe the child's acquisition of language as a kind of theory construction. The child discovers the theory of his language with only small amounts of data from that language. Not only does his "theory of the language" have an enormous predictive scope, but it also enables the child to reject a great deal of the very data on which the theory has been constructed. Normal speech consists, in large part, of fragments, false starts, blends, and other distortions of the underlying idealized forms. Nevertheless, as is evident from a study of the mature use of language, what the child learns is the underlying ideal theory. This is a remarkable fact. We must also bear in mind that the child constructs this ideal theory without explicit instruction, that he acquires this knowledge at a time when he is not capable of complex intellectual achievements in many other domains, and that this achievement is relatively independent of intelligence or the particular course of experience. These are facts that a theory of learning must face.

A scientist who approaches phenomena of this sort without prejudice or dogma would conclude that the acquired knowledge must be determined in a rather specific way by intrinsic properties of mental organization. He would then set himself the task of discovering the innate ideas and principles that make such acquisition of knowledge possible.

It is unimaginable that a highly specific, abstract, and tightly organized language comes by accident into the mind of every four-year-old child. If there were not an innate restriction on the form of grammar, then the child could employ innumerable theories to account for his linguistic experience, and no one system, or even small class of systems, would be found exclusively acceptable or even preferable. The child could not possibly acquire knowledge of a language. This restriction on the form of grammar is a precondition for linguistic experience, and it is surely the critical factor in determining the course and result of language learning. The child cannot know at birth which language he is going to learn. But he must "know" that its grammar must be of a predetermined form that excludes many imaginable languages.

The child's task is to select the appropriate hypothesis from this restricted class. Having selected it, he can confirm his choice with the evidence further available to him. But neither the evidence nor any process of induction (in any well-defined sense) could in themselves have led to this choice. Once the hypothesis is sufficiently well confirmed, the child knows the language defined by this hypothesis; consequently, his knowledge extends vastly beyond his linguistic experience, and he can reject much of this experience as imperfect, as resulting from the interaction of many factors, only one of which is the ideal grammar that determines a sound-meaning connection for an infinite class of linguistic expressions. Along such lines as these one might outline a theory to explain the acquisition of language.

As has been pointed out, both the form and meaning of a sentence are determined by syntactic structures that are not represented directly in the signal and that are related to the signal only at a distance, through a long sequence of interpretive rules. This property of abstractness in grammatical structure is of primary importance, and it is on this property that our inferences about mental processes are based. Let us examine this abstractness a little more closely.

Not many years ago, the process of sentence interpretation might have been described approximately along the following lines. A speech signal is received and segmented into successive units (overlapping at the borders). These units are analyzed in terms of their invariant phonetic properties and assigned to "phonemes." The sequence of phonemes, so constructed, is then segmented into minimal grammatically functioning units (morphemes and words). These are again categorized. Successive operations of segmentation and classification will lead to what I have called "surface structure"—an analysis of a sentence into phrases, which can be represented as a proper bracketing of the sentence, with the bracketed units assigned to various categories (see Figure 4, page 105.) Each segment—phonetic, syntactic or semantic—would be identified in terms of certain invariant properties. This would be an exhaustive analysis of the structure of the sentence.

With such a conception of language structure, it made good sense to look forward hopefully to certain engineering applications of linguistics —for example, to voice-operated typewriters capable of segmenting an expression into its successive phonetic units and identifying these, so that speech could be converted to some form of phonetic writing in a mechanical way; to mechanical analysis of sentence structure by fairly straightforward and well-understood computational techniques; and perhaps even beyond to such projects as machine translation. But these hopes have by now been largely abandoned with the realization that this conception of grammatical structure is inadequate at every level, semantic, phonetic, and syntactic. Most important, at the level of syntactic organization, the surface structure indicates semantically significant relations only in extremely simple cases. In general, the deeper aspects of syntactic organization are representable by labeled bracketing, but of a very different sort from that seen in surface structure.

There is evidence of various sorts, both from phonetics and from experimental psychology, that labeled bracketing is an adequate representation of surface structure. It would go beyond the bounds of this paper to survey the phonetic evidence. A good deal of it is presented in a forthcoming book, *Sound Pattern of English*, by myself and Morris Halle. Similarly, very interesting experimental work by Jerry Fodor and his colleagues, based on earlier observations by D. E. Broadbent and Peter Ladefoged, has shown that the disruption of a speech signal (for example, by a superimposed click) tends to be perceived at the boundaries of phrases rather than at the point where the disruption actually occurred, and that in many cases the bracketing of surface structure can be read directly from the data on perceptual displacement. I think the evidence is rather good that labeled bracketing serves to represent the surface structure that is related to the perceived form of physical signals.

Deep structures are related to surface structures by a sequence of certain formal operations, operations now generally called "grammatical transformations." At the levels of sound, meaning, and syntax, the significant structural features of sentences are highly abstract. For this rea-

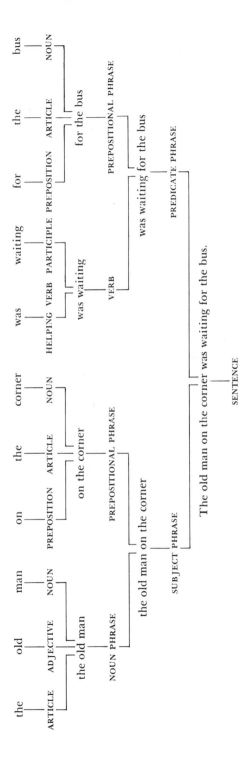

Figure 4. Surface structure analysis. A type of sentence analysis now abandoned as inadequate at every level is this labeled bracketing which analyzes the sentence by successive division into larger units with each unit assigned to its own category.

son they cannot be recovered by elementary data-processing techniques. This fact lies behind the search for central processes in speech perception and the search for intrinsic, innate structure as the basis for language learning.

How can we represent deep structure? To answer this question we must consider the grammatical transformations that link surface structure to the underlying deep structure that is not always apparent.

Consider, for example, the operations of passivization and interrogation. In the sentences (1) John was examined by the doctor, and (2) did the doctor examine John, both have a deep structure similar to the paraphrase of Sentence 1, (3) the doctor examined John. The same network of grammatical relations determines the semantic interpretation in each case. Thus two of the grammatical transformations of English must be the operations of passivization and interrogation that form such surface structures as Sentences 1 and 2 from a deeper structure which in its essentials also underlies Sentence 3. Since the transformations ultimately produce surface structures, they must produce labeled bracketings (see Figure 4, page 105). But notice that these operations can apply in sequence: we can form the passive question "was John examined by the doctor" by passivization followed by interrogation. Since the result of passivization is a labeled bracketing, it follows that the interrogative transformation operates on a labeled bracketing and forms a new labeled bracketing. Thus a transformation such as interrogation maps a labeled bracketing into a labeled bracketing.

By similar argument, we can show that all grammatical transformations are structure-dependent mappings of this sort and that the deep structures which underlie all sentences must themselves be labeled bracketings. Of course, the labeled bracketing that constitutes deep structure will in general be quite different from that representing the surface structure of a sentence. Our argument is somewhat oversimplified, but it is roughly correct. When made precise and fully accurate it strongly supports the view that deep structures, like surface structures, are formally to be taken as labeled bracketings, and that grammatical transformations are mappings of such structures onto other similar structures.

Recent studies have sought to explore the ways in which grammatical structure of the sort just described enters into mental operations. Much of this work has been based on a proposal formulated by George Miller as a first approximation, namely, that the amount of memory used to store a sentence should reflect the number of transformations used in deriving it. For example, H. B. Savin and E. Perchonock investigated this assumption in the following way: they presented to subjects a sentence followed by a sequence of unrelated words. They then determined the number of these unrelated words recalled when the subject attempted to repeat the sentence and the sequence of words. The more words re-called, the less memory used to store the sentence. The fewer words recalled, the more memory used to store the sentence. The results showed a remarkable correlation of amount of memory and number of transfor-mations in certain simple cases. In fact, in their experimental material, shorter sentences with more transformations took up more "space in memory" than longer sentences that involved fewer transformations.

Savin has extended this work and has shown that the effects of deep structure and surface structure can be differentiated by a similar tech-nique. He considered paired sentences with approximately the same deep structure but with one of the pair being more complex in surface struc-ture. He showed that, under the experimental conditions just described, the paired sentences were indistinguishable. But if the sequence of unre-lated words precedes, rather than follows, the sentence being tested, then the more complex (in surface structure) of the pair is more difficult to repeat correctly than the simpler member. Savin's very plausible infer-ence is that sentences are coded in memory in terms of deep structure. When the unrelated words precede the test sentence, these words use up a certain amount of short-term memory, and the sentence that is more complex in surface structure cannot be analyzed with the amount of memory remaining. But if the test sentence precedes the unrelated words, it is, once understood, stored in terms of deep structure, which is about the same in both cases. Therefore the same amount of memory remains, in the paired cases, for recall of the following words. This is a beautiful example of the way creative experimental studies can interweave with theoretical work in the study of language and of mental processes.

In speaking of mental processes we have returned to our original problem. We can now see why it is reasonable to maintain that the lin-guistic evidence supports an "active" theory of acquisition of knowledge. The study of sentences and of speech perception, it seems to me, leads to a perceptual theory of a classical rationalist sort. Representative of this school, among others, were the seventeenth-century Cambridge Platon-ists, who developed the idea that our perception is guided by notions that originate from the mind and that provide the framework for the interpretation of sensory stimuli. It is not sufficient to suggest that this framework is a store of "neural models" or "schemata" which are in some manner applied to perception (as is postulated in some current theories of perception). We must go well beyond this assumption and return to the view of Wilhelm von Humboldt, who attributed to the mind a system of rules that generates such models and schemata under the stimulation of the senses. The system of rules itself determines the content of the percept that is formed.

We can offer more than this vague and metaphoric account. A generative grammar and an associated theory of speech perception provide a concrete example of the rules that operate and of the mental objects that they construct and manipulate. Physiology cannot yet explain the physical mechanisms that affect these abstract functions. But neither physiology nor psychology provides evidence that calls this account into question or that suggests an alternative. As mentioned earlier, the most exciting current work in the physiology of perception shows that even the peripheral systems analyze stimuli into the complex properties of objects, and that central processes may significantly affect the information transmitted by the receptor organs.

The study of language, it seems to me, offers strong empirical evidence that empiricist theories of learning are quite inadequate. Serious efforts have been made in recent years to develop principles of induction, generalization, and data analysis that would account for knowledge of a language. These efforts have been a total failure. The methods and principles fail not for any superficial reason such as lack of time or data. They fail because they are intrinsically incapable of giving rise to the system of rules that underlies the normal use of language. What evidence is now available supports the view that all human languages share deep-seated properties of organization and structure. These properties—these linguistic universals—can be plausibly assumed to be an innate mental endowment rather than the result of learning. If this is true, then the study of language sheds light on certain long-standing issues in the theory of knowledge. Once again, I see little reason to doubt that what is true of language is true of other forms of human knowledge as well.

There is one further question that might be raised at this point. How does the human mind come to have the innate properties that underlie acquisition of knowledge? Here linguistic evidence obviously provides no information at all. The process by which the human mind has achieved its present state of complexity and its particular form of innate organization are a complete mystery, as much of a mystery as the analogous questions that can be asked about the processes leading to the physical and mental organization of any other complex organism. It is perfectly safe to attribute this to evolution, so long as we bear in mind that there is no substance to this assertion—it amounts to nothing more than the belief that there is surely some naturalistic explanation for these phenomena.

There are, however, important aspects of the problem of language and mind that can be studied sensibly within the limitations of present understanding and technique. I think that, for the moment, the most productive investigations are those dealing with the nature of particular grammars and with the universal conditions met by all human languages. I have tried to suggest how one can move, in successive steps of increasing abstractness, from the study of percepts to the study of grammar and perceptual mechanisms, and from the study of grammar to the study of universal grammar and the mechanisms of learning.

In this area of convergence of linguistics, psychology, and philosophy, we can look forward to much exciting work in coming years.

*Recent studies suggest that the process
of learning a language rests more
heavily on other factors than on the
child's ability to imitate, or on parents'
corrections, expansions, or reinforcements of their children's speech.
While these are relevant to the child's
learning, other parts of the process
seem more crucial.*

Learning the Language

URSULA BELLUGI

The question of how the child acquires the ability to
produce and understand an infinite number of sentences
by the time he is, say, four years old is certainly not an easy
question to answer. Nor is it a question for which we now
have a very satisfactory answer. Yet, we do know a great
deal about language generally and about language
acquisition and development specifically. Much of the
insight that we do have has been a direct result of the
research conducted by Ursula Bellugi and her colleagues
on which she reports in this paper. In reporting this
research Bellugi provides us with additional insight into
the nature and structure of language as well as insight into
the mechanism which may account for the child's eventual
mastery of language.

Recent studies suggest that the process of learning a language rests more heavily on other factors than on the child's ability to imitate, or on parents' corrections, expansions or reinforcements of their children's speech. While these are relevant to the child's learning, other parts of the process seem more crucial.

There is evidence that the child discovers quite abstract regularities, analyzes at progressively deeper levels the sentences he hears, and reproduces the results of this analysis in his own speech. From the time he first puts words together, a child's sentences reflect some grammatical regularities and show striking differences from the adult system.

It may not be obvious that, except for a few routine remarks, most sentences we hear and utter are unique. We understand them because we know the rules of combination that make up the syntax of a language. Consider the sentences in this magazine. Although they are easy to understand, probably only a few are *exact* repetitions of sentences you have seen or heard before. It is our knowledge of the rules of combination—the syntax of the language—that governs how we construct and understand an infinite number of sentences from a finite vocabulary. Syntax gives language its power.

ADAM & EVE & SARAH

It is not surprising then, that in the last 10 years researchers have been particularly interested in the child's learning of syntax. During this time, Roger Brown, Colin Fraser and I studied the speech development of three children, Sarah, Adam and Eve. At the start of our study Adam and Sarah were 27 months old, and Eve was 18 months old. We followed Adam and Sarah until they were five years old, but worked with Eve only nine months, after which she moved away. We selected these chil-

Reprinted from Psychology Today *Magazine (December 1970),* pp. 33–35, 66. *Copyright* © *Communications/Research/Machines, Inc.*

dren because they were just beginning to combine words into two-word utterances. We visited Adam and Eve at two- or three-week intervals, spending two hours with each. We visited Sarah every week for a half-hour. During these visits we recorded everything said by and to each child.

Between visits we met in a research seminar to discuss the children's development and to plan small experiments. At one point Adam sometimes pluralized nouns and sometimes not. So on the next visit, we asked, "Adam, which is right, 'two shoes' or 'two shoe'?" His answer, produced with enthusiasm, was "Pop go the weasel!" So much for the two-year-old child as a model informant. We had to devise games and tests to lead him to display his knowledge of language less directly.

Because children cannot tell us the rules they use, we must infer their knowledge of the rules from *indirect* evidence. Children occasionally correct their own speech, thereby displaying their knowledge of the rules ("I seed it in the mirror . . . I saw it").

WHAT HE WANTED?

The richest information so far comes from the children themselves, from the sentences they use at various periods. To discover children's knowledge of regularities, researchers look at patterns of evidence in large samples of children's speech—sets of well-formed utterances, types of omissions, and, most important, sets of utterances the children produce that they probably have not heard. Many constructions in child language are strikingly and characteristically different from the language adults use to children. If you listen carefully to three- and four-year-olds, you may hear sentences like, *Do she don't need that one? Why I can't have it? Why turtles crawled? Where the other Joe will drive? What he wanted?*

A conversation we recorded when Eve was 24 months old shows interesting differences of speech between her and her mother. Certain elements are characteristically and systematically missing from the child's speech—most significantly the auxiliary verbs *may, is, are, am, will, can.*

Eve: *Have that?*
Mother: *No, you may not have it.*
Eve: *Mom, where my tapioca?*
Mother: *It's getting cool. You'll have it in just a minute.*
Eve: *Let me have it.*
Mother: *Would you like to have your lunch right now?*
Eve: *Yeah. My tapioca cool?*
Mother: *Yes, it's cool.*

Eve: *You gonna watch me eat my lunch?*
Mother: *Yeah, I'm gonna watch you eat your lunch.*
Eve: *I eating it.*
Mother: *I know you are.*
Eve: *It time Sarah take a nap.*
Mother: *It's time for Sarah to have some milk, yeah. And then she's gonna take a nap and you're gonna take a nap.*
Eve: *And you?*
Mother: *And me too, yeah.*

WILL

Although both Eve and her mother used declarative sentences, requests, negatives and questions, Eve's sentences omit, among other things, the auxiliary verbs. Just three months later Eve's speech showed a marked change. Within a short time she was using auxiliary verbs in many places where the language required them (*can, will, are, won't, is, did, could, don't, can't*).

Mother: *Come and sit over here.*
Eve: *You can sit down by me. That will make me happy. Ready to turn it.*
Mother: *We're not quite ready to turn the page.*
Eve: *Yep, we are.*
Mother: *Shut the door, we won't hear her then.*
Eve: *Then Fraser won't hear her too. Where he's going? Did you make a great big hole there?*
Mother: *Yes, we made a great big hole in here; we have to get a new one.*
Eve: *Could I get some other piece of paper?*
Mother: *You ask Fraser.*
Eve: *Could I use this one?*
Mother: *I suppose so.*
Eve: *Is Fraser goin' take his pencil home when he goes?*
Mother: *Yes, he is.*
Eve: *Then we don't see him.*
Mother: *Nope, probably not. He'll share the paper with you while he's here.*
Eve: *I will write right here. I will put my pencil right here.*
Mother: *Okay, you do that.*
Eve: *Now let me draw you a lady. I can't. I not know . . . make one.*
Mother: *You don't know how to make one? You look at Fraser's lady and see if you can make one.*
Eve: *I can't. I think I have tear one and I think I can write one.*

This radical change in Eve's language indicates that she had learned many of the English rules for handling auxiliary verbs—but that she had learned them implicitly. Like most of us, Eve would not be able to tell us the rules she knows or uses. During this period her mother used a number of sentences with the auxiliary *will* in talking to her:

> *I'll have to buy a new dishpan.*
> *We'll get it later.*
> *You'll ruin it.*
> *That'll be enough.*
> *Yes, and he'll kick you.*
> *It'll be a little one.*

In each case the mother contracted the auxiliary *will* with the subject pronoun.

But the child produced the full form of *will* in her declarative sentences during this period:

> *I will stand on my knees.*
> *We will buy Becky a new one.*
> *You will gone away.*
> *It will work on here, see?*
> *I will read you book.*

The mother, of course, used the full form of *will* in questions (*Will it be fun?*). In Adam, Eve and Sarah the developments were precisely the same, although at different ages: the mother said *I'll get it*, but the child said *I will get it*. The child's sentences seem more filled-in than the mother's—a switch on what we might expect. The child is clearly not imitating or copying her mother's sentences. The sentences she uses suggest that she has analyzed the underlying *will* in her mother's contracted forms.

GRASP

A child's responses often mislead parents into thinking that he understands most of the language they address to him. The fact is that they usually speak to him in a context that is rich with cues that help him understand what they mean. A mother may say to her small child, *Go over to that chair and bring me my knitting.* The child obeys, but he may have understood only the word *knitting*, and perhaps the word *chair.* The mother may have looked in the direction of the chair on which the knitting lay; she may even have pointed to it and held out her hand.

To test the child's grasp of some grammatical rule, we must eliminate all such cues and construct test sentences carefully. We must set up a situation in which the child can perform correctly *only* if he understands the difference between two sentences that differ only in some minimal grammatical aspect.

Children hear many sentences that contain three basic elements—an actor, an action and the object of that action (simple declarative sentences).

Sarah is eating lunch.

John broke the truck.

In the last sentence there is an actor, *John*, an action, *broke*, and an object of the action, *the truck*. The relation of these (i.e., who does what to whom) is expressed by word order. Rearranging the nouns in these sentences produces strange results:

The truck broke John.

Lunch is eating Sarah.

But we can construct sentences in which both nouns are either animate or inanimate. These are reversible active sentences, such as *The boy feeds the girl* and *The girl feeds the boy.*

WHO WASHES WHOM

Brown, Fraser and I developed some pairs of pictures that test the child's understanding of some grammatical constructs. In one of these tests the child must point to the picture that illustrates the sentence he hears. Another form of the test uses objects instead of pictures. We set toys before the child and asked him to act out *The cat chases the dog* and *The dog chases the cat.* Children of about three perform rather well on these tests with simple declarative sentences.

Not all English sentences have the actor before the verb and the object of the action following the verb. In so-called passive sentences these relations are systematically reversed. Compare: *John broke the truck* and *The truck was broken by John.* These two sentences mean the same but the order of major elements is different. We can test the child's understanding of passive constructions by imposing the same constraints we used before. This time two pictures illustrate the sentences *The boy is washed by the girl* and *The girl is washed by the boy.* In preliminary testing, three-year-old children seldom pointed to the picture described by the sentence they heard. The most common error was to point to the wrong picture each time. Perhaps young children process these passive sentences as if they were active sentences with extra uninterpretable parts. It is not just a matter of understanding the meaning of the main words (*boy, wash, girl*), but how they are related by grammatical rules. Children's systematic errors can provide rich information about their language processing.

DADDY GOED

In most cases English verbs change in form from present tense to simple past tense: *teach, taught.* Although a few English verbs retain their form when tense is changed from present to past (*hit, hit*), most take on a tense marker, usually written *-ed: walk, walked; push, pushed.* Many of the most common verbs, however, form their past tenses irregularly: *go, went; come, came; break, broke; hold, held.* Some children learn a number of these irregular forms early as separate vocabulary items and use them correctly. *He came yesterday. It broke. Daddy went out. I fell.* Later, when the child acquires the rule for forming past tenses, the irregular forms that he has produced correctly may disappear for a period and be replaced by overgeneralized forms. The child now may say: *He comed yesterday. It breaked. Daddy goed out. I falled.*

Clearly, children have not heard these forms from adults but have built them on patterns of regular speech they hear. A change from *went* to *goed* may not be evidence that the child is regressing; on the contrary, it might indicate that the child has discovered a regular pattern in language and is using it in his own speech.

During periods of overregularization, the child's speech may be remarkably impervious to gentle efforts at correction. Jean Berko Gleason reported the conversation at the beginning of this article in which the child telling about a rabbit clings stubbornly to *holded* as the past tense of *hold.*

WUGS

We see the same pattern of overregularization when the child discovers the rules for singular and plural nouns. English shows plural in several ways. The regular written plural ending is, of course, a final *-s* (or *-es*). A modifier may indicate plurality: *many spoons* or *several books.* There are also irregular plurals in English, many of them quite common: *foot, feet; mouse, mice; man, men; deer, deer; child, children;*

tooth, teeth. The irregular forms, like the irregular verb forms, must be learned as separate items.

If someone were to say, "Point to the sheep," it would be as correct to point to one as to many. In English, linguistic context need not indicate whether a singular or plural noun is involved. Researchers have used this flexibility in constructing tests of children's knowledge of rules for forming plurals from singular nouns.

We show a child an object or picture that has no common name. The tester names these objects with monosyllables that are possible combinations of sounds but are not English words. He gives one object to the child and says, *Here is a wug*. Then he puts another next to it and says, *Now there is another wug. There are two* _____. The child obligingly fills in the nonexistent but regular item *wugs*.

As he did with verbs, the child who has been using some irregular noun forms correctly (*feet, mice, men*) may, for a time, overgeneralize his newly discovered rules of plural formation and say *foots, mouses, mans* —or sometimes even *feets, mices, mens*.

ADAM WINNED

We have given some evidence with simple problems to support the claim that children do not copy precisely what they hear but instead construct sentences according to rules of their own that they have extracted from the language around them. We can see this even more clearly in children's acquisition of a late-appearing, complex set of grammatical rules, tag questions.

Tag questions are often thought of as requests for a statement's confirmation.

You'll finish your lunch, *won't you?*
She's here, *isn't she?*
John broke it, *didn't he?*
This can't fall off here, *can it?*

Notice that the tag is different in each question (*won't you? isn't she? didn't he? can it?*). Tag questions are particularly interesting to researchers because the form of the tag is explicitly determined by the syntax of the statement it follows. We can put into words the grammatical processes that are aspects of tag-question formation. They involve copying or supplying a pronoun for the subject of a sentence; copying the auxiliary verb (or some form of *do*); negating the auxiliary verb in an affirmative sentence and vice versa; and inverting the order of the pronoun and auxiliary verb. When Adam was four and a half, he produced a great variety of tag questions. The examples here are from Adam's speech to illustrate the grammatical rules we use in forming tag questions. Adam had to select the correct pronoun that matched the subject of each sentence:

> *The man's* not bad, is *he?*
> *Me and Jim* are working, aren't *we?*
> *Susie* is my sister, isn't *she?*
> *The puzzle* is finished, isn't *it?*

He had to copy the auxiliary verb in the sentence or supply a form of *do*:

> He *was* scared, *was*n't he?
> It's tricking you, *is*n't it?
> He *can* say Adam, *can*'t he?
> Adam winned, *did*n't he?

Now we have four people, *don't* we? Adam had to learn to change the auxiliary verb to the negative form in affirmative sentences and to the positive form in negative sentences:

> I *can* hold on like a monkey, *can't* I?
> He *can't* beat me down, *can* he?

Adam inverted the order of the auxiliary verb and the subject pronoun:

> *He did*n't know, *did he?*

NO PUT

The grammatical processes that form tag questions are complex and rest on basic operations of English: the rules for changing nouns to pronouns, for making assertions, negating and questioning.

How does the child learn to produce tag questions correctly? Children produce many sentences with tags that they have not heard before. The evidence suggests again that they derive the rules from the speech they hear. Sometimes they even supply logical missing forms like *I'm magic, amn't I?*

Tag questions appear rather late in the speech of children who have been studied, but apparently the reason is not just that such sentences are long. Before he was four, Adam said many sentences that were longer than some of his tag-question sentences. Since a number of grammatical processes are combined in forming tag questions, we might look for evidence that the child learns the separate aspects before this period.

For example, a number of intermediate steps—not always resembling the sentences of adult English—precede a child's learning of the rules for negation. Adam when he was 28 months said:

No put glove.
No go back.
Take it, no.
This a radiator, no.

At around 35 months Adam said sentences like these:

You not have one.
He not have hair.
That one not bump that one, no.

Around three months later the child had mastered the rules for simple negation. This occurred at the same time that he began to use auxiliary verbs in affirmative statements and questions.

It's not big enough.
I don't like this one.
This won't work.
I didn't get in the way.
This can't fit.

RULES

If we traced each of the grammatical processes involved in forming tags, we would find that there are rudimentary forms—often different from those the children hear—that are gradually replaced as the child discovers other aspects of the underlying rule system, but we would also find that children master all the basic processes before they go on to the more complicated step of combining these to form tag questions.

From the time they begin to make two-word sentences, children are systematic, regular and productive in their language. The child can analyze regularities in the language, segment novel utterances into their component parts, and invent new combinations at all levels. Children seem to develop rules of maximal generality, often applying them too broadly at first and only later learning the proper restrictions on them. Children develop an implicit knowledge of language structure; they do not need to be taught the rules for making sentences any more than they need to be taught the rules for recognizing the same object under different lights and in different positions.

Although the samples of language we have studied have been from few children and from few languages, the samples show remarkably similar orders of development among children and across languages. It may be, that all languages of the world share certain structural features and that these features develop as a result of relational abilities built into the human brain. Perhaps there are fixed, species-wide processes of information analysis that are released in a relatively fixed order when the growing child encounters any materials having the universal properties of language.

It is the 'plainest' English which contains the greatest number of unconscious assumptions about nature.

Languages and Logic

BENJAMIN LEE WHORF

The central question which Benjamin Lee Whorf raises in this essay is the extent to which a particular language structures the experiences of its speakers. Languages differ, for example, in their vocabularies and in their rules for combining words into sentences and, according to Whorf, these differences have cognitive and behavioral implications. Specifically, "we cut up and organize the spread and flow of events as we do, largely because, through our mother tongue, we are parties to an agreement to do so, not because nature itself is segmented in exactly that way for all to see." According to this Whorfian thesis, speakers of widely differing languages not only speak about the world in different terms but actually experience the world in different ways.

In English, the sentences 'I pull the branch aside' and 'I have an extra toe on my foot' have little similarity. Leaving out the subject pronoun and the sign of the present tense, which are common features from requirements of English syntax, we may say that no similarity exists. Common, and even scientific, parlance would say that the sentences are unlike because they are talking about things which are intrinsically unlike. So Mr. Everyman, the natural logician, would be inclined to argue. Formal logic of an older type would perhaps agree with him.

If, moreover, we appeal to an impartial scientific English-speaking observer, asking him to make direct observations upon cases of the two phenomena to see if they may not have some element of similarity which we have overlooked, he will be more than likely to confirm the dicta of Mr. Everyman and the logician. The observer whom we have asked to make the test may not see quite eye to eye with the old-school logician and would not be disappointed to find him wrong. Still he is compelled sadly to confess failure. "I wish I could oblige you," he says, "but try as I may, I cannot detect any similarity between these phenomena."

By this time our stubborn streak is aroused; we wonder if a being from Mars would also see no resemblance. But now a linguist points out that it is not necessary to go as far as Mars. We have not yet scouted around this earth to see if its many languages all classify these phenomena as disparately as our speech does. We find that in Shawnee these two statements are, respectively, *ni-l'θawa-'ko-n-a* and *ni-l'θawa-'ko-θite* (the θ here denotes *th* as in 'thin' and the apostrophe denotes a breath-catch). The sentences are closely similar; in fact, they differ only at the tail end. In Shawnee, moreover, the beginning of a construction is generally the important and emphatic part. Both sentences start with *ni-* ('I'), which is a mere prefix. Then comes the really important key word, *l'θawa*, a common Shawnee term, denoting a forked outline, like Figure 1, no. 1. The next element, -'ko, we cannot be sure of, but it agrees

Reprinted from Language, Thought, and Reality *by B. L. Whorf, pp. 233–245, by permission of the MIT Press. Copyright © 1956 by the Massachusetts Institute of Technology.*

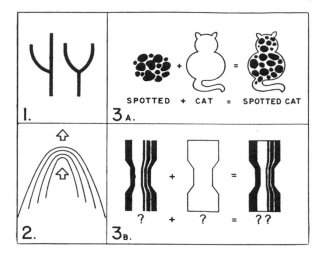

Figure 1. Suggested above are certain linguistic concepts which, as explained in the text, are not easily definable.

in form with a variant of the suffix *-a'kw* or *-a'ko*, denoting tree, bush, tree part, branch, or anything of that general shape. In the first sentence, *-n-* means 'by hand action' and may be either a causation of the basic condition (forked outline) manually, an increase of it, or both. The final *-a* means that the subject ('I') does this action to an appropriate object. Hence the first sentence means 'I pull it (something like branch of tree) more open or apart where it forks.' In the other sentence, the suffix *-θite* means 'pertaining to the toes,' and the absence of further suffixes means that the subject manifests the condition in his own person. Therefore the sentence can mean only 'I have an extra toe forking out like a branch from a normal toe.'

Shawnee logicians and observers would class the two phenomena as intrinsically similar. Our own observer, to whom we tell all this, focuses his instruments again upon the two phenomena and to his joy sees at once a manifest resemblance. Figure 2 illustrates a similar situation: 'I push his head back' and 'I drop it in water and it floats,' though very dissimilar sentences in English, are similar in Shawnee. The point of view of linguistic relativity changes Mr. Everyman's dictum: Instead of saying, "Sentences are unlike because they tell about unlike facts," he now reasons: "Facts are unlike to speakers whose language background provides for unlike formulation of them."

Conversely, the English sentences, "The boat is grounded on the beach' and 'The boat is manned by picked men,' seem to us to be rather

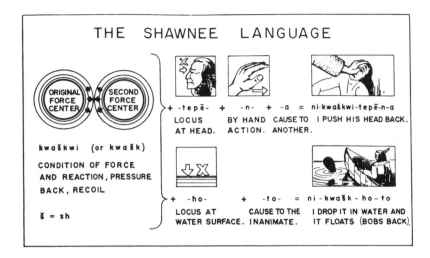

Figure 2. The English sentences 'I push his head back' and 'I drop it in water and it floats' are unlike. But in Shawnee the corresponding statements are closely similar, emphasizing the fact that analysis of nature and classification of events as like or in the same category (logic) are governed by grammar.

similar. Each is about a boat; each tells the relation of the boat to other objects—or that's OUR story. The linguist would point out the parallelism in grammatical pattern thus: "The boat is xed preposition y." The logician might turn the linguist's analysis into "A is in the state x in relation to y," and then perhaps into $fA = xRy$. Such symbolic methods lead to fruitful techniques of rational ordering, stimulate our thinking, and bring valuable insight. Yet we should realize that the similarities and contrasts in the original sentences, subsumed under the foregoing formula, are dependent on the choice of mother tongue and that the properties of the tongue are eventually reflected as peculiarities of structure in the fabric of logic or mathematics which we rear.

In the Nootka language of Vancouver Island, the first "boat" statement is *tlih-is-ma*; the second, *lash-tskwiq-ista-ma*. The first is thus I-II-*ma*; the second, III-IV-V-*ma*; and they are quite unlike, for the final -*ma* is only the sign of the third-person indicative. Neither sentence contains any unit of meaning akin to our word 'boat' or even 'canoe.' Part I, in the first sentence, means 'moving pointwise,' or moving in a way like the suggestion of the outline in Fig. 1, no. 2; hence 'traveling in or as a canoe,' or an event like one position of such motion. It is not a name for what we should call a "thing," but is more like a vector in physics. Part II means 'on the beach'; hence I-II-*ma* means 'it is on the beach pointwise as an event of canoe motion,' and would normally refer to a boat that has come to land. In the other sentence, part III means 'select, pick,' and IV means 'remainder, result,' so that III-IV means 'selected.' Part V means 'in a canoe (boat) as crew.' The whole, III-IV-V-*ma*, means either 'they are in the boat as a crew of picked men' or 'the boat has a crew of picked men.' It means that the whole event involving picked ones and boat's crew is in process.

As a hang-over from my education in chemical engineering, I relish an occasional chemical simile. Perhaps readers will catch what I mean when I say that the way the constituents are put together in these sentences of Shawnee and Nootka suggests a chemical compound, whereas their combination in English is more like a mechanical mixture. A mixture, like the mountaineer's potlicker, can be assembled out of almost anything and does not make any sweeping transformation of the overt appearance of the material. A chemical compound, on the other hand, can be put together only out of mutually suited ingredients, and the result may be not merely soup but a crop of crystals or a cloud of smoke. Likewise the typical Shawnee or Nootka combinations appear to work with a vocabulary of terms chosen with a view not so much to the utility of their immediate references as to the ability of the terms to combine suggestively with each other in manifold ways that elicit novel and useful images. This principle of terminology and way of analyzing events would seem to be unknown to the tongues with which we are familiar.

It is the analysis of nature down to a basic vocabulary capable of this sort of evocative recombination which is most distinctive of polysynthetic languages, like Nootka and Shawnee. Their characteristic quality is not, as some linguists have thought, a matter of the tightness or indissolubility of the combinations. The Shawnee term *l'θawa* could probably be said alone but would then mean 'it (or something) is forked,' a statement which gives little hint of the novel meanings that arise out of its combinations—at least to our minds or our type of logic. Shawnee and Nootka do not use the chemical type of synthesis exclusively. They make large use of a more external kind of syntax, which, however, has no basic structural priority. Even our own Indo-European tongues are not wholly devoid of the chemical method, but they seldom make sentences by it, afford little inkling of its possibilities, and give structural priority to another method. It was quite natural, then, that Aristotle should found our traditional logic wholly on this other method.

Let me make another analogy, not with chemistry but with art—art of the pictorial sort. We look at a good still-life painting and seem to see a lustrous porcelain bowl and a downy peach. Yet an analysis that screened out the totality of the picture—as if we were to go over it carefully, looking through a hole cut in a card—would reveal only oddly shaped patches of paint and would not evoke the bowl and fruit. The synthesis presented by the painting is perhaps akin to the chemical type of syntax, and it may point to psychological fundamentals that enter into both art and language. Now the mechanical method in art and language might be typified by no. 3A in Fig. 1. The first element, a field of spots, corresponds to the adjective 'spotted,' the second corresponds to the noun 'cat.' By putting them together, we get 'spotted cat.' Contrast the technique in Fig. 1, no. 3B. Here the figure corresponding to 'cat' has only vague meaning by itself—"chevron-like," we might say—while the first element is even vaguer. But, combined, these evoke a cylindrical object, like a shaft casting.

The thing common to both techniques is a systematic synthetic use of pattern, and this is also common to all language techniques. I have put question marks below the elements in Fig. 1, no. 3B, to point out the difficulty of a parallel in English speech and the fact that the method probably has no standing in traditional logic. Yet examination of other languages and the possibility of new types of logic that has been advanced by modern logicians themselves suggest that this matter may be significant for modern science. New types of logic may help us eventually to understand how it is that electrons, the velocity of light, and other components of the subject matter of physics appear to behave illogically, or that phenomena which flout the sturdy common sense of yesteryear can nevertheless be true. Modern thinkers have long since pointed out that the so-called mechanistic way of thinking has come to an impasse before the great frontier problems of science. To rid ourselves of this way of thinking is exceedingly difficult when we have no linguistic experience of any other and when even our most advanced logicians and mathematicians do not provide any other—and obviously they cannot without the linguistic experience. For the mechanistic way of thinking is perhaps just a type of syntax natural to Mr. Everyman's daily use of the western Indo-European languages, rigidified and intensified by Aristotle and the latter's medieval and modern followers.

As I said in an article, "Science and linguistics," in the *Review* for April 1940, the effortlessness of speech and the subconscious way we picked up that activity in early childhood lead us to regard talking and thinking as wholly straightforward and transparent. We naturally feel that they embody self-evident laws of thought, the same for all men. We know all the answers! But, when scrutinized, they become dusty answers. We use speech for reaching agreements about subject matter: I say, "Please shut the door," and my hearer and I agree that 'the door' refers to a certain part of our environment and that I want a certain result produced. Our explanations of how we reached this understanding, though quite satisfactory on the everyday social plane, are merely more agreements (statements) about the same subject matter (door, and so on), more and more amplified by statements about the social and personal needs that impel us to communicate. There are here no laws of thought. Yet the structural regularities of our sentences enable us to sense that laws are SOMEWHERE in the background. Clearly, explanations of understanding such as "And so I ups and says to him, says I; see here, why don't you . . . !" evade the true process by which 'he' and 'I' are in communication. Likewise psychological-social descriptions of the social and emotional needs that impel people to communicate with their fellows tend to be learned versions of the same method and, while interesting, still evade the question. In similar case is evasion of the question by skipping from the speech sentence, via physiology and "stimuli" to the social situation.

The WHY of understanding may remain for a long time mysterious; but the HOW or logic of understanding—its background of laws or regularities—is discoverable. It is the grammatical background of our mother tongue, which includes not only our way of constructing propositions but the way we dissect nature and break up the flux of experience into objects and entities to construct propositions about. This fact is important for science, because it means that science CAN have a rational or logical basis even though it be a relativistic one and not Mr. Everyman's natural logic. Although it may vary with each tongue, and a planetary mapping of the dimensions of such variation may be necessitated, it is, nevertheless, a basis of logic with discoverable laws. Science is not compelled to see its thinking and reasoning procedures turned into processes merely subservient to social adjustments and emotional drives.

Moreover, the tremendous importance of language cannot, in my opinion, be taken to mean necessarily that nothing is back of it of the nature of what has traditionally been called "mind." My own studies suggest, to me, that language, for all its kingly role, is in some sense a superficial embroidery upon deeper processes of consciousness, which are necessary before any communication, signaling, or symbolism whatsoever can occur, and which also can, at a pinch, effect communication (though not true AGREEMENT) without language's and without symbolism's aid. I mean "superficial" in the sense that all processes of chemistry, for example, can be said to be superficial upon the deeper layer of physical existence, which we know variously as intra-atomic, electronic, or sub-electronic. No one would take this statement to mean that chemistry is UNIMPORTANT—indeed the whole point is that the more superficial can mean the more important, in a definite operative sense. It may even be in the cards that there is no such thing as "Language" (with a capital L) at all! The statement that "thinking is a matter of LANGUAGE" is an incorrect generalization of the more nearly correct idea that "thinking is a matter of different tongues." The different tongues are the real phenomena and may generalize down not to any such universal as "Language," but to something better—called "sublinguistic" or "superlinguistic"—and NOT ALTOGETHER unlike, even if much unlike, what we now call "mental." This generalization would not diminish, but would rather increase, the importance of intertongue study for investigation of this realm of truth.

Botanists and zoologists, in order to understand the world of living species, found it necessary to describe the species in every part of the globe and to add a time perspective by including the fossils. Then they found it necessary to compare and contrast the species, to work out families and classes, evolutionary descent, morphology, and taxonomy. In linguistic science a similar attempt is under way. The far-off event toward which this attempt moves is a new technology of language and thought. Much progress has been made in classifying the languages of earth into genetic families, each having descent from a single precursor, and in tracing such developments through time. The result is called "comparative linguistics." Of even greater importance for the future technology of thought is what might be called "contrastive linguistics." This plots the outstanding differences among tongues—in grammar, logic, and general analysis of experience.

As I said in the April 1940 *Review*, segmentation of nature is an aspect of grammar—one as yet little studied by grammarians. We cut up and organize the spread and flow of events as we do, largely because, through our mother tongue, we are parties to an agreement to do so, not because nature itself is segmented in exactly that way for all to see. Languages differ not only in how they build their sentences but also in how they break down nature to secure the elements to put in those sentences. This breakdown gives units of the lexicon. "Word" is not a very good "word" for them; "lexeme" has been suggested, and "term" will do for the present. By these more or less distinct terms we ascribe a semifictitious isolation to parts of experience. English terms, like 'sky, hill, swamp,' persuade us to regard some elusive aspect of nature's endless variety as a distinct THING, almost like a table or chair. Thus English and similar tongues lead us to think of the universe as a collection of rather distinct objects and events corresponding to words. Indeed this is the implicit picture of classical physics and astronomy—that the universe is essentially a collection of detached objects of different sizes.

The examples used by older logicians in dealing with this point are usually unfortunately chosen. They tend to pick out tables and chairs and apples on tables as test objects to demonstrate the object-like nature of reality and its one-to-one correspondence with logic. Man's artifacts and the agricultural products he severs from living plants have a unique degree of isolation; we may expect that languages will have fairly isolated terms for them. The real question is: What do different languages do, not with these artificially isolated objects but with the flowing face of nature in its motion, color, and changing form; with clouds, beaches, and yonder flight of birds? For, as goes our segmentation of the face of nature, so goes our physics of the Cosmos.

Here we find differences in segmentation and selection of basic terms. We might isolate something in nature by saying 'It is a dripping spring.' Apache erects the statement on a verb *ga*: 'be white (including clear, uncolored, and so on). With a prefix *nō-* the meaning of downward motion enters: 'whiteness moves downward.' Then *tó*, meaning both 'water' and 'spring' is prefixed. The result corresponds to our 'dripping spring,' but synthetically it is 'as water, or springs, whiteness moves downward.' How utterly unlike our way of thinking! The same verb, *ga*, with a prefix that means 'a place manifests the condition' becomes *gohlga*: 'the place is white, clear; a clearing, a plain.' These examples show that some languages have means of expression—chemical combination, as I called it—in which the separate terms are not so separate as in English but flow together into plastic synthetic creations. Hence such languages, which do not paint the separate-object picture of the universe to the same degree as English and its sister tongues, point toward possible new types of logic and possible new cosmical pictures.

The Indo-European languages and many others give great prominence to a type of sentence having two parts, each part built around a class of word—substantives and verbs—which those languages treat differently in grammar. As I showed in the April 1940 *Review*, this distinction is not drawn from nature; it is just a result of the fact that every tongue must have some kind of structure, and those tongues have made a go of exploiting this kind. The Greeks, especially Aristotle, built up this contrast and made it a law of reason. Since then, the contrast has been stated in logic in many different ways: subject and predicate, actor and action, things and relations between things, objects and their attributes, quantities and operations. And, pursuant again to grammar, the notion became ingrained that one of these classes of entities can exist in its own right but that the verb class cannot exist without an entity of the other class, the "thing" class, as a peg to hang on. "Embodiment is necessary," the watchword of this ideology, is seldom STRONGLY questioned. Yet the whole trend of modern physics, with its emphasis on "the field," is an implicit questioning of the ideology. This contrast crops out in our mathematics as two kinds of symbols—the kind like 1, 2, 3, x, y, z and the kind like $+$, $-$, $\div$, $\sqrt{\ \ }$, log $-$, though, in view of 0, $\frac{1}{2}$, $\frac{3}{4}$, π, and others, perhaps no strict two-group classification holds. The two-group notion, however, is always present at the back of the thinking, although often not overtly expressed.

Our Indian languages show that with a suitable grammar we may

have intelligent sentences that cannot be broken into subjects and predi-
cates. Any attempted breakup is a breakup of some English translation
or paraphrase of the sentence, not of the Indian sentence itself. We
might as well try to decompose a certain synthetic resin into Celluloid
and whiting because the resin can be imitated with Celluloid and whiting. The Algonkian language family, to which Shawnee belongs, does
use a type of sentence like our subject and predicate but also gives prominence to the type shown by our examples in the text and in Figure 1. To
be sure, *ni-* is represented by a subject in the translation but means 'my'
as well as 'I,' and the sentence could be translated thus: 'My hand is
pulling the branch aside.' Or *ni-* might be absent; if so, we should be apt
to manufacture a subject, like 'he, it, somebody,' or we could pick out
for our English subject an idea corresponding to any one of the Shawnee
elements.

When we come to Nootka, the sentence without subject or predicate
is the only type. The term "predication" is used, but it means "sentence."
Nootka has no parts of speech; the simplest utterance is a sentence, treat-
ing of some event or event-complex. Long sentences are sentences of sentences (complex sentences), not just sentences of words. In Figure 3 we
have a simple, not a complex, Nootka sentence. The translation, he invites people to a feast,' splits into subject and predicate. Not so the native
sentence. It begins with the event of 'boiling or cooking,' *tl'imsh*; then
comes *-ya* ('result') = 'cooked'; then *-'is* 'eating' = 'eating cooked food';
then *-ita* ('those who do') = 'eaters of cooked food'; then *-'itl* ('going for');
then *-ma*, sign of third-person indicative, giving *tl'imshya'isita'itlma*,
which answers to the crude paraphrase, 'he, or somebody, goes for (invites) eaters of cooked food.'

The English technique of talking depends on the contrast of two
artificial classes, substantives and verbs, and on the bipartitioned ideology of nature, already discussed. Our normal sentence, unless imperative,
must have some substantive before its verb, a requirement that corresponds to the philosophical and also naïve notion of an actor who produces an action. This last might not have been so if English had had
thousands of verbs like 'hold,' denoting positions. But most of our verbs
follow a type of segmentation that isolates from nature what we call
"actions," that is, moving outlines.

Following majority rule, we therefore read action into every sentence,
even into 'I hold it.' A moment's reflection will show that 'hold' is no
action but a state of relative positions. Yet we think of it and even see
it as an action because language formulates it in the same way as it formulates more numerous expressions, like 'I strike it,' which deal with
movements and changes.

We are constantly reading into nature fictional acting entities, simply

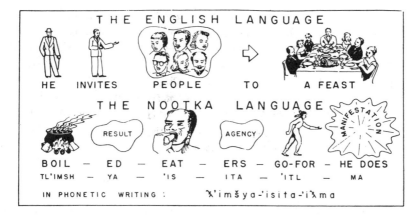

THE ENGLISH LANGUAGE

HE   INVITES   PEOPLE   TO   A FEAST

THE NOOTKA LANGUAGE   MANIFESTATION

RESULT   AGENCY

BOIL — E D — EAT — ERS — GO-FOR — HE DOES

TL'IMSH — YA — 'IS — ITA — 'ITL — MA

IN PHONETIC WRITING :   ƛ'imšya-'isita-'iƛma

Figure 3. Here are shown the different ways in which English and Nootka formulate the same event. The English sentence is divisible into subject and predicate; the Nootka sentence is not, yet it is complete and logical. Furthermore, the Nootka sentence is just one word, consisting of the root *tl'imsh* with five suffixes.

because our verbs must have substantives in front of them. We have to say 'It flashed' or 'A light flashed,' setting up an actor, 'it' or 'light,' to perform what we call an action, "to flash." Yet the flashing and the light are one and the same! The Hopi language reports the flash with a simple verb, *rehpi*: 'flash (occurred).' There is no division into subject and predicate, not even a suffix like *-t* of Latin *tona-t* 'it thunders.' Hopi can and does have verbs without subjects, a fact which may give that tongue potentialities, probably never to be developed, as a logical system for understanding some aspects of the universe. Undoubtedly modern science, strongly reflecting western Indo-European tongues, often does as we all do, sees actions and forces where it sometimes might be better to see states. On the other hand, 'state' is a noun, and as such it enjoys the superior prestige traditionally attaching to the subject or thing class; therefore science is exceedingly ready to speak of states if permitted to manipulate the concept like a noun. Perhaps, in place of the 'states' of an atom or a dividing cell, it would be better if we could manipulate as readily a more verblike concept but without the concealed premises of actor and action.

I can sympathize with those who say, "Put it into plain, simple English," especially when they protest against the empty formalism of loading discourse with pseudolearned words. But to restrict thinking to the patterns merely of English, and especially to those patterns which represent the acme of plainness in English, is to lose a power of thought which, once lost, can never be regained. It is the "plainest" English which contains the greatest number of unconscious assumptions about nature. This is the trouble with schemes like Basic English, in which an eviscerated British English, with its concealed premises working harder than ever, is to be fobbed off on an unsuspecting world as the substance of pure Reason itself. We handle even our plain English with much greater effect if we direct it from the vantage point of a multilingual awareness. For this reason I believe that those who envision a future world speaking only one tongue, whether English, German, Russian, or any other, hold a misguided ideal and would do the evolution of the human mind the greatest disservice. Western culture has made, through language, a provisional analysis of reality and, without correctives, holds resolutely to that analysis as final. The only correctives lie in all those other tongues which by aeons of independent evolution have arrived at different, but equally logical, provisional analyses.

In a valuable paper, "Modern logic and the task of the natural sciences," Harold N. Lee says: "Those sciences whose data are subject to quantitative measurement have been most successfully developed because we know so little about order systems other than those exemplified in mathematics. We can say with certainty, however, that there are other kinds, for the advance of logic in the last half century has clearly indicated it. We may look for advances in many lines in sciences at present well founded if the advance of logic furnishes adequate knowledge of other order types. We may also look for many subjects of inquiry whose methods are not strictly scientific at the present time to become so when new order systems are available."[1] To which may be added that an important field for the working out of new order systems, akin to, yet not identical with, present mathematics, lies in more penetrating investigation than has yet been made of languages remote in type from our own.

[1]*Sigma Xi Quart.*, 28:125 (Autumn 1940).

*Whatever we call a thing, whatever
we say it is, it is not. For whatever
we say is words, and words are words
and not things. The words are maps,
and the map is not the territory.*

Some Limitations of Language

HARRY L. WEINBERG

"Like any tool," says Weinberg, "language has its
limitations. There are certain things we cannot do with it,
and the attempt to make it do what it cannot do often
leads to trouble." In this brief paper Weinberg elaborates
on some of the limitations of language: what language
cannot do, the problems created when language is used
inappropriately or unscientifically, the difficulties which
arise when we fail to recognize the different functions of
language, and the importance of the distinction between
signal versus symbol reactions. Perhaps most important is
Weinberg's discussion of the semantic devices—the date,
the index, and the *etc. "Theoretically,"* argues Weinberg,
"if we could learn to introduce these devices into all our
evaluations and have the habit sink down to the feeling
level, we could never become neurotic or psychotic; we
would never indulge in the wrong kind of worry." This
is a particularly powerful claim but a most provocative one.

Irving J. Lee often likened language to a tool, perhaps man's most important one, more useful than fire, the wheel, or atomic energy. It is most likely that none of these, most certainly not the latter, could ever have been put to use by a non-symbol-using creature. But, like any tool, language has its limitations. There are certain things we cannot do with it, and the attempt to make it do what it cannot do often leads to trouble.

In expanding upon this, Lee compared language with a fish net. The very small fish escape from the web; the very large ones cannot be encircled. In the case of language, the small fry are the infinite details of the material world; no matter how fine we weave the mesh, an infinity escape. We can never describe completely even the simplest bit of matter. We can never exhaust what could be said about a single grain of sand. For convenience, and by utter necessity, we concentrate on a large number (though relatively few) of the characteristics of grains of sand, noting those similarities important to us at the moment and neglecting differences which seem to make no difference for our generalizations. In this way we come to talk about "properties" of sand. These are the fish—descriptions and inferences—for which the net of language is most suited.

But there is something very peculiar about the catch: it is nonexistent. It is as though the fish had slipped from their skins and what we have left is lifeless and unchanging, a dull and hazy replica of the ones that got away. For words are *about things*; they are *not* the things themselves. The world of things is constantly changing; it "is" bright, hard, soft, green, rosy, acrid, black, burnt, rubbery, loud, sharp, velvety, bitter, hot, freezing, silent, flowing, massive, ephemeral, wispy, granitic. Or rather, these are the names we use for the way it seems to us. Above all, it appears "real"; it is not words. Whatever we call a thing, whatever we say it is, it is not. For whatever we *say* is words, and words are words and not things. The words are maps, and the map is not the territory.

From "Some Limitations of Language" from LEVELS OF KNOWING AND EXISTENCE by Harry L. Weinberg, pp. 34–47. Copyright © 1959, by Harry L. Weinberg. Reprinted by permission of Harper & Row, Publishers, Inc.

The map is static; the territory constantly flows. Words are always about the past or the unborn future, never about the living present. The present is ever too quick for them; by the time the words are out, it is gone. When we forget this, we tend to act as if words were things, and because they are so much more easily manipulated and molded to our desires, there is the danger of building maps that fit no known territory and the greater danger of not caring whether or not they do. We then tend more and more to live in the past and the future and we lose the present, the sense of nowness, the feeling of the immediacy, mystery, and flow of the sensory world; we drift into the gray, dead world of words.

THE QUEERNESS OF THINGNESS:
WHAT IS RED LIKE, "REALLY"?

The non-verbal quality of the sensory world—the world of thingness —is the large fish which escapes the net of language. If you were asked to describe the color "red" to a man blind from birth, you would very quickly discover that this is an absolute impossibility. No matter what you said, you could never convey to him the sensation you experience when you see a color called red. The same observation applies to smells, tastes, sounds—any sensory perceptions. They are literally unspeakable, as are all feelings and emotions. During his lectures, Alfred Korzybski would ask the members of the audience to pinch themselves, to concentrate on the feeling, and then try to describe the pain. It does no good to say sharp, dull, or prickly, for then you have to describe these words, *ad infinitum*. Incidentally, it might interest the reader to know that it is quite difficult to get some people, especially the more sophisticated intellectuals, to perform this little experiment. It is silly, childish, and obvious. They "know" words are not things. But to really know it on all levels of abstraction, one must actually do and experience this non-verbal act. If not, then one is acting as if his words were the actual sensations.

All that words—descriptions and labels—can do is evoke sensations and feelings which the reader or listener has already experienced. They can never transmit new experience. If one has never experienced what is described, one is absolutely incapable of experiencing it through description alone. No woman can make me feel what it is like to give birth to a child. I may infer it is similar to a bad case of cramps, but I will never know, no matter what she says. Since I know that a toothache differs in "quality" from a headache, and that a burn does not feel like bruised skin, it is a reasonable inference on my part that birth pains are different in some respects from anything I have ever experienced or ever will.

This poses an interesting question. If you feel a pain in your jaw and say, "I have a toothache," have you made an inferential or factual statement? Certainly it has been made after observation, but what about verification by accepted standards? What is the accepted standard for sensations, feelings, emotions? It can only be the person experiencing them. Only you can feel your pain and the experience itself represents the verification. Your statement is a factual one for you and inferential for everyone else. We can only guess that you are reporting the "truth" about your feelings.

The limitations of language go even further. I have no way of knowing what "red" looks like even to another sighted person. He cannot tell me; I cannot check. I can only infer that what he experiences is similar to what I experience. It cannot be identical because our nervous systems are different, and an experience is a product of both what is "out there" and the way the organism reacts to it. But in order to get on with the business of living together and reaching some kind of agreement, we are forced to assume a similarity in response. The danger lies in our forgetting that this similarity is only a convenient inference. There may be important differences in what different people perceive in the "same" situation or in what one individual perceives at different moments. Hundreds of experiments designed by psychologists, physiologists, and others demonstrate this dependence of perception upon both the structure of the stimulus and the structure and state of the responding organ.

Let us take a simple example. Eat a lump of sugar and concentrate on the taste. Then take another and another. After a few lumps, the sweetness changes. It may become cloying or its sweetness may be diminished. What has happened? Has the sugar changed its taste? If you say no, you have become satiated, but the sweetness of the sugar is the same, why do you assume that the first taste of sugar is the "real" taste, and that after six lumps it is less "real"?

Or place a piece of red paper on a gray background. Place another piece of the same paper on a bright green background. Compare the two and you will find that the pieces of red paper look different. Which is the "real" color? It won't do to say that the real color is that of the red paper by itself. It is never by itself; there is always a background. Which is the right background? One is as arbitrary as the other.

We could go on and on with this. How about the color-blind man who presumably sees only a shade of gray when he looks at your red sheet? Who is seeing the correct, the "real" color? If you say you are because your range of color perception is greater than his, consider these facts: The majority of people cannot see ultraviolet light. If we filter out light in the range of the visible spectrum, red to violet, in an ultraviolet lamp, the average person would see nothing and would say that the lamp is not lit. However, it has been discovered that a few people do see a fraction of the ultraviolet range. This means that they see a color they cannot describe to us if we are one of the majority who cannot see ultraviolet light, and we cannot imagine what the color is like. It is no good to say it is like violet; that would be like saying green must be like yellow because it follows it in the spectrum. If you have seen yellow but never green, you cannot imagine, on the basis of yellow, what green is like.

Now, since there is, normally, ultraviolet light in daylight, it will be reflected from the "red" sheet of paper, so that the person who can see ultraviolet light will see a different shade of "red," that is, red and ultraviolet. Which is the "real" color of "red," his or ours?

We met this problem before when we tried to find the "real" height of the table, which upon analysis we found to be a meaningless, unanswerable question. A similar solution can be found in this case by tracing the sequence of events. Light waves (shower of particles?), reflected from the paper to our eyes, are electromagnetic waves and have no color. These waves hit our eyes and give rise to a series of complex psychophysical responses, resulting in the sensation red, gray, or some other color. Two things should be noted here. First, the electromagnetic (light) waves have no qualities (no color, sounds, smells) and their existence is inferred. Second, when a response is aroused in an organism, that response is in terms of some sensation like red, gray, etc. The particular quality of the response depends upon the structure and condition of the organ and the organism. Given a different organism, a different sensation arises in response to the "same" electromagnetic waves. Thus, the light *waves* produce this sensation of *light* in the organism, but one is not the other.

Incidentally, by distinguishing between sound waves and sound, we can speedily dispatch that old riddle concerning the tree that falls in the forest when no one is about. Does it make a sound? The answer is no! We infer that the tree produces sound waves, a reasonable inference based on past factual data on falling objects. But sound is sensation produced in and by an organism as a result of being stimulated by sound waves (which are not sound) and until such an organism is present, the tree makes no sound. If a man is present when the tree falls, it is a factual statement for him to say, "I hear a sound," provided he is not deaf. But any statement I make about his hearing it is purely inferential.

WHAT IS A QUALITY?: TO-ME-NESS

In asking what is the "real" color of a piece of paper, we imply that color is *in* the paper, that it exists independently of the responding organism. But since the color, or any quality for that matter, is a product of both the observer and the observed, in order to make language fit these facts as discovered by science, we must change the question to, "What color does it appear to me at this moment?" In this way, the structure of the language fits the structure of reality. By adding "to me at this time," we imply in our language a universe characterized by constant change, one whose qualities are given it, projected upon it, by a responding organism. By omitting these words, we imply a simple, absolute, static world where the organism is simply a mirror, largely a distorting one, of an ideal world whose qualities are independent of and unchanged by the observer.

This may not matter much when talking about color, taste, or sound, but when we are evaluating the realm of the social it makes quite a difference whether one says "Johnny is bad" or "Johnny appears bad to me now." If he *is* bad, he has badness in him; it is a part of him, and he is always bad in everything he does and will appear that way to every "normal" observer. When we add "to me, now," we imply there is a possibility that he may not appear that way to everyone else. We are more prepared to consider other evaluations of his behavior, on the possibility that they may be more accurate than our own. Actually, if I tell you Johnny is bad, I tell you very little about him other than that I probably dislike him if I dislike those I label bad. If I say that he appears bad to me, I invite the obvious questions, "What kind of behavior do you call bad? What did Johnny do?" If I then describe what he did, we might discover that you do not consider such behavior bad; rather, to you, it may show that Johnny is independent and self-reliant. To Mr. X, this behavior may mean Johnny is trying to hide his insecurity and lack of parental affection. Who is right? All may be partly right and partly wrong, but at least the situation can be discussed on a much more objective, descriptive level. The probability of agreement and of more appropriate behavior with respect to Johnny is much greater. When we say *and mean,* "It appears this way to me," we invite checking, discussion, reëvaluation. When we say, "It is," we cut off further investigation. It is the contention of the general semanticist that the constant, conscious use of the "to me" will help make proper evaluation more likely, for language structure influences thought, behavior, and feelings. Constant talking in absolute terms produces a feeling of the "rightness" of such patterns of evaluation, and this emotional barrier is most difficult to crack in attempting to change behavior. It stifles questioning the appropriateness of patterns of evaluation and talking both by the speaker himself and by others, and is one of the foundation stones in man's grimmest prison—prejudice.

CRACKING THE LANGUAGE
BARRIER: PHATIC COMMUNION

Because feelings, sensations, and emotions cannot be transmitted by language, but only evoked in the listener, and because of our great need to find out how others feel and to communicate our own feelings to them, we spend much time trying to crack this sound barrier. A writer uses hundreds of examples, descriptions, image-evoking words, hoping they will be similar enough to past experiences of the reader to provoke his memory and recreate a similar non-verbal reaction in him. For this reason it may take an entire novel or play to make a simple point. One of the themes of the play, *Death Takes a Holiday*, is that love is stronger than the fear of death. Why doesn't the author simply make the statement and call it quits? Obviously because it doesn't work; we don't "feel" this by reading one sentence. It takes the writer with his shotgun loaded with pellets of description to wing the emotions of the reader.

Another technique we use in our attempt to overcome this linguistic barrier, interestingly enough, involves the use of non-symbolic language, the language of sound as such. This is the language of lovers and infants and animals, and we all use it in addition to symbolic language. Bronislaw Malinowski called it "phatic communion."

When Fido growls and bares his teeth, he is letting us and other animals know that he is angry. When the baby howls and bares his gums, he communicates to us his unhappiness. And Fido and the baby are equally adept at reading our feelings by the tone of our voice totally apart from the verbal meanings of the words used. All of us gather our impressions of a person's sincerity, for example, by the inflections of his voice, not by any protestation by him.

Not only do sounds serve to convey expressions of feelings, but also the general musculature of the body plays a part in this type of communication. The good poker player "reads" the faces (the tiny movements of the muscles around the eyes and mouth) of the other players to see if they are bluffing or suppressing excitement. Indeed, there is evidence to suggest that the very young infant is frighteningly adept at picking up the "true" feelings of his mother toward him, which she herself may have repressed. Thus, if she unconsciously rejects him and, feeling guilty, talks fondly or rather, uses fond language, he will feel this rejection by "reading" the inflections in her voice and the tensions in her muscles.

WHEN SENSE IS NONSENSE

Much social talk is in the same category. It is our attempt to escape the desperate loneliness that is, in a sense, our lot. No one can know how we feel, what we see; nor we, they. Each is a solitude. No logic or analysis or theorizing is nearly as effective in softening this aloneness as phatic communion. Misevaluation enters when we expect them to. It has been stated that a bore is a man who, when you greet him with, "How are you?" tells you. You are not really asking about his health but saying, "Let's be friends." If you are fixing a flat tire on a hot day and a passerby asks, "Got a flat?", he is asking you to be friendly. If you take his words literally, you are likely to become angry and say, "Any damn fool can see I have."

It is often a temptation to snicker or feel very superior to the logically absurd "itsy bitsy boo" talk of lovers. But if we remember that it is the sound, not the literal meaning that conveys the affection in this case, then any attempt to talk "sense" in this kind of situation is itself a form of nonsense. Consequently the general semanticist does not demand that we talk sense all the time. All he asks is that we distinguish between situations that call for big talk and those that do better with small talk, and not confuse the two or try to pass off one as the other. Small talk is the oil in social machinery. Big talk—logic, theorizing, factual statements—will help solve the problems; small talk eases the way.

Most commonly both types of communication occur simultaneously and in varying degrees, which serves to complicate mutual understanding and gives the lie to the assertion that facts speak for themselves. Meaning occurs on all levels of abstraction, and differs in character at each level. At the feeling level it is a diffuse, deep, primitive, alogical meaning expressed in the scream of anguish, the coo of affection, the snarl of hatred, the *tra la la* of the poet.

SIGNAL "VERSUS" SYMBOL REACTIONS:
DELAYED REACTIONS

Subverbal responses, called signs by some writers and signal reactions by Alfred Korzybski, must be distinguished from verbal or symbol responses or reactions. When you hit your thumb and howl with pain, the howl is a sign of the pain, an undelayed signal reaction. When the lookout crow gives a danger "caw" at the approach of the farmer, it is a sign that he senses danger. In these cases the distinguishing characteristic is that the vocal or other signal response is undelayed. The feeling and sign of it are almost synchronous.

Symbol reactions, on the other hand, are delayed responses. "It hurts" are words *about* feelings or a painful occurrence and are of a higher order of abstraction than the undelayed howl. They require some "thinking." An infant jabbed with a pin will scream—a signal reaction; the scream is a sign of his pain. It does not take long, however, before he learns to howl deliberately to attract attention; the scream is now a symbol response. Just where the dividing line is we cannot say. There is probably a continuum from the undelayed signal response to the delayed symbol reaction which may even involve a delay of years. For example, a student may feel that he is unjustly treated by a teacher. But he delays his response until he graduates and then goes back to give the teacher a piece of his mind.

One of the aims of general semantics training is the development of the habit of delaying responses, thus increasing the chances that our responses will be more appropriate for the situation. The delay does not have to be more than a fraction of a second in many cases, just enough to pass from the unmediated signal reaction to the modified, thought-out symbol behavior. This may mean the difference between acting like an animal and behaving like a man. The man who "blows his top" at the drop of a hat, who gets fighting mad at the mention of a word like yellow, chicken, or Communist, never gives the higher orders of abstraction a chance to operate, so his responses are less likely to fit the occasion. He is at the mercy of his feelings and may soon regret his actions. Of course, there are some occasions where "instantaneous" response is most appropriate. When a brick is falling from a building and you are under it, if someone yells, "Look out!" there doesn't seem to be much time for evaluating the situation. Yet even here a quick glance might tell you which way to jump or you might jump under the brick.

SOME DEVICES FOR DELAYING RESPONSES: THE INDEX, THE DATE, THE ETC.

The general semanticist contends that too often signal responses are made where symbol reactions would be more appropriate. Learning a general pattern of delaying response is more likely to produce proper evaluation. Three semantic devices for achieving this end are the date, the index, and the *etc.* Korzybski was fond of repeating that if one could just learn to use these three in all situations, he could forget all of general semantics theory and still have the most important part of the system. *Theoretically*, if we could learn to introduce these devices into all our evaluations and have the habit sink down to the feeling level, we could never become neurotic or psychotic; we would never indulge in the wrong kind of worry. We shall have much to say about this later, but one example, which we shall bring up again, will suffice at this point. This is the classical case of the young man who comes to the psychiatrist because, among other things, he hates women. After some probing, the psychiatrist discovers that his trouble began in childhood when his mother maltreated and rejected him. He soon both hated her and felt guilty about it. This hatred was soon generalized to all women. After perhaps a year of treatment, or two or three, after much difficult and trying work on the part of both patient and therapist, he is "cured." In effect, he is "cured" when he can apply the three devices to his illness. As a result of therapy he learns to index his hatred. On the insight, feeling level, he "sees" that woman $_1$, his mother, is not woman $_{2, 3, 4}$. He then learns to put a date on his hatred. It was proper to hate his mother as a child; twenty years later, both he, she, and times have changed. Finally he learns to add the *etc.* to his evaluation of her actions; that is, he learns there is more to be said about the situation. Maybe she couldn't help what she did, or she didn't realize the significance of her actions, or maybe he was expecting too much of her or maybe. . . .

The general semanticist does not maintain that merely by saying "person $_1$ isn't person $_2$, time $_1$ isn't time $_2$, and there is more to be said," this young man could cure himself. But we do think that if over a long period of time, preferably from childhood, we are trained to talk this way, there is more chance that we will not wind up on the psychiatrist's couch. The time to make the use of these devices habitual is not when the pinch is on, but over the long run of relatively unstressed situations.

These devices make the structure of the language fit the structure of reality. As far as proper evaluation is concerned, the three basic characteristics of the world around us are that events are infinitely complex, they are changing all the time, and no two are identical. If this is so, then dating statements implies a constantly changing in-process reality. Indexing referents implies non-identity of events. The addition of an *etc.* to statements indicates that in the face of the complexity of things and the limitations of our knowledge, there is always more to be said. This practice cannot help but have some inhibiting effect upon the tendency in all of us to be dogmatic and absolutistic. The constant use of these devices makes it "feel right" and obvious to do so; this in turn increases the chances of our using them and producing maps that fit the territory.

When we fail to use these semantic devices we fall into the "allness" pattern of evaluation characterized by statements such as, "Everyone knows Negroes are inferior people," "You can't tell me anything about Mexicans. I was brought up among them," "Once a criminal, always a criminal."

Consider the difference it would have made if Senator McCarthy had been taught to use these devices so that he and others of his ilk could have been able to say, "The fact that this man joined the Communist Party in 1934 does not necessarily mean he is a Communist today." Or, "Not all of those who joined movements to the left of my political position are necessarily Communist Party members." Or, perhaps best of all, "Perhaps my definition of a Communist is not the only possible valid and useful one." Now it is quite possible that a man who joined the Party in 1934 is still a member today and just as possible that many liberals are being deceived by Communist front organizations. But we can't be sure until we do some careful checking. If we are victims of the "allness pattern," verification and the more mature pattern of behavior will be automatically and effectively short-circuited. Our language patterns then do the thinking for us.

Reports of marriage counselors are filled with remarks flung at one another by couples whose marriages are on the rocks: "You always burn the toast," "You always make a fool of yourself at parties," "You never think about what I want," "You never really loved me," "Your mother always tries to get me," "All men are alike; you can't trust them." Granted such statements may be motivated by factors other than conscious evaluation of the marital situation. They may reflect conscious hatreds, projections, etc., but it would be much more difficult for a person to speak this way if he had consciously acquired the habit of indexing and dating his statements.

Constant failure to use these semantic devices invites further use of the "allness pattern" and reinforces the unconscious drives which help sustain it. We shall have more to say about the mutual interaction of conscious and unconscious factors in later chapters. We shall conclude this chapter by repeating something we have already emphasized and shall continue to emphasize throughout this book: Although everyone knows this stuff, all of us at one time or another act as if we don't. Nobody really believes that words are things, that things never change. Still, in hundreds of ways we act as if we do. Read the letters sent to the editors of newspapers and magazines or to "advice to the lovelorn" columnists, for example, and note how frequently are found the words "never," "all," "everyone knows," "they say." Such letters imply a simplicity not to be found in the people and situations they presume to describe. Nor is this failing limited to the few who write letters. The editors and columnists themselves are frequently as guilty as their correspondents—

often, I presume, deliberately and with malice aforethought. We are surrounded by tabloids, digests, summaries, condensations of all types which presume to give "all" the "really important" news that is fit (and fitted) to print.

The complexity and variety of daily events does necessitate some selection and condensation. Nevertheless an awareness on our part that something important probably has been left out, that distortion and bias most likely are present, can, perhaps, diminish the chances of a misevaluation of important events. The deliberate and constant use of semantic devices helps to provoke and maintain the vitally important awareness of the dangers of oversimplification, dogmatism, and static-mindedness, and aids in the development of that sophisticated innocence which enables us to look with a fresh and inquiring eye upon the world around us.

Each of us has learned to see the world not as it is but through the distorting glass of our words. It is through words that we are made human, and it is through words that we are dehumanized.

The Language of Self-Deception

ASHLEY MONTAGU

Ashley Montagu here analyzes the terms "human nature," "instinct," "aggressiveness," "the law of the jungle," "the 'lower' animals," "heredity," "blood and consanguinity," "miscegenation," and "atavism." These terms are often employed as if they were valid biological and/or social descriptions with the effect that they "have conditioned and confused and misdirected the thinking and conduct of men in the Western world." Montague attempts to demonstrate that the words we use serve as psychophysical conditioners, influencing the ways in which we think, feel, and behave.

The way we talk about ourselves and our institutions, the way in which we use long-established "respectable" terms, leads us to make unrealistic and destructive evaluations of ourselves, of others, of the man-made world, and of the world of nature. It is seldom understood that the world we perceive is the world we see through words, that the world of experience is the world of arbitrarily conferred meanings. Each of us has learned to see the world not as it is but through the distorting glass of our words. It is through words that we are made human, and it is through words that we are dehumanized.

The meaning of a word is the action it produces. That is the operational definition of a word. Every member of a culture becomes a functioning member of that culture as a consequence of the behavior of others acting upon him. During the socialization process, that is, the process of being turned into a human being, the words are directed toward him with specific ends in view, and as the child becomes increasingly aware of the world around him, words, even though they are not specifically directed at him, continue to be the principal instruments which turn him upon the lathe of language into a growing human being. His behavior is shaped by words.

Words consist not merely of chopped-up segments of sounds having conventionalized meanings, but also of their accompaniments, such as kinesic movements of the body, principally of the face. Part or even the whole of the meaning of a word may be derived from the expression, the inflection, associated with it. Furthermore, words also derive a considerable part of this meaning from the environmental contexts in which they occur. For example, take the term *race*. When uttered with the malice, bigotry, and hatred of a Southern racist, the term differs very greatly from the meaning with which it is endowed when uttered by a scientist, however insubstantially, as a classificatory device. The term

Ashley Montague, "The Language of Self-Deception," in LAN-GUAGE IN AMERICA, eds. Neil Postman, Charles Weingartener, and Terence P. Moran (New York: Pegasus, 1969), pp. 82–95.

has a very different meaning in the home of a Georgia cracker from that which it has in a university classroom in which it is undergoing prolonged and critical examination. Words, in short, are the repositories of our experience. Their private and their public faces do not necessarily correspond, and they are accommodatable to changes in time and place. "Race" is a good example of such a word, for it is characterized by all sorts of private and public meanings, when in fact it corresponds to nothing whatever in reality. But no matter how confused or unreal the idea, a word can always be found to give a habitation and a name. The ambiguity of language is uniquely helpful in promoting confusion of thought, for with its assistance men are able to build their logic to fit their rationalizations, and most men's words are nothing but pseudo-logical rationalizations based on unanalyzed systems of values.

Men measure the value of words by the realities in which they believe, and since those realities are determined by the very words they believe in, the process is tautologically very satisfactory indeed. When the unreal is acted upon as if it were real it becomes, for all practical purposes, just as real as the real.

For most people, whether they are racists or not, the term "race" means that there exists something called "race" which determines the mental, behavioral, cultural abilities, and physical traits of different peoples. This colligation of differences is what the "true believer" understands by "race." The erroneous beliefs, attitudes, and conclusions and violent emotions that are enshrined in this term serve not only to maintain the doctrine of the inequality of man, but also to perpetuate the irrational practices which maintain the barriers between men. The fact that "race" corresponds to nothing in reality, that it represents a purely arbitrary classificatory device at best which many authorities consider wholly inapplicable to man, not to mention other creatures,[1] and at worst a wholly untenable confusion of ideas concerning the nature of the physical traits, and the meaning of differences in individual and cultural achievement, is something that is wholly unknown to the hundreds of millions who believe in "race" as a real entity. Furthermore, when such "true believers" are exposed to the facts they are often utterly unimpressed by them. When exposed to the light their minds, like the pupils of their eyes, automatically contract. In addition, there are those who are able to accept the facts intellectually, but not emotionally. "I don't believe in ghosts," remarked Madame de Staël, "but I'm afraid of them." It is a common human response.

[1]Ashley Montagu (ed.), *The Concept of Race*, New York, The Free Press, 1964; Ashley Montagu, *Man's Most Dangerous Myth: The Fallacy of Race* (4th ed.), Cleveland and New York, World Publishing Company, 1964.

In what follows I shall consider a selection of words and phrases which are commonly used as if they had a biological or social validity or both; words and phrases which are more or less pervasive in their influence upon the thinking and the conduct mostly of the educated; words which for too long have conditioned and confused and misdirected the thinking and conduct of men in the Western world. There are literally hundreds of such words, phrases, and metaphors. I discuss here only a few of those with which I have myself been involved in attempting to clarify and criticize in the past.

HUMAN NATURE

Since people are so much in the midst of human nature most of us are authorities on the subject. The first of the errors almost universally committed is the assumption that human nature is something with which one is born. The fact is that one is no more born with human nature than one is born with speech. Both are potentialities which have to be learned. There are, of course, genetic limits, which are associated with those potentialities, but allowing for the full range of those limits, all members of the species *Homo sapiens* are capable of being humanized. And they are humanized according to the patterns of conditioning they undergo within their particular social group or culture. The enculturation of the individual is a continuous process of growth and development in the ability to interact with the world in which one develops, according to and with the learned forms of behavior prevailing in the culture. *That* is human nature. Hence, the vulgar practice of attributing a variety of usually unpleasant forms of human behavior to "human nature," as if that "human nature" constituted an hereditary or inborn endowment from which one cannot escape, is quite unsound.

What man is born with is a highly generalized capacity for learning, for educability. Educability is, indeed, the species characteristic of man. But what he will learn will depend, allowing for his genetic limitations, entirely upon the man-made part of the environment into which he is born and the manner in which it acts upon him to tailor him according to the pattern prevailing in that culture. Man, in short, is custom made.

It is not his nature, therefore, that requires attention, but his nurture. Let us cease blaming his faults upon the former, when they are in fact due to the latter.

INSTINCT

When one asks most people to define what they mean by "instinct" it is my experience that they are seldom able to do so and make any sense at all. The nearest most people get to a definition is to say that an instinct is an automatic response to a stimulus. This is incorrect. That is the definition of a reflex—a very different thing. Yet most people are sure that man is driven by many instincts. But the truth is that man has no instincts. An instinct is an inherited psychophysical disposition causing the organism to react upon the perception of a particular stimulus with a particular behavior or series of behaviors accompanied by a particular emotion. Man has no such endowments.

It makes things a lot easier to be able to attribute complex forms of behavior to innate mechanisms like "instincts," but while this may be satisfying to many people, it is very unsatisfying to those who are interested in discovering what the truth really is. And the truth, as is always the case, is vastly more interesting than the mythology which serves to obscure it.

Again, allowing for the genetic limits and differences which characterize every individual, all human behavior has to be learned. If we would understand any of man's behaviors our task must then be to study the conditions in which he acquired those behaviors. To attempt to trace those behaviors back to "instinctive" causes would be like searching for a nonexistent cat in a big dark room. It would divert attention from the real causes and focus them on an attention- and time-wasting procedure which would only lead to deeper confusion. This is precisely what such writers as Robert Ardrey, Konrad Lorenz, and Desmond Morris are succeeding in doing in their widely read books.[2] These books enjoy the wide appeal they do, not only because they serve to "explain" the aggressiveness of man, but because by attributing that aggressiveness to "human nature" and to "instinct," they relieve the reader of the burden of guilt he may have been carrying around for being as aggressive as he knows himself to be. For, he reasons, if he was born so, he can hardly be blamed for being so.

AGGRESSIVENESS

Aggressiveness is behavior designed to inflict pain upon another. The "authorities," such as Ardrey, Lorenz, and Morris, have informed us, as have innumerable "authorities" before them, that aggressive behavior is part of human nature, that it is instinctive. Hence, wars, juvenile delinquents, murderers, rapists, and violence will always be with us. Again,

[2]Robert Ardrey, *African Genesis*, New York: Atheneum, 1961; Robert Ardrey, *The Territorial Imperative*, New York, Atheneum, 1966; Konrad Lorenz, *On Aggression*, New York, Harcourt, Brace & World, 1966; Desmond Morris, *The Naked Ape*, New York, McGraw-Hill, 1968.

the truth is that aggressive behavior is always learned behavior provided by aggressive models who, under the appropriate conditions, are imitated. Aggression is almost invariably the response to frustration and, especially in the young, a reaction to the frustrated need for love.[3]

Misinterpretations of Darwin's discussions of "the struggle for existence," to which Darwin undeliberately contributed by the careless use of such phrases as "the warfare of nature," "the survival of the fittest," and the like, helped to create a pseudo-scientific basis for the belief that "Nature" was, as Tennyson had put, "red in tooth and claw."[4] "Nature," actually the projection of nineteenth-century industrial Europe upon the screen of "the jungle" and "the wild," was conceived to be an arena in which the most successfully competitive reaped the rewards and the weakest went to the wall. This fitted very well the Protestant ethic of wealth as evidence of divine grace, and poverty the station to which its occupiers had been divinely appointed. It also fitted, like a glove, the world of laissez-faire competition, and the Social Darwinists' views of the relations of men, classes, and nations to each other.[5]

Hence, it was clear that aggression was virtually part of the nature of things. Aggression was a law of nature. This only goes to show how easily men mistake their prejudices for the laws of nature, and how seldom they realize that all the laws of nature are man-made laws, and only too often are completely artifactual.

The belief in "innate depravity," in the natural aggressiveness of man, has influenced religious teachings and practice, education, law, military theoreticians, and would-be reformers, not to mention businessmen in their relations with their competitors and their employers, as well as their customers.

It is perhaps significant that criminologists, one of the few professional people who have been disinclined to believe in "innate depravity," enjoy possibly the best of opportunities to know what a large part environmental factors have played in the history of the lives of those convicted of aggressive crimes.

If any progress is ever to be made in controlling and reducing the development of aggressive behavior in man, it will be necessary to recognize its causes for what they are. Those causes are mainly, if not entirely, environmental. To divert attention from this fact is to do a disservice to the cause of human progress.

[3]Ashley Montagu, *The Direction of Human Development*, New York, Harper, 1955.

[4]Ashley Montagu, *Darwin, Competition, and Cooperation*, New York, Schuman, 1953.

[5]Richard Hofstadter, *Social Darwinism in American Thought 1860–1915*, Boston, Beacon Press, 1965.

THE LAW OF THE JUNGLE

This Victorian idea is closely associated with the rise of Darwinism and such other related ideas as "The Struggle for Existence," "The Survival of the Fittest," "The race is to the swift," "The strongest survive; the weakest go to the wall," "Might is Right," and many others of a similar sort. "Nature" was conceived to be in a continuous state of conflict, and "the jungle," a gladiatorial struggle in which no quarter was given.

We see, it has been said, according to the kingdom that is within us, and as I have already remarked, this view of "Nature," of "the jungle," represented nothing more nor less than the projection of man's own crippled image of himself and the frightfulness of his own societies upon the screen of "Nature." Such a view of Nature not only justified the ways of man to his fellow men, not only served to explain them, even though deprecatorily, but also served to justify the ways of man in his ruthless destruction of "Nature" for his own ends. Thus, the application of "The Law of the Jungle" against its inhabitants was considered a just punishment for their brutishness and cruelty, and the cropping out of such behavior toward his fellow man was considered one of those unavoidable expressions of "human nature" due to man's own ancestry of brutishness and cruelty. "The Law of the Jungle" seemed to be a "Law of Nature" which, do what he would, man found difficulty in escaping.

These misbegotten ideas are closely related to that other confusion of pathogenic ideas enshrined in what I have called "The Myth of the Beast." This is the idea that "lower" animals are cruel and ferocious by "nature." Hence, their extermination is an act of grace which serves to reduce the quantity of cruelty and danger that exists in the world. Hence, anyone who chooses to do so may arm himself with some lethal weapon and take the life of any number of "wild" animals he chooses.

The truth is that there are no jungles or wild animals except in the cities which men have created; that the view of "nature," of "the wild," and of "wild animals" that men have created represents a libel and a caricature of the realities. These views serve to distort and impoverish the world of humanity and of nature, and what is worse, to justify the destruction of both humanity and nature.

THE "LOWER" ANIMALS

Other animals by virtue of the fact that they are different are classified as "lower." But they are not "lower," they are merely different. Certainly men can do some things better than other animals, but then virtually every other animal can do a great many things a great deal better than any man can do. Every animal is adapted to its particular niche, and most animals have occupied their particular niches considerably longer than man has his. Man's anthropocentrism, however, is such that, having awarded himself all the prizes and elected himself to the topmost rung of the "scale of nature," he can afford to look down with pride in himself and contempt for all other animals, for is he not *Homo sapiens,* the "wise guy," the first amidst the Order of Mammals, *Primates*? It was Oscar Wilde who described man's naming himself *Homo sapiens* as perhaps the most oafishly arrogant definition of a species ever given. However that may be, man combining his myth making with his taxonomic faculty has become the creator and caretaker of his own classificatory system in which he has elected himself to the top and placed other animals on a descending series of rungs upon the "scale of nature."

The conception of "lower animals" is closely related to the idea of "lower races." Because other ethnic groups differ in various ways from ourselves they are therefore regarded as "inferior" and we, the classifiers, as "superior." When we inquire into the causes of the differences we find that the classifier's prejudices enable him to find a ready explanation for them in "heredity" or "innate factors," when, in fact, the differences have a vastly more interesting explanation than that, and have nothing whatever to do with questions of superiority or inferiority. Both physical and behavioral traits are due to differences in the physical and cultural history of the different groups.

Differences in the challenges of the physical environment have elicited genetic reactions which have adaptively served to fit the organism to live in an environment of such challenges, whether of sunlight intensity, humidity, the presence of malaria-bearing mosquitoes, and the like. Dark-pigmented skin is at an advantage in high-sunlight areas. In such areas it is definitely adaptively superior to white skin. But a highly developed intelligence enables light-skinned people to stay out of the sun. Such intelligence is also an evolutionary product of adaptive value.

Similarly, differences in behavior and in cultural achievement are due not to differences in genes but to differences in the history of experience which each group and each individual has undergone, to differences in the storage of acquired traits, namely, culture.

It is not to genetic heredity but to social heredity that man owes his equipment of behavioral traits. That equipment will differ according to the characteristics of the culture in which it has been acquired. There is no such thing as the inheritance of acquired physical characteristics. But behaviorally there is very definitely such a thing as the inheritance of acquired social traits—not from a genetic heredity but from a social heredity.

HEREDITY

Most people take "heredity" to mean something equivalent to predestination—a view which has done a considerable amount of harm. More explicitly, what "heredity" has been taken to mean by many who should have known better is that it is something that is determined at fertilization; something we derive from our parents in our genes which determines our physical traits and largely our behavioral characteristics.

This is a wholly confused and unsound view of heredity.

Heredity is neither something that is determined at conception nor something that we are born with. In fact, heredity determines nothing. What the genes do, *under the stimulation of the environments in which they interact and develop,* is influence the physiological and behavioral development of traits. Genes do not act, they interact with one another and in the environments which act upon them. There is no interaction of genes with anything unless there are environmental actions upon them. Thus, what the organism develops as is dependent upon two principal interactive factors: 1) the genes, and 2) the environments. Heredity is the expression of the interaction between genes and environments in which they have undergone development. Hence, the end result of that expression, the phenotype, is not something that has been determined by genes or by anything else, but has been *influenced* to develop as it has as a consequence of the differences in the interactions which have occurred between unique aggregates of genes and particular kinds of environments.

Heredity is a dynamic interactive series of processes, *not* a static condition. Heredity is *not* predestination. It is not something about which one can do nothing. On the contrary, it is something about which one can do a great deal. By varying either the genes or the environments or both, one can greatly influence the expression of traits. This is readily seen in matters of health, growth, development, intelligence, learning ability, behavior, achievement, and the like.[6]

Discussions as to whether heredity or environment is "stronger" are, in the light of the facts, completely nonsensical. What is important always to remember is that there are no genes without an environment,

[6]Ashley Montagu, *Human Heredity,* Cleveland and New York, World Publishing Company, 1965; Gladys C. Schwesinger, *Heredity and Environment,* New York, Macmillan, 1933; Jenny Hirsch (ed.), *Behavior—Genetic Analysis,* New York, McGraw-Hill, 1967; Max Levitan and Ashley Montagu, *Fundamentals of Human Genetics,* New York, Oxford University Press, 1968.

and what the genes can do the environment can also do, but alone neither can do anything.

BLOOD AND CONSANGUINITY

Blood as the quintessential element of the body which carries, and through which are transmitted, the hereditary qualities of the stock is a persisting archaism which has, for example, forced the Red Cross to segregate Negro blood banks from white blood banks, and societies to distinguish between "royal blood," "blue blood," "foreign blood," and the blood of commoners. Except for the great variability in its groups, types, and other serological characters, all human blood is of one and the same kind, and no blood carries hereditary "determinants." The hereditary factors are carried in the genes, which are situated in the chromosomes, and nowhere else. The blood of aristocrats, royalty, foreigners, and ordinary men and women is of the same kind and indistinguishable from one another. There is no such thing as blue blood. Nor is there any such thing as "consanguinity," for the simple reason that human beings cannot be related by "blood" but only by genes.

"Good blood, "bad blood," "fullblood," "halfblood," are all scientifically nonsensical terms. The official philosopher of the Nazis, Alfred Rosenberg, declared that "this recognition of the profound significance of blood is now mysteriously encircling our planet, irresistibly gripping one nation after the other."[7] And, indeed, with this belief the Nazis carried out a murderous blood bath such as the world had never even imagined possible. As Voltaire remarked, those who believe in absurdities will not find it difficult to commit atrocities.

MISCEGENATION

The term *miscegenation* provides a remarkable exhibit in the natural history of nonsense. The term is used in a pejorative sense as referring to "race mixture." The prefix *mis* (from the Latin *miscere*, mix) has probably contributed its share to the misunderstanding of the nature of "race" mixture. Words that begin with the prefix *mis* suggest "mistake," "misuse," "mislead," and similar erroneous ideas implying wrong conduct.

The word *miscegenation* was invented as a hoax, and published in an anonymous pamphlet in New York in 1864, with the title *Miscegenation: The Theory of the Blending of the Races, Applied to the White Man*

[7] *Vossiche Zeitung*, September 3, 1933.

and Negro.[8] The pamphlet was almost certainly the joint product of two members of the New York *World* staff, David Goodman Croly, an editor, and George Wakeman, one of the reporters. The purpose of the authors was to raise the "race" issue in aggravated form in the 1864 presidential campaign by attributing to the abolitionist Republican party the views set forth in *Miscegenation*. The pamphlet was intended to commit the Republican leaders to "the conclusions to which they are brought by their own principles," without any hope of success but in the expectation that their folly would be made all the more clear to them in granting the Negro the franchise. The brief introduction sets the tone of the whole pamphlet.

"The word is spoken at last. It is Miscegenation—the blending of the various races of men—the practical recognition of all the children of the common father. While the sublime inspirations of Christianity have taught this doctrine, Christians so-called have ignored it in denying social equality to the colored man; while democracy is founded upon the idea that all men are equal, democrats have shrunk from the logic of their own creed, and refuse to fraternize with the people of all nations. . . ." And much else, with tongue in cheek, to the same effect.

The word *miscegenation* is defined by the authors as follows: "*Miscegenation*—from the Latin *Miscere*, to mix, and *Genus*, race, is used to denote the abstract idea of the mixture of two or more races."

Thus, the word *miscegenation* was invented by satirists to replace the vulgar term *amalgamation*, as not being sufficiently elevated or distinguished.

Indeed, the word does carry with it a sort of authoritative aura, implying, however, a certain lack of respectability and even responsibility. The extent of the prejudice inherent in and engendered by this word may be gathered from the fact that Webster's New International Dictionary (Second Edition) defines "miscegenator" as "one who is *guilty* of miscegenation." The italics are mine. Former President Harry S Truman, when asked whether he thought "racial" intermarriages would become widespread in the United States, replied, "I hope not. I don't believe in it. What's that word about four feet long? Miscegenation?"[9]

ATAVISM

As a sorry example of the folly of falling into folk error, Webster scores again with *atavism*. Webster attributes the occurrence of an ata-

---

[8]This pamphlet is the subject of an excellent little book by J. M. Bloch, *Miscegenation, Meloleukation, and Mr. Lincoln's Dog*, Schaum, 1958.

[9]*The New York Times*, September 12, 1963.

vism to "recombination of ancestral genes." This lends the definition an aura of scientific respectability which it in fact wholly lacks. Such a "recombination of ancestral genes" simply never occurs and atavisms are simply creations of the imagination. Derived from the Latin *atavus,* an ancestor, the word appears to have been first used in English by James Rennie in 1833, writing, "Children often resemble their grandfathers or grandmothers more than their immediate parents. . . . This propensity is termed Atavism by Duchesne."[10] In this sense the word would have had a perfectly legitimate meaning and usage. But it suffered a change during the rise of evolutionary biology in the later half of the nineteenth century when it came to have the meaning of a reversion or throwback to an ancestral evolutionary condition. From biology the term was taken over for further service by literary men and writers in general. This is unfortunate because the word refers to a purely mythical series of events as if they were matters of fact.

When structures or functions occur which resemble those which existed among ancestral groups, but have been lost by descendant groups, the trait, like a fistula in the neck which is homologized with the gill slits of a fish, or a tail-like structure, is not due to a "recombination of ancestral genes" but to abnormal developmental changes resulting in either persistence, suppression, reduction, hypertrophy, duplication, or multiplication of structures. A fistula in the neck has nothing to do developmentally or in any other way with the gill slits of fishes, but everything to do with an arrest of development at an early embryonic stage of the branchial arches.

It is apparent, then, that the words we use act as psychophysical conditioners which determine the manner in which the individual shall think, feel, and behave. Hence, the importance of sound-thinking and right-feeling, familial and educational goals. Hence, also, the importance of teaching language not so much as grammar but as behavior, of teaching language as a fine and delicate instrument of expression designed to put man into touch with his fellow man.

[10] James Rennie, *The Science of Gardening,* Condon, 1833, p. 113.

Among the many problems of effective communication none is more subtle or more widespread than the problem of prejudice.

The Language of Prejudice

ELDON L. SEAMANS

Here Eldon Seamans considers five "languages" of prejudice: the languages of benevolence, concern, self-disparagement, self-reproach, and directed response. The assumption Seamans makes—and I think it's a valid one—is that if we understand our prejudices and the way in which we manifest them we will be in a better position to prevent them from becoming barriers to communication. The prior problem, however, is to recognize and admit that prejudice (both positive and negative) is a universal tendency and that the task is, as Seamans puts it, "to live with our prejudices and understand them."

Among the many problems of effective communication none is more subtle or more widespread than the problem of prejudice. The subtlety lies in the fact that the average man seems to feel he is free of prejudice as he makes his decisions. This failure to recognize his prejudices is further complicated by the widespread notion that prejudices are always of a negative character. If a man is "for" something he automatically considers himself free from prejudice. Only when he is "against" something does he feel any compulsion to admit that he may be issuing a prejudiced opinion.

The universality of prejudicial judgment and expression is found in the fact that life is a constant chain of decisions. Whether a man chooses to wear a red necktie or a blue one may be of little importance to the world, but a decision it is. And the process of choosing is a constant factor in man's life, involving every area of human conduct and philosophy. From the life of the garbage collector to that of the president of the large corporation this decision-making goes on continually, and the decisions always involve man's prejudices.

If this is true, we must learn to live with our prejudices and understand them. Basic to this understanding is the realization that every prejudice has both positive and negative sides. When a man chooses to wear his red necktie instead of his blue one he is prejudiced *in favor of* the one and *against* the other. When he makes any statement regarding his choice, both the positive and the negative elements are inherent in the communicative process.

All this brings us to a consideration of some of the ways in which men express their prejudices. Sometimes these expressions are spoken with conviction; sometimes they are apologetically set forth. Yet it appears to me that there are several common modes of communication which are found in what I have called "the language of prejudice."

In the first place men often express their prejudices by using what

From Eldon L. Seamans, "The Language of Prejudice," Etc. 23 (June 1966), pp. 216–224, by permission of the International Society for General Semantics.

may be called "the language of benevolence." I recently heard a conversation which is illustrative of this type of communication. Two men were discussing Little League baseball in a community in which feelings regarding both baseball and race run high. One of the men made this observation: "Those Negro boys walk clear across town for Little League practice, and some of those kids are among the best players we have!" A casual auditor might feel that these words are indicative of an openminded attitude toward both Little League and race relations, but a closer look reveals a subtle prejudice for Little League and against the Negro. The program is important enough to warrant letting these boys participate if they are a help to the team. At the same time one is made to feel it is surprising that "those kids" should be "among the best ball players we have."

The language of benevolence in this instance does three things, the first of which is to indicate an equalitarian spirit. My first reaction to the statement was, "How nice that this man accepts these boys as a part of the baseball program in the community." His commendation of their ambition and ability rings of good will. A moment's thought, however, makes us realize that this good will is conditional.

This leads us to the second aspect of the statement: the benevolent expression carries the notion that the burden of proof lies with these boys from the minority group. While the language expresses recognition of the boys' achievement, it also carries a note of surprise which seems to say, "As long as you keep up the good work we shall be on your side."

It also must be noted that the speaker of these benevolent words is the judge of the boys' success or failure. What he is really saying is, "I approve of these boys because they are interested enough in Little League to walk across town to practice every day. Also, in my opinion, they are valuable to the team." On this basis this particular man accepts them, but he reserves the right to change his opinion. In this case, at least, the language of benevolence is based on a personal—and, I fear, a fickle—opinion.

A general summary of this type of language of prejudice can be stated in the following manner: the language of benevolence, while professing an equalitarian spirit, suggests that the individual or group possesses unrealized potential, the realization of which is dependent solely on this individual or group. Also, the evaluation of the subject's progress in the achievement of the potential lies in the hands of the speaker.

The second type of expression found in the language of prejudice may be called the "language of concern." This type is characterized by generalizations which fail to relate themselves to a specific frame of reference. One of the most common examples of this type of language is found in the statement, "Some of my best friends are. . . ."

In areas in which racial tensions are the most pronounced, another example of language of concern is often heard. Even in heated arguments over the rights of the Negro citizen, opponents of civil and social liberty programs have been heard to voice their vehement protests against the actions and then conclude by saying of the Negro, "But we love them!" I am convinced that, in spite of its incongruous nature, this statement is often made in sincerity. It is possible for men to profess such a concern without implementing their words with action and to feel that they have been freed from their prejudice against their dark-skinned neighbors. The reasons for this are three in number.

First of all, the statement "We love them!" expresses its concern by witnessing to a "love in general." The impression which the statement leaves is that the speaker feels the same degree of concern for every member of the minority group. At no point does this attitude take into consideration such matters as individual differences among the persons to be loved and the varieties of environments within which this concern must be administered.

Out of this initial ambiguity the second characteristic of the language of concern arises. This is found in the fact that the expression of concern is ill-defined in regard to both the object of its interest and the goals of its anxiety. Just as the love of which it speaks is defined only in the most general terms, so is the object of concern seen only in terms of a group image. No specific goals for realizing this love are defined. The language of concern makes no attempt to define what love is or how it acts. Yet this love-in-general, with its ill-defined object and goals, appears to bring great comfort to the individual who makes use of it.

Such language of concern is a comfort to the prejudiced man because it minimizes his sense of guilt. Everyone in his right mind agrees that love is a good thing. It is as bad to be against love as it is to frown on motherhood or endorse sin. The fact that a man says he loves his dark-skinned neighbor indicates that he is not prejudiced against him—or so he reasons as he expresses himself by using the language of concern. And with the power such language possesses to minimize one's sense of guilt it is not difficult to see why it has gained its wide popularity.

Moving on to the third type of the language of prejudice we discover a mode of speech which may be designated as the "language of self-disparagement." This type of speech is as valuable in expressing man's positive prejudices as it is in revealing his negative ones. I remember a professor of mine who occasionally used to find himself in disagreement with the author of our textbook. He used to say, "I guess I'm not very bright, but I simply can't agree with this author." Even his young students were aware that he was seeking to impress them with his own view (the positive prejudice) while belittling the text's point of view (the negative one). Nor were his classes fooled into thinking their professor really thought of himself as an idiot.

The language of self-disparagement is an effective tool when used skillfully—a fact of which Benjamin Franklin was quite aware. In his *Autobiography* Franklin tells of his use of humility in the conduct of his daily affairs. He says, "I made it a rule to forbear all direct contradiction to the sentiments of others, and all positive assertion of my own. I even forbade myself . . . the use of every word or expression in the language that imparted a fixed opinion, such as *certainly*, I *apprehend*, or I *imagine* a thing to be so or so; or it so appears to me at present." Here we see a profound insight into the language of self-disparagement. Franklin had learned that dogmatic pronouncements make enemies. So he covered his prejudices with language designed to soften his opinions while still presenting them to those who heard his voice.

The effect of the language of self-disparagement is two-fold. First, it conveys a sense of humility on the part of the speaker. This is the impression which Franklin set out to create. It may be a mock humility, but it is useful in catching men's attention. There is something about arrogance which places its hearers on the defensive. The person who speaks humbly leaves the impression that he is so deeply convinced of the truth of his opinion that he cannot help speaking, even though he "is not very bright."

In the second place, the language of self-disparagement plays on the sympathy of its audience. When the speaker talks disparagingly of himself the listener's imagination tries to discover why this unfounded sense of inferiority should plague the speaker's thoughts. Why should the professor say, "I guess I'm not very bright"? He has a doctoral degree. He has written many books. He is sought after as a lecturer. Who has given him this groundless inferiority complex? So it is that we listen to the statement of prejudice which he speaks and feel sorry for him as he speaks of himself disparagingly. And by thus playing on our sympathy he opens our minds to a careful consideration of his point of view.

Closely related to the language of self-disparagement is a style of speaking which we may call the "language of self-reproach." In this instance the speaker does not convey humility or inferiority. He gives the opposite impression of himself. As he expresses his opinions he indicates that he is self-confident and astute. In argumentation he gives his opponent the idea that he has honestly tried to see his correspondent's point of view, but that he cannot accept so shallow an opinion.

I remember a man who took violent exception to an opinion I had expressed in an article I had written. In response to his criticisms I sought to explain my position. His reply was, "I appreciate your attempt to answer my criticism, but I regret to say that you have failed completely." The desired effect was to indicate that, in spite of every effort on his part, my opinion was obviously untenable. Actually he was pleased to find that his prejudice was not changed in the slightest by my prejudice. But the language of self-reproach, in expressing regret, leaves two impressions.

First of all, it implies that there has been a sincere effort on the part of the critic to understand his opponent's point of view. An open-mindedness is indicated. The speaker has done his level best to put himself in the place of the other fellow. Yet even such an effort to understand the opposition has resulted in failure.

By using the language of self-reproach he appears to place the blame for his failure on his own short-comings while retaining his former prejudice.

This brings us to the second effect of the language of self-reproach. From the implication of a sincere but unsuccessful effort to be persuaded, it is now easy to intimate that the failure to change one's mind stems from the weakness of the efforts of one's opponent. As my friend put it, although he was appreciative of my efforts to answer his criticisms my attempt simply was not good enough.

This approach, like the language of benevolence, throws the burden of proof on the shoulders of those who are the object of the prejudice.

The last type of language—and perhaps the most effective—in the expression of prejudice is the "language of directed response." This mode of expression is most often found in the form of a question. While its approach may vary, the basic question always takes the "Don't you think. . . ?" form. Examples of the language of directed response are legion. Among the more common of them are questions which begin, Don't you think. . . ? Isn't it true. . . ? Do you agree. . . ? Such expressions as these have a tendency to do two things.

The first result of the language of directed response is to outline in the question the answer which is expected. Such a use of language constitutes a strong motivation for an agreeable answer. The desire for popularity, for friendship, and for approval prompts a reply to the language of directed response in terms agreeable to the questioner. The one who uses this mode of expression sets the climate for any response which may be given to his prejudice, and this climate is favorable to his own viewpoint.

In addition to outlining the expected answer to its statements the language of directed response also puts its respondent in a defensive position. Any man who is faced with the necessity of replying to a prejudice expressed in a statement of the "Don't you think. . . ?" variety can choose to disagree. But if he follows this course he is placed in the position of defending his own prejudice. The language of directed response states what his answer ought to be. If he does not agree with the implied viewpoint it becomes his duty to prove that his prejudice is more tenable than the one that has been voiced in the implication.

Prejudicial statements are inevitable. Any definite opinion is a prejudice in favor of some idea or thing and a prejudice against something else. It is therefore absurd for any man to say he is without prejudice. Yet if men are to communicate effectively they must find a way of overcoming their preconceived notions to a degree which will enable them at least to listen to and understand other points of view. The various modes of the language of prejudice which we have outlined tend to make effective communication difficult.

The task is not impossible, and recognizing that there is a language of prejudice is a beginning. If we remember that benevolence is a method of compensating for our prejudices; if we understand that love—to have meaning—must be accompanied by action; if we recognize that our opinions are the product of a healthy self-esteem; then the modes of benevolence, concern, and self-disparagement will be seen in their true light. If, instead of using the language of self-disparagement, we admit our inability to be completely objective in our treatment of the views of others we shall be able to communicate more truthfully with one another. If we repudiate the use of the language of directed response, thus refraining from imposing our rationalizations on others, we shall be better able to speak with and understand one another.

In short, the language of prejudice will remain with us. But as we understand our prejudices better they will be less able to confuse our communications.

*The English language must become
democratic. It must become respectful
of the possibilities of the human spirit.*

The English Language Is My Enemy

OSSIE DAVIS

The problems faced by minority groups are here
described by actor-writer Ossie Davis who argues that the
English language is "one of the prime carriers of racism
from one person to another in our society." Davis makes
a number of assumptions which many would question; for
example, that education is "the act or process of imparting
or communicating a culture, developing the powers of
reasoning and judgment and generally preparing oneself
and others intellectually for a mature life" or that
"thinking itself is subvocal speech (in other words, one
must use words in order to think at all)." The principle
value of this article, I think, is in raising the question of
the relationship between language and social attitudes,
beliefs, and values not in an abstract theoretical model but
in a real and present and important context.

I stand before you, a little nervous, afflicted to some degree with stage fright. Not because I fear you, but because I fear the subject.

The title of my address is, "Racism in American Life—Broad Perspectives of the Problem," or, "The English Language is My Enemy."

In my speech I will define culture as the sum total of ways of living built up by a group of human beings and transmitted by one generation to another. I will define education as the act or process of impairing and communicating a culture, developing the powers of reasoning and judgment and generally preparing oneself and others intellectually for a mature life.

AN EDUCATION IN WORDS

I will define communication as the primary means by which the process of education is carried out.

I will say that language is the primary medium of communication in the educational process and, in this case, the English language. I will indict the English language as one of the prime carriers of racism from one person to another in our society and discuss how the teacher and the student, especially the Negro student, are affected by this fact.

The English language is my enemy.

Racism is a belief that human races have distinctive characteristics, usually involving the idea that one's own race is superior and has a right to rule others. Racism.

The English language is my enemy.

But that was not my original topic—I said that English was my goddamn enemy. Now why do I use "goddamn" to illustrate this aspect of the English language? Because I want to illustrate the sheer gut power of words. Words which control our action. Words like "nigger," "kike," "sheeny," "Dago," "black power"—words like this. Words we don't use

Ossie Davis, "The English Language Is My Enemy," American Teacher *(American Federation of Teachers, AFL-CIO), (April 1967), pp. 13-15.*

in ordinary decent conversation, one to the other. I choose these words deliberately, not to flaunt my freedom before you. If you are a normal human being these words will have assaulted your senses, may even have done you physical harm, and if you so choose, you could have me arrested.

Those words are attacks upon your physical and emotional well being; your pulse rate is possibly higher, your breath quicker; there is perhaps a tremor along the nerves of your arms and your legs; sweat begins in the palms of your hands, perhaps. With these few words I have assaulted you. I have damaged you, and there is nothing you can possibly, possibly do to control your reactions—to defend yourself against the brute force of these words.

There words have a power over us; a power that we cannot resist. For a moment you and I have had our deepest physical reaction controlled, not by our own wills, but by words in the English language.

WHAT ROGET REVEALS

A superficial examination of Roget's Thesaurus of the English Language reveals the following facts: The word "whiteness" has 134 synonyms, 44 of which are favorable and pleasing to contemplate. For example: "purity," "cleanness," "immaculateness," "bright," "shiny," "ivory," "fair," "blonde," "stainless," "clean," "clear," "chaste," "unblemished," "unsullied," "innocent," "honorable," "upright," "just," "straightforward," "fair," "genuine," "trustworthy,"—and only 10 synonyms of which I feel to have been negative and then only in the mildest sense, such as "gloss-over," "whitewash," "gray," "wan," "pale," "ashen," etc.

The word "blackness" has 120 synonyms, 60 of which are distinctly unfavorable, and none of them even mildly positive. Among the offending 60 were such words as "blot," "blotch," "smut," "smudge," "sullied," "begrime," "soot," "becloud," "obscure," "dingy," "murky," "low-toned," "threatening," "frowning," "foreboding," "forbidding," "sinister," "baneful," "dismal," "thundery," "wicked," "malignant," "deadly," "unclean," "dirty," "unwashed," "foul," etc. In addition, and this is what really hurts, 20 of those words—and I exclude the villainous 60 above—are related directly to race, such as "Negro," "Negress," "nigger," "darkey," "blackamoor," etc.

'THINKING IS SUBVOCAL SPEECH'

If you consider the fact that thinking itself is subvocal speech (in other words, one must use words in order to think at all), you will appreciate the enormous trap of racial prejudgment that works on any child who is born into the English language.

Any creature, good or bad, white or black, Jew or Gentile, who uses the English language for the purposes of communication is willing to force the Negro child into 60 ways to despise himself, and the white child, 60 ways to aid and abet him in the crime.

Language is a means of communication. This corruption, this evil of racism, doesn't affect only one group. It doesn't take white to make a person a racist. Blacks also become inverted racists in the process.

A part of our function, therefore, as teachers, will be to reconstruct the English language. A sizeable undertaking, but one which we must undertake if we are to cure the problems of racism in our society.

DEMOCRATIZING ENGLISH

The English language must become democratic. It must become respectful of the possibilities of the human spirit. Racism is not only reflected in words relating to the color of Negroes. If you will examine some of the synonyms for the word Jew you will find that the adjectives and the verb of the word Jew are offensive. However, if you look at the word Hebrew you will see that there are no offensive connotations to the word.

When you understand and contemplate the small difference between the meaning of one word supposedly representing one fact, you will understand the power, good or evil, associated with the English language. You will understand also why there is a tremendous fight among the Negro people to stop using the word "Negro" altogether and substitute "Afro-American."

You will understand, even further, how men like Stokely Carmichael and Floyd McKissick can get us in such serious trouble by using two words together: Black Power. If Mr. McKissick and Mr. Carmichael had thought a moment and said Colored Power, there would have been no problem.

We come today to talk about education. Education is the only valid transmitter of American values from one generation to another. Churches have been used from time immemorial to teach certain values to certain people, but in America, as in no other country, it is the school that bears the burden of teaching young Americans to be Americans.

Schools define the meaning of such concepts as success. And education is a way out of the heritage of poverty for Negro people. It's the way we can get jobs.

THE ONE-BY-ONE ROUTE

Education is that which opens that golden door that was so precious to Emma Lazarus. But education in the past has basically been built on the theory that we could find those gifted individuals among the Negro people and educate them out of their poverty, out of their restricted conditions, and then, they would, in turn, serve to represent the best interests of the race; and if we concentrated on educating Negroes as individuals, we would solve the problem of discrimination by educating individual Negroes out of the problem. But I submit that that is a false and erroneous function and definition of education. We can no longer, as teachers, concentrate on finding the gifted black child in the slums or in the middle-class areas and giving him the best that we have. This no longer serves the true function of education if education indeed is to fulfill its mission to assist and perpetuate the drive of the Negro community to come into the larger American society on the same terms as all other communities have come.

Let us look for a brief moment at an article appearing in *Commentary* in February, 1964, written by the associate director of the American Jewish Committee. "What is now perceived as the revolt of the Negro amounts to this," he says. "The solitary Negro seeking admission into the white world through unusual achievement has been replaced by the organized Negro insisting upon a legitimate share for his group of the goods of American society. The white liberal, in turn, who, whether or not he is fully conscious of it, has generally conceived of progress in race relations as the one-by-one assimilation of deserving Negroes into the larger society, now finds himself confused and threatened by suddenly having to come to terms with an aggressive Negro community that wishes to enter en masse.

"Accordingly, in the arena of civil rights, the Negro revolution has tended to take the struggle out of the courts and bring it to the streets and the negotiating tables. Granting the potential for unprecedented violence that exists here, it must also be borne in mind that what the Negro people are now beginning to do, other ethnic minorities who brought to America their strong traditions of communal solidarity did before them. With this powerful asset, the Irish rapidly acquired political strength and the Jews succeeded in raising virtually an entire immigrant population into the middle class within a span of two generations. Viewed in this perspective, the Negroes are merely the last of America's significant ethnic minorities to achieve communal solidarity and to grasp the role of the informal group power structure in protecting the rights and advancing the opportunities of the individual members of the community."

LIBERAL 'GRADUALISM'

Teachers have a very important function. They have before them the raw materials of the future. And if we were satisfied by the job that was being done in our country and in our culture it would not be necessary to call a protest conference. It would be necessary only to call a conference to celebrate.

I submit that racism is inherent in the English language because the language is an historic expression of the experience of a people; that racism, which is the belief that one group is superior to the other and has the right to set the standards for the other, is still one of the main spiritual policies of our country as expressed in the educational process.

Those of us who are concerned, those of us who are caught up, those of us who really want to be involved, must be prepared at this conference to tear aside our most private thoughts and prejudices, remembering that we have been taught them because we are all born to the English language.

Let us not feel personally guilty or personally responsible for the fact that we may not like Negroes. Let us remember that we are participating in the culture which has taught us not to like them, so that, when we are tempted to teach a child from above his position, or to say that "I represent white Anglo-Saxon gentility and culture, and out of the gratitude and graciousness of my heart I am going to reach down and lift you up to my level," we know that is the incorrect attitude.

We cannot reach down and lift up anymore, we must all get down together and reciprocate one to the other and come up together.

Let us, above all, be honest one to the other. Let us pursue truth though it makes us bleed. I said in the beginning that my purpose in using those lacerating words was to expose our innermost feeling. We must dig even deeper for the roots in our own consciousness, black and white, or the real fact of racism in our culture, and having faced that in ourselves, go back to the various schools from which we came and look upon the children before us as an opportunity, not only to practice the craft of teaching and the imparting of knowledge but, equally important, as an opportunity to learn from a subjugated people what its value, its history, its culture, its wealth as an independent people are. Let there be in our classrooms a sharing of the wealth of American democracy.

WHY TEACHERS FAIL

Liberal opinion in the North and in the South thus continues to stand upon its traditions of gradualism—that of one-by-one admission of deserving Negroes into the larger society and rejection of the idea that to help the Negro it must help first the Negro community.

Today in America, as elsewhere, the Negro has made us forcefully aware of the fact that the rights and privileges of an individual rest upon the status obtained by the group to which he belongs.

In the American pattern, where social power is distributed by groups, the Negro has come to recognize that he can achieve equal opportunities only through concerted action of the Negro community. We can't do it one by one anymore, we must do it as a group.

Now, how is education related to the process not of lifting individuals but of lifting a whole group by its bootstraps and helping it climb to its rightful place in American society?

One of the ways is by calling such meetings as this to discuss Negro history—to discuss those aspects of Negro culture which are important for the survival of the Negro people as a community. There is nothing in the survival of the Negro people as a community that is inherently hostile to the survival of the interests of any other group.

So when we say Black Power and Black Nationalism we do not mean that that is the only power or that that is the only nationalism that we are concerned about or that it is to predominate above all others. We merely mean that it should have the right of all other groups and be respected as such in the American way of life.

'A BOOTLEG TEACHER'

I have had occasion (and with this I'll come to a close) to function as a teacher—I'm a bootleg teacher, I teach Sunday school, it's the closest I can get to the process—I teach boys from nine to 12, and I have the same problem with getting them to appreciate the spoken and written word, as you do, in your daily classrooms. Most of them can't read. I don't see how they're going to get, not only to Heaven—I don't see how they're going to get to the next grade unless they can command some of these problems that we have.

But, more importantly, I am also involved in the educational process. And those of us who are involved in culture and cultural activities, do ourselves and our country and our cause a great injustice not to recognize that we, too, are communicators and have therefore a responsibility in the process of communication. I could be hired today to communicate to the great American public my great delight in smoking a cigarette, but I know that a cigarette would cause you cancer and I could be paid for that. I could be used to do many other things in the process of communications from the top to the bottom.

I have a responsibility to show that what I do, what is translated through me, is measured by the best interest of my country and my people and my profession. And in that I think we are all together.

*Sexist language is any language that
expresses such stereotyped attitudes
and expectations, or assumes the
inherent superiority of one sex over
the other.*

One Small Step for Genkind

CASEY MILLER AND KATE SWIFT

Betty Friedan, Kate Millett, Germaine Greer, Ti-Grace
Atkinson, Gloria Steinem, and various others have
articulately argued the cause of Women's Liberation. In
politics, in religion, in education, and in business women
are not granted equal rights. In this article Casey Miller
and Kate Swift argue that one of the most discriminating
institutions is language itself. The authors here illustrate
some of the specifics of the discriminatory nature of
language and present some suggestions for changes which
they claim would bring language to reflect women's equal
status with men.

A riddle is making the rounds that goes like this: A man and his young son were in an automobile accident. The father was killed and the son, who was critically injured, was rushed to a hospital. As attendants wheeled the unconscious boy into the emergency room, the doctor on duty looked down at him and said, "My God, it's my son!" What was the relationship of the doctor to the injured boy?

If the answer doesn't jump to your mind, another riddle that has been around a lot longer might help: The blind beggar had a brother. The blind beggar's brother died. The brother who died had no brother. What relation was the blind beggar to the blind beggar's brother?

As with all riddles, the answers are obvious once you see them: The doctor was the boy's mother and the beggar was her brother's sister. Then why doesn't everyone solve them immediately? Mainly because our language, like the culture it reflects, is male oriented. To say that a woman in medicine is an exception is simply to confirm that statement. Thousands of doctors are women, but in order to be seen in the mind's eye, they must be called women doctors.

Except for words that refer to females by definition (mother, actress, Congresswoman), and words for occupations traditionally held by females (nurse, secretary, prostitute), the English language defines everyone as male. The hypothetical person ("If a man can walk 10 miles in two hours . . ."), the average person ("the man in the street") and the active person ("the man on the move") are male. The assumption is that unless otherwise identified, people in general—including doctors and beggars—are men. It is a semantic mechanism that operates to keep women invisible: *man* and *mankind* represent everyone; *he* in generalized use refers to either sex; the "land where our fathers died" is also the land of our mothers—although they go unsung. As the beetle-browed and mustachioed man in a Steig cartoon says to his two male drinking companions, "When I speak of mankind, one thing I *don't* mean is womankind."

172

Semantically speaking, woman is not one with the species of man, but a distinct subspecies. "Man," says the 1971 edition of the Britannica Junior Encyclopedia, "is the highest form of life on earth. His superior intelligence, combined with certain physical characteristics, have enabled man to achieve things that are impossible for other animals." (The prose style has something in common with the report of a research team describing its studies on "the development of the uterus in rats, guinea pigs and men.") As though quoting the Steig character, still speaking to his friends in McSorley's, the Junior Encyclopedia continues: "Man must invent most of his behavior, because he lacks the instincts of lower animals. . . . Most of the things he learns have been handed down from his ancestors by language and symbols rather than by biological inheritance."

Considering that for the last 5,000 years society has been patriarchal, that statement explains a lot. It explains why Eve was made from Adam's rib instead of the other way around, and who invented all those Adam-rib words like *fe*male and *wo*man in the first place. It also explains why, when it is necessary to mention woman, the language makes her a lower caste, a class separate from the rest of man; why it works to "keep her in her place."

This inheritance through language and other symbols begins in the home (also called a man's castle) where man and wife (not husband and wife, or man and woman) live for a while with their children. It is reinforced by religious training, the educational system, the press, government, commerce and the law. As Andrew Greeley wrote not long ago in this magazine, "man is a symbol-creating animal. He orders and interprets his reality by his symbols, and he uses the symbols to reconstruct that reality."

Consider some of the reconstructed realities of American history. When school children learn from their textbooks that the early colonists gained valuable experience in governing themselves, they are not told that the early colonists who were women were denied the privilege of self-government; when they learn that in the 18th century the average man had to manufacture many of the things he and his family needed, they are not told that this "average man" was often a woman who manufactured much of what she and her family needed. Young people learn that intrepid pioneers crossed the country in covered wagons with their wives, children and cattle: they do not learn that women themselves were intrepid pioneers rather than part of the baggage.

In a paper published this year in Los Angeles as a guide for authors and editors of social-studies textbooks, Elizabeth Burr, Susan Dunn and Norma Farquhar document unintentional skewings of this kind that occur either because women are not specifically mentioned as affecting or being affected by historical events, or because they are discussed in terms of outdated assumptions. "One never sees a picture of women captioned simply 'farmers' or 'pioneers,'" they point out. The subspecies nomenclature that requires a caption to read "women farmers" or "women pioneers" is extended to impose certain jobs on women by definition. The textbook guide gives as an example the word *housewife*, which it says not only "suggests that domestic chores are the exclusive burden of females," but gives "female students the idea that they were born to keep house and teaches male students that they are automatically entitled to laundry, cooking and housecleaning services from the women in their families."

Sexist language is any language that expresses such stereotyped attitudes and expectations, or that assumes the inherent superiority of one sex over the other. When a woman says of her husband, who has drawn up plans for a new bedroom wing and left out closets, "Just like a man," her language is as sexist as the man's who says, after his wife has changed her mind about needing the new wing after all, "Just like a woman."

Male and female are not sexist words, but masculine and feminine almost always are. Male and female can be applied objectively to individual people and animals and, by extension, to things. When electricians and plumbers talk about male and female couplings, everyone knows or can figure out what they mean. The terms are graphic and culture free.

Masculine and feminine, however, are as sexist as any words can be, since it is almost impossible to use them without invoking cultural stereotypes. When people construct lists of "masculine" and "feminine" traits they almost always end up making assumptions that have nothing to do with innate differences between the sexes. We have a friend who happens to be going through the process of pinning down this very phenomenon. He is 7 years old and his question concerns why his coats and shirts button left over right while his sister's button the other way. He assumes it must have something to do with the differences between boys and girls, but he can't see how.

What our friend has yet to grasp is that the way you button your coat, like most sex-differentiated customs, has nothing to do with real differences but much to do with what society wants you to feel about yourself as a male or female person. Society decrees that it is appropriate for girls to dress differently from boys, to act differently, and to think differently. Boys must be masculine, whatever that means, and girls must be feminine.

Unabridged dictionaries are a good source for finding out what society decrees to be appropriate, though less by definition than by their choice of associations and illustrations. Words associated with males— *manly, virile* and *masculine*, for example—are defined through a broad range of positive attributes like strength, courage, directness and independence, and they are illustrated through such examples of contemporary usage as "a manly determination to face what comes," "a virile literary style," "a masculine love of sports." Corresponding words associated with females are defined with fewer attributes (though weakness is often one of them) and the examples given are generally negative if not clearly pejorative: "feminine wiles," "womanish tears," "a womanlike lack of promptness," "convinced that drawing was a waste of time, if not downright womanly."

Male associated words are frequently applied to females to describe something that is either incongruous ("a mannish voice") or presumably commendable ("a masculine mind," "she took it like a man"), but female-associated words are unreservedly derogatory when applied to males, and are sometimes abusive to females as well. The opposite of "masculine" is "effeminate," although the opposite of "feminine" is simply "unfeminine."

One dictionary, after defining the word *womanish* as "suitable to or resembling a woman," further defines it as "unsuitable to a man or to a strong character of either sex." Words derived from "sister" and "brother" provide another apt example, for whereas "sissy," applied either to a male or female, conveys the message that sisters are expected to be timid and cowardly, "buddy" makes clear that brothers are friends.

The subtle disparagement of females and corresponding approbation of males wrapped up in many English words is painfully illustrated by "tomboy." Here is an instance where a girl who likes sports and the out-of-doors, who is curious about how things work, who is adventurous and bold instead of passive, is defined in terms of something she is not—a boy. By denying that she can be the person she is and still be a girl, the word surreptitiously undermines her sense of identity; it says she is unnatural. A "tomboy," as defined by one dictionary, is a "girl, especially a young girl, who behaves like a spirited boy." But who makes the judgment that she is acting like a spirited boy, not a spirited girl? Can it be a coincidence that in the case of the dictionary just quoted the editor, executive editor, managing editor, general manager, all six members of the Board of Linguists, the usage editor, science editor, all six general editors of definitions, and 94 out of the 104 distinguished experts consulted on usage—are men?

It isn't enough to say that any invidious comparisons and stereotypes lexicographers perpetuate are already present in the culture. There are ways to define words like womanly and tomboy that don't put women down, though the tradition has been otherwise. Samuel Johnson, the lexicographer, was the same Dr. Johnson who said. "A woman preaching is like a dog's walking on his hind legs. It is not done well; but you are surprised to find it done at all."

Possibly because of the negative images associated with womanish and woman-like, and with expressions like "woman driver" and "woman of the street," the word woman dropped out of fashion for a time. The women at the office and the women on the assembly line and the women one first knew in school all became ladies or girls or gals. Now a counter-movement, supported by the very term women's liberation, is putting back into words like woman and sister and sisterhood the meaning they were losing by default. It is as though, in the nick of time, women had seen that the language itself could destroy them.

Some long-standing conventions of the news media add insult to injury. When a woman or girl makes news, her sex is identified at the beginning of a story, if possible in the headline or its equivalent. The assumption, apparently, is that whatever event or action is being reported, a woman's involvement is less common and therefore more newsworthy than a man's. If the story is about achievement, the implication is: "pretty good for a woman." And because people are assumed to be male unless otherwise identified, the media have developed a special and extensive vocabulary to avoid the constant repetition of "woman." The results, "Grandmother Wins Nobel Prize," "Blonde Hijacks Airliner," "Housewife to Run for Congress," convey the kind of information that would be ludicrous in comparable headlines if the subjects were men. Why, if "Unsalaried Husband to Run for Congress" is unacceptable to editors, do women have to keep explaining that to describe them through external or superficial concerns reflects a sexist view of women as decorative objects, breeding machines and extensions of men, not real people?

Members of the Chicago chapter of the National Organization for Women recently studied the newspapers in their area and drew up a set of guidelines for the press. These include cutting out descriptions of the "clothes, physical features, dating life and marital status of women where such references would be considered inappropriate if about men"; using language in such a way as to include women in copy that refers to homeowners, scientists and business people where "newspaper descriptions often convey the idea that all such persons are male"; and displaying the same discretion in printing generalizations about women as would be shown toward racial, religious and ethnic groups. "Our concern with what we are called may seem trivial to some people," the women said, "but we regard the old usages as symbolic of women's position within this society."

The assumption that an adult woman is flattered by being called a girl is matched by the notion that a woman in a menial or poorly paid job finds compensation in being called a lady. Ethel Strainchamps has pointed out that since lady is used as an adjective with nouns designating both high and low occupations (lady wrestler, lady barber, lady doctor, lady judge), some writers assume they can use the noun form without betraying value judgments. Not so, Strainchamps says, rolling the issue into a spitball: "You may write, 'He addressed the Republican ladies,' or 'The Democratic ladies convened' . . . but I have never seen 'the Communist ladies' or 'the Black Panther ladies' in print."

Thoughtful writers and editors have begun to repudiate some of the old usages. "Divorcée," "grandmother" and "blonde," along with "vivacious," "pert," "dimpled" and "cute," were dumped by The Washington Post in the spring of 1970 by the executive editor, Benjamin Bradlee. In a memo to his staff, Bradlee wrote, "The meaningful equality and dignity of women is properly under scrutiny today . . . because this equality has been less than meaningful and the dignity not always free of stereotype and condescension."

What women have been called in the press—or at least the part that operates above ground—is only a fraction of the infinite variety of alternatives to "woman" used in the subcultures of the English-speaking world. Beyond "chicks," "dolls," "dames," "babes," "skirts" and "broads" are the words and phrases in which women are reduced to their sexuality and nothing more. It would be hard to think of another area of language in which the human mind has been so fertile in devising and borrowing abusive terms. In "The Female Eunuch," Germaine Greer devotes four pages to anatomical terms and words for animals, vegetables, fruits, baked goods, implements and receptacles, all of which are used to dehumanize the female person. Jean Faust, in an article aptly called "Words That Oppress," suggests that the effort to diminish women through language is rooted in a male fear of sexual inadequacy. "Woman is made to feel guilty for and akin to natural disasters," she writes; "hurricanes and typhoons are named after her. Any negative or threatening force is given a feminine name. If a man runs into bad luck climbing up the ladder of success (a male-invented game), he refers to the 'bitch goddess' success."

The sexual overtones in the ancient and no doubt honorable custom of calling ships "she" have become more explicit and less honorable in an age of air travel: "I'm Karen. Fly me." Attitudes of ridicule, contempt and disgust toward female sexuality have spawned a rich glossary of insults and epithets not found in dictionaries. And the usage in which four-letter words meaning copulate are interchangeable with cheat, attack and destroy can scarcely be unrelated to the savagery of rape.

In her updating of Ibsen's "A Doll House," Clare Booth Luce has Nora tell her husband she is pregnant—"in the way only men are supposed to get pregnant." "Men, pregnant?" he says, and she nods: "With ideas. Pregnancies there [*she taps his head*] are masculine. And a very superior form of labor. Pregnancies here [*taps her tummy*] are feminine —a very inferior form of labor."

Public outcry followed a revised translation of the New Testament describing Mary as "pregnant" instead of "great with child." The objections were made in part on esthetic grounds: there is no attractive adjective in modern English for a woman who is about to give birth. A less obvious reason was that replacing the euphemism with a biological term undermined religious teaching. The initiative and generative power in the conception of Jesus are understood to be God's; Mary, the mother, was a vessel only.

Whether influenced by this teaching or not, the language of human reproduction lags several centuries behind scientific understanding. The male's contribution to procreation is still described as though it were the entire seed from which a new life grows: the initiative and generative power involved in the process are thought of as masculine, receptivity and nurturance as feminine. "Seminal" remains a synonym for "highly original," and there is no comparable word to describe the female's equivalent contribution.

An entire mythology has grown from this biological misunderstanding and its semantic legacy; its embodiment in laws that for centuries made women nonpersons was a key target of the 19-century feminist movement. Today, more than 50 years after women finally won the basic democratic right to vote, the word "liberation" itself, when applied to women, means something less than when used of other groups of people. An advertisement for the N.B.C. news department listed Women's Liberation along with crime in the streets and the Vietnam war as "bad news." Asked for his views on Women's Liberation, a highly placed politician was quoted as saying, "Let me make one thing perfectly clear. I wouldn't want to wake up next to a lady pipe-fitter."

One of the most surprising challenges to our male-dominated culture is coming from within organized religion, where the issues are being stated, in part, by confronting the implications of traditional language. What a growing number of theologians and scholars are saying is that the myths of the Judeo-Christian tradition, being the products of patriarchy, must be re-examined, and that the concept of an exclusively male ministry and the image of a male god have become idolatrous.

Women are naturally in the forefront of this movement, both in their efforts to gain ordination and full equality and through their contributions to theological reform, although both these efforts are often subtly diminished. When the Rev. Barbara Anderson was ordained by the American Lutheran Church, one newspaper printed her picture over a caption headed "Happy Girl." Newsweek's report of a protest staged last December by women divinity students at Harvard was jocular ("another tilt at the windmill") and sarcastic: "Every time anyone in the room lapsed into what [the students] regarded as male chauvinism—such as using the word 'mankind' to describe the human race in general—the outraged women . . . drowned out the offender with earpiercing blasts from party-favor kazoos. . . . What annoyed the women most was the universal custom of referring to God as 'He.' "

The tone of the report was not merely unfunny; it missed the connection between increasingly outmoded theological language and the accelerating number of women (and men) who are dropping out of organized religion, both Jewish and Christian. For language, including pronouns, can be used to construct a reality that simply mirrors society's assumptions. To women who are committed to the reality of religious faith, the effect is doubly painful. Professor Harvey Cox, in whose classroom the protest took place, stated the issue directly: The women, he said, were raising the "basic theological question of whether God is more adequately thought of in personal or suprapersonal terms."

Toward the end of Don McLean's remarkable ballad "American Pie," a song filled with the imagery of abandonment and disillusion, there is a stanza that must strike many women to the quick. The church bells are broken, the music has died; then:

And the three men I admire most,
The Father, Son and Holy Ghost,
They caught the last train for the Coast—
The day the music died.

Three men I admired most. There they go, briefcases in hand and topcoats buttoned left over right, walking down the long cold platform under the city, past the baggage wagons and the hissing steam onto the Pullman. Bye, bye God—all three of you—made in the image of male supremacy. Maybe out there in L.A. where the weather is warmer, someone can believe in you again.

The Roman Catholic theologian Elizabeth Farians says "the bad theology of an overmasculinized church continues to be one of the root causes of women's oppression." The definition of oppression is "to crush or burden by abuse of power or authority; burden spiritually or mentally as if by pressure."

When language oppresses, it does so by any means that disparage and belittle. Until well into the 20th-century, one of the ways English was manipulated to disparage women was though the addition of feminine endings to nonsexual words. Thus a woman who aspired to be a poet was excluded from the company of real poets by the label poetess, and a woman who piloted an airplane was denied full status as an aviator by being called an aviatrix. At about the time poetess, aviatrix, and similar Adam-ribbisms were dropping out of use, H. W. Fowler was urging that they be revived. "With the coming expansion of women's vocations," he wrote in the first edition (1926) of "Modern English Usage," "femininies for vocation-words are a special need of the future." There can be no doubt he subconsciously recognized the relative status implied in the -ess designations. His criticism of a woman who wished to be known as an author rather than an authoress was that she had no need "to raise herself to the level of the male author by asserting her right to his name."

Who has the prior right to a name? The question has an interesting bearing on words that were once applied to men alone, or to both men and women, but now, having acquired abusive associations, are assigned to women exclusively. Spinster is a gentle case in point. Prostitute and many of its synonyms illustrate the phenomenon better. If Fowler had chosen to record the changing usage of harlot from hired man (in Chaucer's time) through rascal and entertainer to its present definition, would he have maintained that the female harlot is trying to raise herself to the level of the male harlot by asserting her right to his name? Or would he have plugged for harlotress?

The demise of most -ess endings came about before the start of the new feminist movement. In the second edition of "Modern English Usage," published in 1965, Sir Ernest Gowers frankly admitted what his predecessors had been up to. "Feminine designations," he wrote, "seem now to be falling into disuse. Perhaps the explanation of this paradox is that it symbolizes the victory of women in their struggle for equal rights; it reflects the abandonment by men of those ideas about women in the professions that moved Dr. Johnson to his rude remark about women preachers."

If Sir Ernest's optimism can be justified, why is there a movement back to feminine endings in such words as chairwoman, councilwoman and congresswoman? Betty Hudson, of Madison, Conn., is campaigning for the adoption of "selectwoman" as the legal title for a female member of that town's executive body. To have to address a woman as "Selectman," she maintains, "is not only bad grammar and bad biology, but it implies that politics is still, or should be, a man's business." A valid argument, and one that was, predictably, countered by ridicule, the sure-fire weapon for undercutting achievement. When the head of the Federal Maritime Commission, Helen D. Bentley, was named "Man of the Year" by an association of shipping interests, she wisely refused to be drawn into lighthearted debate with interviewers who wanted to make the award's name a humorous issue. Some women, of course, have yet to learn they are invisible. An 8-year-old who visited the American Museum of Natural History with her Brownie scout troop went through the impressive exhibit on pollution and overpopulation called "Can Man Survive?" Asked afterward, "Well, can he?" she answered, "I don't know about him, but we're working on it in Brownies."

Nowhere are women rendered more invisible by language than in politics. The United States Constitution, in describing the qualifications for Representative, Senator and President, refers to each as *he*. No wonder Shirley Chisholm, the first woman since 1888 to make a try for the Presidential nomination of a major party, has found it difficult to be taken seriously.

The observation by Andrew Greeley already quoted—that "man" uses "his symbols" to reconstruct "his reality"—was not made in reference to the symbols of language but to the symbolic impact the "nomination of a black man for the Vice-Presidency" would have on race relations in the United States. Did the author assume the generic term "man" would of course be construed to include "woman"? Or did he deliberately use a semantic device to exclude Shirley Chisholm without having to be explicit?

Either way, his words construct a reality in which women are ignored. As much as any other factor in our language, the ambiguous meaning of *man* serves to deny women recognition as people. In a recent magazine article, we discussed the similar effect on women of the generic pronoun *he*, which we proposed to replace by a new common gender pronoun *tey*. We were immediately told, by a number of authorities, that we were dabbling in the serious business of linguistics, and the message that reached us from these scholars was loud and clear: It - is - absolutely - impossible - for - anyone - to - introduce - a - new - word - into - the language - just - because - there - is - a - need - for - it, so - stop - wasting - your - time.

When words are suggested like "herstory" (for history), "sportsoneship" (for sportsmanship) and "mistresspiece" (for the work of a Virginia Woolf) one suspects a not-too-subtle attempt to make the whole language problem look silly. But unless Alexander Pope, when he wrote "The proper study of mankind is man," meant that women should be relegated to the footnotes (or, as George Orwell might have put it, "All men are equal, but men are more equal than women"), viable new words will surely someday supersede the old.

Without apologies to Freud, the great majority of women do not wish in their hearts that they were men. If having grown up with a language that tells them they are at the same time men and not men raises psychic doubts for women, the doubts are not of their sexual identity but of their human identity. Perhaps the present unrest surfacing in the Women's Movement is part of an evolutionary change in our par-

ticular form of life—the one form of all in the animal and plant king-
doms that orders and interprets its reality by symbols. The achievements
of the species called man have brought us to the brink of self-destruction.
If the species survives into the next century with the expectation of going
on, it may only be because we have become part of what Harlow Shapley
calls the psychozoic kingdom, where brain overshadows brawn and ra-
tionality has replaced superstition.

Searching the roots of Western civilization for a word to call this
new species of man and woman, someone might come up with *gen*, as in
genesis and generic. With such a word, *man* could be used exclusively
for males as *woman* is used for females, for gen would include both sexes.
Like the words deer and bison, gen would be both plural and singular.
Like progenitor, progeny, and generation, it would convey continuity.
Gen would express the warmth and generalized sexuality of generous,
gentle, and genuine; the specific sexuality of genital and genetic. In the
new family of gen, girls and boys would grow to genhood, and to speak
of genkind would be to include all the people of the earth.

The purpose of Newspeak was not only to provide a medium of expression for the world-view and mental habits proper to the devotees of Ingsoc, but to make all other modes of thought impossible.

The Principles of Newspeak

GEORGE ORWELL

In *1984* George Orwell describes the futuristic state of Oceania where everyone's behavior and ultimately even thought are controlled by the Party whose slogans are "War is Peace," "Freedom is Slavery," and "Ignorance is Strength." In *1984* control of the people is seen as being effected largely by the language, Newspeak. "It was intended," says Orwell, "that when Newspeak had been adopted once and for all and Oldspeak forgotten, a heretical thought . . . should be literally unthinkable, at least so far as thought is dependent on words." The extent to which the language we speak influences the thoughts we have or may have is a much argued and little agreed upon question. But it is a question which has intrigued man from the earliest times—probably from the time man began to speak. Here Orwell describes in considerable detail the workings of Newspeak and provides us with unusual insight not only into the structure of language and languages but also into the relationship between language and thought, thought and behavior.

Newspeak was the official language of Oceania and had been devised to meet the ideological needs of Ingsoc, or English Socialism. In the year 1984 there was not as yet anyone who used Newspeak as his sole means of communication, either in speech or writing. The leading articles in the *Times* were written in it, but this was a tour de force which could only be carried out by a specialist. It was expected that Newspeak would have finally superseded Oldspeak (or Standard English, as we should call it) by about the year 2050. Meanwhile it gained ground steadily, all Party members tending to use Newspeak words and grammatical constructions more and more in their everyday speech. The version in use in 1984, and embodied in the Ninth and Tenth Editions of the Newspeak dictionary, was a provisional one, and contained many superfluous words and archaic formations which were due to be suppressed later. It is with the final, perfected version, as embodied in the Eleventh Edition of the dictionary, that we are concerned here.

The purpose of Newspeak was not only to provide a medium of expression for the world-wide and mental habits proper to the devotees of Ingsoc, but to make all other modes of thought impossible. It was intended that when Newspeak had been adopted once and for all and Oldspeak forgotten, a heretical thought—that is, a thought diverging from the principles of Ingsoc—should be literally unthinkable, at least so far as thought is dependent on words. Its vocabulary was so constructed as to give exact and often very subtle expression to every meaning that a Party member could properly wish to express, while excluding all other meanings and also the possibility of arriving at them by indirect methods. This was done partly by the invention of new words, but chiefly by eliminating undesirable words and by stripping such words as remained of unorthodox meanings, and so far as possible of all secondary meanings whatever. To give a single example. The word *free* still existed in Newspeak, but it could be used in such statements as "This dog is free from lice" or "This field is free from weeds." It could not be used in its old sense of "politically free" or "intellectually free," since political and intellectual freedom no longer existed even as concepts, and were therefore of necessity nameless. Quite apart from the suppression of definitely heretical words, reduction of vocabulary was regarded as an end in itself, and no word that could be dispensed with was allowed to survive. Newspeak was designed not to extend but to *diminish* the range of thought, and this purpose was indirectly assisted by cutting the choice of words down to a minimum.

Newspeak was founded on the English language as we now know it, though many Newspeak sentences, even when not containing newly created words, would be barely intelligible to an English-speaker of our own day. Newspeak words were divided into three distinct classes, known as the A vocabulary, the B vocabulary (also called compound words), and the C vocabulary. It will be simpler to discuss each class separately, but the grammatical peculiarities of the language can be dealt with in the section devoted to the A vocabulary, since the same rules held good for all three categories.

THE A VOCABULARY

The A vocabulary consisted of words needed for the business of everyday life—for such things as eating, drinking, working, putting on one's clothes, going up and down stairs, riding in vehicles, gardening, cooking, and the like. It was composed almost entirely of words that we already possess—words like *hit, run, dog, tree, sugar, house, field*—but in comparison with the present-day English vocabulary, their number was extremely small, while their meanings were far more rigidly defined. All ambiguities and shades of meaning had been purged out of them. So far as it could be achieved, a Newspeak word of this class was simply a staccato sound expressing *one* clearly understood concept. It would have been quite impossible to use the A vocabulary for literary purposes or for political or philosophical discussion. It was intended only to express simple, purposive thoughts, usually involving concrete objects or physical actions.

The grammar of Newspeak had two outstanding peculiarities. The first of these was an almost complete interchangeability between different parts of speech. Any word in the language (in principle this applied even to very abstract words such as *if* or *when*) could be used either as verb, noun, adjective, or adverb. Between the verb and the noun form, when they were of the same root, there was never any variation, this rule of itself involving the destruction of many archaic forms. The word *thought*, for example, did not exist in Newspeak. Its place was taken by *think*, which did duty for both noun and verb. No etymological principle was involved here; in some cases it was the original noun that was chosen for retention, in other cases the verb. Even where a noun and verb of kindred meaning were not etymologically connected, one or other of them was frequently suppressed. There was, for example, no such word as *cut*, its meaning being sufficiently covered by the noun-verb *knife*. Adjectives were formed by adding the suffix *-ful* to the noun-verb, and adverbs by adding *-wise*. Thus, for example, *speedful* meant "rapid" and *speedwise* meant "quickly." Certain of our present-day adjectives, such as *good, strong, big, black, soft*, were retained, but their total number was very small. There was little need for them, since almost any adjectival meaning could be arrived at by adding *-ful* to a noun-verb. None of the now-existing adverbs was retained, except for a very few already ending in *-wise*; the *-wise* termination was invariable. The word *well*, for example, was replaced by *goodwise*.

In addition, any word—this again applied in principle to every word in the language—could be negatived by adding the affix *un-*, or could be strengthened by the affix *plus-*, or, for still greater emphasis *doubleplus-*. Thus, for example, *uncold* meant "warm," while *pluscold* and *doublepluscold* meant, respectively, "very cold" and "superlatively cold." It was also possible, as in present-day English, to modify the meaning of almost any word by prepositional affixes such as *ante-, post-, up-, down-*, etc. By such methods it was found possible to bring about an enormous diminution of vocabulary. Given, for instance, the word *good*, there was no need for such a word as *bad*, since the required meaning was equally well—indeed, better—expressed by *ungood*. All that was necessary, in any case where two words formed a natural pair of opposites, was to decide which of them to suppress. *Dark*, for example, could be replaced by *unlight*, or *light* by *undark*, according to preference.

The second distinguishing mark of Newspeak grammar was its regularity. Subject to a few exceptions which are mentioned below, all inflections followed the same rules. Thus, in all verbs the preterite and the past participle were the same and ended in *-ed*. The preterite of *steal* was *stealed*, the preterite of *think* was *thinked*, and so on throughout the language, all such forms as *swam, gave, brought, spoke, taken*, etc., being abolished. All plurals were made by adding *-s* or *-es* as the case might be. The plurals of *man, ox, life* were *mans, oxes, lifes*. Comparison of adjectives was invariably made by adding *-er, -est* (*good, gooder, goodest*), irregular forms and the *more, most* formation being suppressed.

The only classes of words that were still allowed to inflect irregularly were the pronouns, the relatives, the demonstrative adjectives, and the auxiliary verbs. All of these followed their ancient usage, except that *whom* had been scrapped as unnecessary, and the *shall, should* tenses had been dropped, all their uses being covered by *will* and *would*. There were also certain irregularities in word-formation arising out of the need for rapid and easy speech. A word which was difficult to utter, or was liable to be incorrectly heard, was held to be ipso facto a bad word; occasionally therefore, for the sake of euphony, extra letters were inserted into a word or an archaic formation was retained. But this need made itself felt chiefly in connection with the B vocabulary. *Why* so great an importance was attached to ease of pronounciation will be made clear later in this essay.

THE B VOCABULARY

The B vocabulary consisted of words which had been deliberately constructed for political purposes: words, that is to say, which not only had in every case a political implication, but were intended to impose a desirable mental attitude upon the person using them. Without a full understanding of the principles of Ingsoc it was difficult to use these words correctly. In some cases they could be translated into Oldspeak, or even into words taken from the A vocabulary, but this usually demanded a long paraphrase and always involved the loss of certain overtones. The B words were a sort of verbal shorthand, often packing whole ranges of ideas into a few syllables, and at the same time more accurate and forcible than ordinary language.

The B words were in all cases compound words.* They consisted of two or more words, or portions of words, welded together in an easily pronounceable form. The resulting amalgam was always a noun-verb, and inflected according to the ordinary rules. To take a single example: the word *goodthink*, meaning, very roughly, "orthodoxy," or, if one chose to regard it as a verb, "to think in an orthodox manner." This inflected as follows: noun-verb, *goodthink*; past tense and past participle, *goodthinked*; present participle, *goodthinking*; adjective, *goodthinkful*; adverb, *goodthinkwise*; verbal noun, *goodthinker*.

The B words were not constructed on any etymological plan. The words of which they were made up could be any parts of speech, and could be placed in any order and mutilated in any way which made them easy to pronounce while indicating their derivation. In the word

*Compound words, such as *speakwrite*, were of course to be found in the A vocabulary, but these were merely convenient abbreviations and had no special ideological color.

crimethink (thoughtcrime), for instance, the *think* came second, whereas in *thinkpol* (Thought Police) it came first, and in the latter word *police* had lost its second syllable. Because of the greater difficulty in securing euphony, irregular formations were commoner in the B vocabulary than in the A vocabulary. For example, the adjectival forms of *Minitrue, Minipax,* and *Miniluv* were, respectively, *Minitruthful, Minipeaceful,* and *Minilovely,* simply because *-trueful, -paxful,* and *-loveful* were slightly awkward to pronounce. In principle, however, all B words could inflect, and all inflected in exactly the same way.

Some of the B words had highly subtilized meanings, barely intelligible to anyone who had not mastered the language as a whole. Consider, for example, such a typical sentence from a *Times* leading article as *Oldthinkers unbellyfeel Ingsoc.* The shortest rendering that one could make of this in Oldspeak would be: "Those whose ideas were formed before the Revolution cannot have a full emotional understanding of the principles of English Socialism." But this is not an adequate translation. To begin with, in order to grasp the full meaning of the Newspeak sentence quoted above, one would have to have a clear idea of what is meant by Ingsoc. And, in addition, only a person thoroughly grounded in Ingsoc could appreciate the full force of the word *bellyfeel,* which implied a blind, enthusiastic acceptance difficult to imagine today; or of the word *oldthink,* which was inextricably mixed up with the idea of wickedness and decadence. But the special function of certain Newspeak words, of which *oldthink* was one, was not so much to express meanings as to destroy them. These words, necessarily few in number, had had their meanings extended until they contained within themselves whole batteries of words which, as they were sufficiently covered by a single comprehensive term, could now be scrapped and forgotten. The greatest difficulty facing the compilers of the Newspeak dictionary was not to invent new words, but, having invented them, to make sure what they meant: to make sure, that is to say, what ranges of words they canceled by their existence.

As we have already seen in the case of the word *free,* words which had once borne a heretical meaning were sometimes retained for the sake of convenience, but only with the undesirable meanings purged out of them. Countless other words such as *honor, justice, morality, internationalism, democracy, science,* and *religion* had simply ceased to exist. A few blanket words covered them, and, in covering them, abolished them. All words grouping themselves round the concepts of liberty and equality, for instance, were contained in the single word *crimethink,* while all words grouping themselves round the concepts of objectivity and rationalism were contained in the single word *oldthink.* Greater precision would have been dangerous. What was required in a Party member was an outlook similar to that of the ancient Hebrew who knew, without knowing much else, that all nations other than his own worshipped "false gods." He did not need to know that these gods were called Baal, Osiris, Moloch, Ashtaroth, and the like; probably the less he knew about them the better for his orthodoxy. He knew Jehovah and the commandments of Jehovah; he knew, therefore, that all gods with other names or other attributes were false gods. In somewhat the same way, the Party member knew what constituted right conduct, and in exceedingly vague, generalized terms he knew what kinds of departure from it were possible. His sexual life, for example, was entirely regulated by the two Newspeak words *sexcrime* (sexual immorality) and *goodsex* (chastity). *Sexcrime* covered all sexual misdeeds whatever. It covered fornication, adultery, homosexuality, and other perversions, and, in addition, normal intercourse practiced for its own sake. There was no need to enumerate them separately, since they were all equally culpable, and in principle, all punishable by death. In the C vocabulary, which consisted of scientific and technical words, it might be necessary to give specialized names to certain sexual aberrations, but the ordinary citizen had no need of them. He knew what was meant by *goodsex*—that is to say, normal intercourse between man and wife, for the sole purpose of begetting children, and without physical pleasure on the part of the woman; all else was *sexcrime*. In Newspeak it was seldom possible to follow a heretical thought further than the perception that it *was* heretical; beyond that point the necessary words were nonexistent.

No word in the B vocabulary was ideologically neutral. A great many were euphemisms. Such words, for instance, as *joycamp* (forced-labor camp) or *Minipax* (Ministry of Peace, i.e., Ministry of War) meant almost the exact opposite of what they appeared to mean. Some words, on the other hand, displayed a frank and contemptuous understanding of the real nature of Oceanic society. An example was *prolefeed*, meaning the rubbishy entertainment and spurious news which the Party handed out to the masses. Other words, again, were ambivalent, having the connotation "good" when applied to the Party and "bad" when applied to its enemies. But in addition there were great numbers of words which at first sight appeared to be mere abbreviations and which derived their ideological color not from their meaning but from their structure.

So far as it could be contrived, everything that had or might have political significance of any kind was fitted into the B vocabulary. The name of every organization, or body of people, or doctrine, or country, or institution, or public building, was invariably cut down into the familiar shape; that is, a single easily pronounced word with the smallest number of syllables that would preserve the original derivation. In the Ministry of Truth, for example, the Records Department, in which

Winston Smith worked, was called *Recdep*, the Fiction Department was called *Ficdep*, the Teleprograms Department was called *Teledep*, and so on. This was not done solely with the object of saving time. Even in the early decades of the twentieth century, telescoped words and phrases had been one of the characteristic features of political language; and it had been noticed that the tendency to use abbreviations of this kind was most marked in totalitarian countries and totalitarian organizations. Examples were such words as *Nazi, Gestapo, Comintern, Inprecorr, Agitprop.* In the beginning the practice had been adopted as it were instinctively, but in Newspeak it was used with a conscious purpose. It was perceived that in thus abbreviating a name one narrowed and subtly altered its meaning, by cutting out most of the associations that would otherwise cling to it. The words *Communist International*, for instance, call up a composite picture of universal human brotherhood, red flags, barricades, Karl Marx, and the Paris Commune. The word Comintern, on the other hand, suggests merely a tightly knit organization and a well-defined body of doctrine. It refers to something almost as easily recognized, and as limited in purpose, as a chair or a table. *Comintern* is a word that can be uttered almost without taking thought, whereas *Communist International* is a phrase over which one is obliged to linger at least momentarily. In the same way, the associations called up by a word like *Minitrue* are fewer and more controllable than those called up by *Ministry of Truth*. This accounted not only for the habit of abbreviating whenever possible, but also for the almost exaggerated care that was taken to make every word easily pronounceable.

In Newspeak, euphony outweighed every consideration other than exactitude of meaning. Regularity of grammar was always sacrificed to it when it seemed necessary. And rightly so, since what was required, above all for political purposes, were short clipped words of unmistakable meaning which could be uttered rapidly and which roused the minimum of echoes in the speaker's mind. The words of the B vocabulary even gained in force from the fact that nearly all of them were very much alike. Almost invariably these words—*goodthink, Minipax, prolefeed, sexcrime, joycamp, Ingsoc, bellyfeel, thinkpol,* and countless others— were words of two or three syllables, with the stress distributed equally between the first syllable and the last. The use of them encouraged a gabbling style of speech, at once staccato and monotonous. And this was exactly what was aimed at. The intention was to make speech, and especially speech on any subject not ideologically neutral, as nearly as possible independent of consciousness. For the purposes of everyday life it was no doubt necessary, or sometimes necessary, to reflect before speaking, but a Party member called upon to make a political or ethical judgment should be able to spray forth the correct opinions as automatically as a machine gun spraying forth bullets. His training fitted him to do this, the language gave him an almost foolproof instrument, and the texture of the words, with their harsh sound and a certain willful ugliness which was in accord with the spirit of Ingsoc, assisted the process still further.

So did the fact of having very few words to choose from. Relative to our own, the Newspeak vocabulary was tiny, and new ways of reducing it were constantly being devised. Newspeak, indeed, differed from almost all other languages in that its vocabulary grew smaller instead of larger every year. Each reduction was a gain, since the smaller the area of choice, the smaller the temptation to take thought. Ultimately it was hoped to make articulate speech issue from the larynx without involving the higher brain centers at all. This aim was frankly admitted in the Newspeak word *duckspeak*, meaning "to quack like a duck." Like various other words in the B vocabulary, *duckspeak* was ambivalent in meaning. Provided that the opinions which were quacked out were orthodox ones, it implied nothing but praise, and when the *Times* referred to one of the orators of the Party as a *doubleplusgood duckspeaker* it was paying a warm and valued compliment.

THE C VOCABULARY

The C vocabulary was supplementary to the others and consisted entirely of scientific and technical terms. These resembled the scientific terms in use today, and were constructed from the same roots, but the usual care was taken to define them rigidly and strip them of undesirable meanings. They followed the same grammatical rules as the words in the other two vocabularies. Very few of the C words had any currency either in everyday speech or in political speech. Any scientific worker or technician could find all the words he needed in the list devoted to his own specialty, but he seldom had more than a smattering of the words occurring in the other lists. Only a very few words were common to all lists, and there was no vocabulary expressing the function of Science as a habit of mind, or a method of thought, irrespective of its particular branches. There was, indeed, no word for "Science," any meaning that it could possibly bear being already sufficiently covered by the word *Ingsoc*.

From the foregoing account it will be seen that in Newspeak the expression of unorthodox opinions, above a very low level, was well-nigh impossible. It was of course possible to utter heresies of a very crude kind, a species of blasphemy. It would have been possible, for example, to say *Big Brother is ungood*. But this statement, which to an orthodox ear merely conveyed a self-evident absurdity, could not have been sustained by reasoned argument, because the necessary words were not available. Ideas inimical to Ingsoc could only be entertained in a vague wordless form, and could only be named in very broad terms which lumped together and condemned whole groups of heresies without defining them in doing so. One could, in fact, only use Newspeak for unorthodox purposes by illegitimately translating some of the words back into Oldspeak. For example, *All mans are equal* was a possible Newspeak sentence, but only in the same sense in which *All men are redhaired* is a possible Oldspeak sentence. It did not contain a grammatical error, but it expressed a palpable untruth, i.e., that all men are of equal size, weight, or strength. The concept of political equality no longer existed, and this secondary meaning had accordingly been purged out of the word *equal*. In 1984, when Oldspeak was still the normal means of communication, the danger theoretically existed that in using Newspeak words one might remember their original meanings. In practice it was not difficult for any person well grounded in *doublethink* to avoid doing this, but within a couple of generations even the possibility of such a lapse would have vanished. A person growing up with Newspeak as his sole language would no more know that *equal* had once had the secondary meaning of "politically equal," or that *free* had once meant "intellectually free," than, for instance, a person who had never heard of chess would be aware of the secondary meanings attaching to *queen* and *rook*. There would be many crimes and errors which it would be beyond his power to commit, simply because they were nameless and therefore unimaginable. And it was to be foreseen that with the passage of time the distinguishing characteristics of Newspeak would become more and more pronounced—its words growing fewer and fewer, their meanings more and more rigid, and the chance of putting them to improper uses always diminishing.

When Oldspeak had been once and for all superseded, the last link with the past would have been severed. History had already been rewritten, but fragments of the literature of the past survived here and there, imperfectly censored, and so long as one retained one's knowledge of Oldspeak it was possible to read them. In the future such fragments, even if they chanced to survive, would be unintelligible and untranslatable. It was impossible to translate any passage of Oldspeak into Newspeak unless it either referred to some technical process or some very simple everyday action, or was already orthodox (*goodthinkful* would be the Newspeak expression) in tendency. In practice this meant that no book written before approximately 1960 could be translated as a whole. Prerevolutionary literature could only be subjected to ideological translation—that is, alteration in sense as well as language. Take for example the well-known passage from the Declaration of Independence:

We hold these truths to be self-evident, that all men are created equal, that they are endowed by their Creator with certain inalienable rights, that among these are life, liberty and the pursuit of happiness. That to secure these rights, Governments are instituted among men, deriving their powers from the consent of the governed. That whenever any form of Government becomes destructive of those ends, it is the right of the People to alter or abolish it, and to institute new Government. . . .

It would have been quite impossible to render this into Newspeak while keeping to the sense of the original. The nearest one could come to doing so would be to swallow the whole passage up in the single word *crimethink*. A full translation could only be an ideological translation, whereby Jefferson's words would be changed into a panegyric on absolute government.

A good deal of the literature of the past was, indeed, already being transformed in this way. Considerations of prestige made it desirable to preserve the memory of certain historical figures, while at the same time bringing their achievements into line with the philosophy of Ingsoc. Various writers, such as Shakespeare, Milton, Swift, Byron, Dickens and some others were therefore in process of translation; when the task had been completed, their original writings, with all else that survived of the literature of the past, would be destroyed. These translations were a slow and difficult business, and it was not expected that they would be finished before the first or second decade of the twenty-first century. There were also large quantities of merely utilitarian literature—indispensable technical manuals and the like—that had to be treated in the same way. It was chiefly in order to allow time for the preliminary work of translation that the final adoption of Newspeak had been fixed for so late a date as 2050.

LANGUAGE AND COMMUNICATION

*"Language not only reveals a person's
identity, who he is, but in some way it
makes him the person he is."*

Logos: Man's Translation of
Himself into Language

GERARD EGAN

The language used in small group communication,
particularly in encounter or sensitivity groups, is often
revealing of the feelings and attitudes of the individuals
involved. Here Gerard Egan examines some aspects of this
language which might be considered and experimented
with in such groups. Egan's concepts of *logos*, languages
used to reveal one's real self, and *antilogos*, language used
to destroy healthful interpersonal contact, are especially
significant today, it seems, when so many persons have
difficulty relating to each other on a meaningful level.
Language, as Egan clearly demonstrates, is a powerful
means for establishing and maintaining meaningful
interpersonal relationships.

197

INTRODUCTION

The contract group* places emphasis on *logos*, effective interpersonal communication through human language. It has been assumed above that a great number of men suffer from emasculation in their emotional life. Now it is also assumed that many men suffer a concomitant emasculation in the quality of their verbal communication, in their ability to use language as a mode of interpersonal contact.

Logos, when used as a generic term, refers to man's interaction with man in terms of human language, the way a man translates himself into language. Both philosophers and behavioral scientists have theorized about the phenomenon of language as a form of what Lorenz (1955) calls "expressive behavior"—that is, as a reflection of the structure of personality (e.g., Buhler, 1934; Cassirer, 1953; Hodges, 1952; Honigfeld, Platz, & Gillis, 1964; Moscovici, 1967; Piaget, 1952; Stout, 1902; Von Hartmann, 1884; Wittgenstein, 1922). There have always been people interested in the language differences between psychiatric and normal populations (e.g., Forrest, 1965 Glauber, 1944; Gottschalk, 1961; Lorenz, 1955; Newman & Mather, 1938; Sanford, 1942; Spiegel, 1959; Wender, 1967), and more or less molecular psychological studies are increasing man's understanding of the phenomenon of language and verbal behavior (e.g., Cofer & Musgrave, 1963; Dixon & Horton, 1968; Kansler, 1966; Mehrabian, 1966; Salzinger, 1967; Wiener & Mehrabian, 1968). Still, little of

From Gerard Egan, Encounter: Group Processes for Interpersonal Growth, pp. 159–175. *Copyright 1970 by Wadsworth Publishing Co., Inc. Reprinted by permission of the publisher, Brooks/Cole Publishing Co., Monterey, California.*

*The author has kindly supplied the following definition of contract group: "A contract group is a human relations training group (encounter group) governed by a contract which specifies the goals of the group and the means (interactions and processes) deemed essential to achieving these goals. The participants enter the group by choosing to observe the contract. All members are held accountable to the stipulations of the contract."

this theorizing and research has been translated in such a way as to be useful in dealing with people, either normal or abnormal, on a clinical or applied level. More attention must be given to such molar dimensions of language as the quality of man's verbal expression in his interpersonal contacts.

As Wiener and Mehrabian (1968) note, it is too fruitful an area of interpersonal discovery to ignore:

> Anyone who listens carefully to the way people say things quickly learns that the particular words a speaker uses to describe an event or experience can be a rich source of information about his feelings and attitudes. The bases for making these kind of inferences are not usually explicit, although members of a communication group appear to respond regularly to these subtle variations in word usage [p. 1].

Laboratory learning situations seem to provide excellent opportunities for research on this subject and for the application of research findings. What follows is a brief indication of the aspects of language that might be profitably considered and experimented with in a sensitivity laboratory. The laboratory experience is an opportunity for the participants to examine man as one who speaks by subjecting their own verbal interactions to the scrutiny of the group.

THE PROBLEMS AND POTENTIAL
OF LANGUAGE

Problems

There are various ways in which people underuse or abuse language in interpersonal situations and many reasons why they do so. Some language problems stem directly from, and reflect varying degrees of, psychopathology. Bettelheim (1967) discusses children who have surrendered the use of language because of parental disapproval, their mutism being an indication that they have given up any hope of influencing their world. This surrender of speech closes a vicious circle:

> Once the child has even stopped communicating with others, his self becomes impoverished, the more so the longer his mutism lasts, and the more so the longer his personality remains underdeveloped at the time of the onset of withdrawal [p. 56].
> If this [mutism] happens before he has fully learned to manip-

ulate symbolic forms, before the age of three or four, then the child also fails to develop the higher intellectual processes. [p. 57].

Erikson (1954) discovered that one of the outcomes of traumatic war experiences was a distrust and devaluation of language. Meerloo (1956) found neurosis manifested in language-use disturbances: "The insecure neurotic shrinks from free word-play he tries to manipulate words mechanically, like machinery. He fears the adventure of communication [p. 87]." Ruesch (1957) sees the origin of communication problems in parents' inability to adapt themselves to the maturation level of their children. According to Ruesch, three types of language are learned in succession: somatic, action, and verbal. If parents do not adapt their language to the developmental stage of their children, while at the same time offering encouragement to improve verbal-language proficiency, then communication disturbances may arise in their children.

Language problems arise from and reflect not only psychopathology in the strict sense; they reflect also the psychopathology of the average. Many normal men fear the communication process because of more or less normal fears of involving themselves deeply with others. They neither pour themselves into their language in interpersonal situations nor expect others to do so. Language must remain on a safe level. They habitually put filters between what they really think and feel and what they say. This results in exsanguinated or muddied, but safe, communication. Some men engage in language that is overly precise—they ask too much of language—while others engage in language that is too vague—that is, they ask too little of language. Both extremes are usually defensive measures, ways of keeping interpersonal contacts at acceptable levels of intensity. Some men are victims of poor education in language. They have lived in families or in societies that are afraid of open communication, with the result that patterns of language are not available to them to express what they would like to express. This conversational or language anemia is recognized by the novel writer:

> Even in modern-novel dialogue the most real is not the most conformable to actual current speech. One has only to read a transcribed tape of actual conversation to realize that it is, in the literary context, not very real. Novel dialogue is a form of shorthand, an impression of what people actually say; and besides that, it has to perform other functions—to keep the narrative moving (which real conversation rarely does), to reveal character (real conversation often hides it), and so on [Fowles, 1968, p. 89].

Men read novels not only for vicarious *pathos* but also for vicarious *logos*, the meaningful talk that is missing from their lives.

In societies that subtly discourage or limit conversational freedom and deeper interpersonal contact through language, some men abandon language (at least in a relative sense) either because it is useless as an instrument of deep human communication or because the patterns of language allowed are identified with the establishment that is being rejected. In the case of the present "hippie" culture, this flight from language involves both (1) the creation of an argot reflecting a break from the values of society seen as useless or oppressive, while emphasizing the values of the subculture and (2) an often irresponsible immersion in the *pathos* dimensions of living. A counter language evolves, and a counter *pathos* society is established, parallel to or outside the confines of the society being rejected.

Potentialities

Despite the problems involved in using exsanguinated language and communication, language is still one of the most dramatic ways in which man differs from other animals. Stout (1902) sees language as an instrument by means of which man examines the world around him. If he is afraid of this world, his language will be anemic and feeble, but if he loves the world and is challenged by it, his language will be strong and searching. To adapt a phrase from Wittgenstein (1922), the limits of a person's language are the limits of his world. Cioran (1968) sees silence as unbearable and says he would find it easier to renounce bread than speech. He claims that one cannot withdraw one's confidence from words "without setting one's foot in the abyss." Language exposes, reveals both individuals and societies: "Words, at least in traditional societies, often express far more than feelings or ideas. The way words are used—in tales, riddles, proverbs, and typical modes of address and conversation—can reveal a great deal about the structure and values of a society [Abrahams, 1968, p. 62]."

Novelists and writers frequently have, if not deeper insights, at least more striking, distinctive, and challenging insights into the nature and force of human language than do behavioral scientists. Writers continually try to enlarge the possibilities of language. D. H. Lawrence, Virginia Woolf, and James Joyce never hesitated to experiment with verbal symbols that would most fully convey what they experienced. As Burgess (1968) notes: "Language, of its very nature, resists tautology; it wants to launch out, risk lies, say the thing which is not."

Brian Friel's entire play *Philadelphia Here I Come* is based on the distinction between what the leading character really thinks, feels, and would like to say and what he actually says. In the play, there are two levels of conversation—the vague, hesitant, compliant, failed bravado of the son about to leave his father in Ireland to seek a new way of life in the United States, and the vigorous speech of the son's "inner core" (played by a separate character). The pity of it all is that, although the audience is electrified by what the "inner man" says, it knows that his speech really dies (and in a sense the son dies with it) because it is never spoken. The man who chains his language chains himself.

The contract group is a laboratory in which the participants can experiment with the potential of language. The purpose of what is said here is not to apotheosize language, for, as Lynd (1958) notes, language is sometimes a sensitive instrument and sometimes a clumsy tool of communication. But when a man enlarges the possibilities of his language, he enlarges his own possibilities. The laboratory gives him the opportunity to extend the range of language in order to contact himself and others at deeper levels. In the safety of the laboratory, he can run risks in his use of language that he could not take in everyday life. The following discussion of language might serve as a basis for experimentation.

DIFFERENT KINDS OF LANGUAGE

In keeping with the consideration of language from a molar, interactional point of view, the following distinctions—again, despite the fact that they are somewhat abstractive—might give direction to the discussion that follows.

Logos

Logos, in the strict or restricted sense, refers to man's ability to translate his real self into language. *Logos* is language filled with the person who is speaking, and therefore refers to his ability to use speech to express his identity. It also refers to the use man makes of speech in order to establish some kind of growthful interpersonal contact. Negatively, it is the refusal to use speech merely to fill interactional space and time or as a smoke screen or shield behind which to hide.

Just as there are different kinds of truly human contact and various degrees or levels of such contact, so there are different kinds of *logos*. If a man talks meaningfully about his political or religious beliefs, this is *logos*. *Logos* need not be self-disclosure in the sense discussed in Chapter 7, but, in that it is meaningful speech, it will always provide some insight into the identity of the speaker. Meaningful speech with an intimate friend will be on a different level from meaningful speech with one's fellow workers. The special ability to allow one's language to express not only one's thoughts but also the feelings and the emotions that surround these thoughts is a special kind of *logos* called *poiesis*. *Poiesis* will be treated separately.

Logos must be clearly differentiated from the ability to speak fluently and elegantly, for both fluency and elegance are at times used to camouflage, rather than reveal, one's identity. It also seems necessary to distinguish *logos* from the ability to speak with insight about oneself. This ability has traditionally been seen as a favorable condition, if not a prerequisite, for effective participation in psychotherapy—an hypothesis that is being seriously challenged today (Carkhuff & Berenson, 1967, London, 1964). *Logos* here means translating oneself, or handing oneself over to others, through the medium of speech, whatever the esthetic value of the language used.

Logos implies a respect for language as a form of communication and contact. It implies dialogue, and, as Matson and Montagu (1967) point out, for certain contemporary existentialist thinkers, authentic existence *is* communication, life *is* dialogue. Dialogue is certainly the life of the contract group. That is why the group member, by contract, is expected to examine his use of speech. If he is to develop new ways of being present to the members of the group, he must discover new ways of speaking and perhaps develop a new respect for language.

Dialogue, in the sense in which it is used here, is opposed to "game" communication. Dialogue is game-free, or at least an attempt to make communication game-free. Rapoport (1964) and Wiener (1950), both of whom have made significant contributions to the mathematical theory of games, caution against the use of game theory as a basis for human communication. Rapoport finds dialogue with the "strategist" impossible, for the basic question in the strategist's mind is: In a conflict, how can I gain an advantage over my opponent? Rapoport thinks that the much more basically human question is: If I can gain an advantage over another, *what sort of person* will I become? The "cybernetic" man is basically monological, not dialogical, and for him, communication is intimately wedded to control—the control of the other.

Berne (1966) uses "game" in a somewhat different sense. The "games people play" are ways of avoiding intimacy in human relationships. The game prevents dialogue. Berne goes so far as to say that the most that one can expect in a psychotherapeutic group is the discovery and analysis of the games played there. Real intimacy, he says, is almost never found in such group situations. It is the contention of this book that the members of a contract interpersonal-growth group can establish dialogue, can free themselves, to a great extent, from a game approach to one another, and can establish not just the social imitation of intimacy that Berne speaks of, but real human intimacy.

Commercial Speech

"Commercial speech" refers to the language of the marketplace, the use of language in the commercial transactions of men. Such language is lean, utilitarian, pragmatic; it deals with objects rather than persons, for it is a medium of exchange rather than of interpersonal contact. Much of such language today is left to computers. It would be of no interest to us here were it not for the fact that there are people who use commercial speech as their principal mode of speech in interpersonal transactions. They see people as objects to be manipulated, rather than person to be contacted, and this is reflected in the quality of their speech.

If speech is principally commercial, then, as McLuhan (1964) suggests, it can be dispensed with: "Electric technology does not need words any more than the digital computer needs numbers [p. 80]." However, the utopia he envisions, characterized by a "speechlessness that could confer a perpetuity of collective harmony and peace" arising from a "collective awareness that may have been the preverbal condition of man [p. 80]," is antithetical to man himself. Speech defines man. It is just strange that he makes such poor use of it in his effort to humanize himself.

Cliché Talk

"Cliché talk" refers to anemic language, talk for the sake of talk, conversation without depth, language that neither makes contact with the other nor reveals the identity of the speaker (except negatively, in the sense that he is revealed as one who does not want to make contact or does not want to be known). Cliché talk fosters ritualistic, rather than fully human, contact ("Do you think that it is really going to rain?"—"The way they're playing, they'll be in first place by the first of September!"). Cliché talk fills interactional space and time without adding meaning, for it is superficial and comes without reflection. Perhaps it is the person who is overcommitted to maintenance functions, a person who is either unaware (because he lacks the requisite social intelligence) or afraid of possibilities for further interpersonal growth, whose speech will be predominantly cliché talk.

People usually listen politely to cliché talk, especially when it is pseudo-*logos*—that is, dressed up or doctored to sound important:

> When a conversation fails to capture the spontaneous involvement of an individual who is obliged to participate in it, he is likely to contrive an appearance of being involved. This he must do to save the feelings of the other participants and their good opinion of him, regardless of his motives for wanting to effect this saving [Goffman, 1967, p. 126].

If the needs of the listener are such that he is willing to put up with the boredom of cliché talk in order to enjoy the safety that is found in ritual, then the circle is complete and the field is wide open for such conversation.

One of the most common forms of cliché talk in our culture (and perhaps this is a transcultural phenomenon) is "griping," a more or less superficial communication of dissatisfaction with persons, institutions, or things outside oneself. It is one of the few verbal expressions of feeling allowed in public, and it is probably allowed because it is a ritual and most rituals are safe. The trouble with chronic griping is that it is a fixative. As Ellis (1962) points out, a person's verbalizations to himself and others often stand in the way of change: "Forces outside me control me"; "I can do nothing to change."

Cliché talk is just words, while *logos* always connotes human contact. Some people speak endlessly about themselves and say nothing (if they were really disclosing themselves, others would not find it boring). They say nothing about themselves because they have no real feeling for themselves—they are deficient in the *pathos* dimension of life—and could hardly be expected to relate what they do not experience. Such people simply are not using speech as a mode of contact. For them, speech is solipsistic, self-centered, centripetal. It is monologue rather than dialogue.

Anti-logos

When language is actually used to destroy growthful interpersonal contact rather than to foster it, then it is *anti-logos*. There are a number of forms of speech that are really violations, rather than uses, of language. For instance, in the heat of anger, language can be used as a weapon, a tool of destruction rather than an instrument of growthful encounter. When a married couple stand shouting at each other (often saying things they do not really mean), language becomes completely swallowed up in emotion; it loses its identity as language. At such times it has more in common with a sledgehammer than with speech. Lying, too, can be a form of *anti-logos*, for deception cannot be the basis of growthful interpersonal contact. The speech of the psychopath, for example, is frequently, if not continually, *anti-logos*, for he uses speech to create situations, to manipulate others rather than to engage in growthful encounters with them. Finally, the language of the psychotic, while it might have its own peculiar logic (and without discounting the possibility that a psychosis may be a desperate form of revolt against a sick family or society—see Laing, 1967), is frequently *anti-logos* The psychotic, at least at times, appears to use language to drive others away. He fears human contact so deeply that he reverses the function of language, making it a barrier instead of a bridge.

Another way of conceptualizing *anti-logos* is to see it as the kind of expression that stems from high deficiency functioning. The stronger the influence of deficiency needs in a person's life, the more likely he is to engage in some form of *anti-logos.*

Most men engage in all four kinds of speech at one time or another. They not only use commercial speech in strictly commercial transactions, but also allow it to slip occasionally into interpersonal encounters. Indeed, life without some cliché talk would be intolerably intense for most men. It is a question, however, of proportion, and most men need to find ways of increasing the amount of *logos* (in the restricted sense) in their lives. The sensitivity laboratory affords an opportunity of discovering ways to do that.

References

Abrahams, R. D. Public drama and common values in two Caribbean islands. *Trans-action,* 1968, 5 (8), 62–71.

Berne, E. *Principles of group treatment.* New York: Oxford University Press, 1966.

Bettelheim, B. *The empty fortress.* New York: Collier-Macmillan, 1967.

Buhler, K. *Sprach theorie.* Jena: Gustav Fisher, 1934.

Burgess, A. The future of Anglo-American. *Harper's,* 1968, 236, 53–56.

Carkhuff, R. R., & Berenson, B. G. *Beyond counseling and psychotherapy.* New York: Holt, Rinehart and Winston, 1967.

Cassirer, E. *The philosophy of symbolic forms. I: Language.* New Haven: Yale University Press, 1953.

Cioran, E. M. *The temptation to exist.* R. Howard (Trans.). Chicago: Quadrangle, 1968.

Cofer, C. N., & Musgrave, B. S. (Eds.). *Verbal behavior and learning problems and processes.* New York: McGraw-Hill, 1963.

Dixon, T. R., & Horton, D. L. (Eds.). *Verbal behavior and general behavior theory.* Englewood Cliffs, N.J.: Prentice-Hall, 1968.

Ellis, A. *Reason and emotion in psychotherapy.* New York: Lyle Stuart, 1962.

Erikson, E. H. On the sense of inner identity. In R. P. Knight & C. R. Friedman (Eds.). *Psychoanalytical psychiatry and psychology: Clinical and theoretical papers.* Vol. I. New York: International Universities Press, 1954.

Forrest, D. V. Poiesis and the language of schizophrenia. *Psychiatry,* 1965, 28, 1–18.

Glauber, I. P. Speech characteristics of psychoneurotic patients. *Journal of Speech Disorders,* 1944, 9, 18–30.

Goffman, E. *Interaction ritual: Essays on face-to-face behavior.* Garden City, N.Y.: Anchor Books (Doubleday), 1967.

Gottschalk, L. A. (Ed.) *Comparative psycholinguistic analysis of two psychotherapeutic interviews.* New York: International Universities Press, 1961.

Hodges, H. A. *The philosophy of Wilhem Dilthey.* London: Routledge & Kegan Paul, 1952.

Honigfeld, G., Platz, A., & Gillis, R. D. Verbal style and personality authoritarianism. *Journal of Communication,* 1964, 14, 215–218.

Kansler, D. H. (Ed.). *Readings in verbal learning: Contemporary theory and research.* New York: Wiley, 1966.

Laing, R. D. *The politics of experience.* New York: Pantheon Books (Random House), 1967.

London, P. *The modes and morals of psychotherapy.* New York: Holt, Rinehart and Winston, 1964.

Lorenz, M. Expressive behavior and language patterns. *Psychiatry,* 1955, 18, 353–366.

Lynd, H. M. *On shame and the search for identity.* New York: Science Editions, 1958.

Matson, F. W., & Montagu, A. (Eds.). *The human dialogue.* New York: Free Press, 1967.

McLuhan, M. *Understanding media: The extensions of man.* New York: McGraw-Hill, 1964.

Meerloo, J. *The rape of the mind.* Cleveland: World, 1956.

Mehrabian, A. Immediacy: An indicator of attitudes in linguistic communication. *Journal of Personality,* 1966, 34, 26–34.

Moscovici, S. Communication processes and the properties of language. In L. Berkowitz (Ed.), *Advances in experimental social psychology.* Vol. 3. New York: Academic Press, 1967. Pp. 225–270.

Newman, S., & Mather, V. G. Analysis of spoken language of patients with affective disorders. *American Journal of Psychiatry*, 1938, 94, 913–942.

Piaget, J. *The language and thought of the child.* London: Routledge & Kegan Paul, 1952.

Rapoport, A. *Strategy and conscience.* New York: Harper & Row, 1964.

Ruesch, J. *Disturbed communication.* New York: Norton, 1957.

Salzinger, K. (Ed.) *Research in verbal behavior and some neurophysiological implications.* New York: Academic Press, 1967.

Sanford, F. H. Speech and personality: A comparative case study. *Character and Personality*, 1942, 10, 169–198.

Spiegel, R. Specific problems of communication in psychiatric conditions. In S. Arieti (Ed.), *American handbook of psychiatry.* New York: Basic Books, 1959. Pp. 909–949.

Stout, G. F. *Analytic psychology.* Vol. 2. New York: Macmillan, 1902.

Von Hartmann, E. *Philosophy of the unconscious.* New York: Macmillan, 1884.

Wender, P. H. Communication unclarity: Some comments on the rhetoric of confusion. *Psychiatry*, 1967, 30, 332–349.

Wiener, N. *The human use of human beings.* New York: Discuss Books (Avon), 1967 (original Houghton Mifflin, 1950).

Wiener, M., & Mehrabian, A. *Language within language: Immediacy, a channel in verbal communication.* New York: Appleton-Century-Crofts, 1968.

Wittgenstein, L. *Tractatus logico-philosophicus.* London: Routledge & Kegan Paul, 1955 (originally published in 1922).

*"I think our news media should for
once not trail the Government but
declare their own peace of semantics
there right now."*

The Semantics of War

HANS KONING

In this brief and timely essay Hans Koning indicates
how the media may use language to slant the news and
distinguish the "good guys" from the "bad guys" without
ever explicitly stating such. The techniques used seem so
obvious when explained but they are probably hardly
noticed in our daily consumption of news. Yet, they very
likely communicate a position and an attitude just as surely
as would explicit statements. Koning's suggestion to try
transcribing Indochina bulletins while accepting the facts
as reported but recalling that, for example, there is only
one country Vietnam and that the terrorists are the type of
men we call resistance fighters in other situations, is well
worth following.

Boston—Last summer, Mr. Kissinger flew to Peking to explore the possibilities arising from the Soviet-China rift; a few weeks ago, Mr. Gromyko flew to Tokyo to exploit the coldness between the U.S. and Japan. The choice of verbs is not mine, but as found in various reports in this newspaper. There's just that nice distinction of sinister purpose, of the now somewhat dated "fishing in troubled waters" that used to be the standard description of any Red diplomatic voyage.

We are too sophisticated to use the obvious loaded words of the Eastern world such as "lackey" or the one-time Chinese favorite "running dog." We deal in nuances. The point (the fun, I'd almost write) of our loaded words is precisely that they never need retraction; they are never untrue per se. I'm not thinking here of Newspeak, of the crude intention to twist facts (we have more of it than Orwell ever had nightmares about); I am thinking of the well-nigh unconscious daily mobilization of words by our news media. The U-2 overflight with its concomitant Washingtonian lies ended, for many of us at least, the innocent idea that the American Government is somehow different from all those foreigners. But oh, how we still cling to an innate good guys-bad guys worldwide dichotomy!

Take as an example that U-2 flight and the Paris summit crisis that followed it. Time magazine used the following words, among others, to describe Khrushchev and his reactions: intransigent, belligerent, almost incredible, bellowing like a wounded rogue elephant, intemperate ramblings, diatribe. The U.S., on the other hand, replied tartly, asserted coolly, and was stern. Russians, in Time, when not bellowing, are inevitably dour: a stern American politician becomes a dour Russian politico. Dour Russian diplomats hustled Kurashvill (the student who recently tried to cut his own throat here) through Kennedy Airport. Really? Hustled? The same story said in its bottom line that he left voluntarily. But "to hustle" is here unmistakably used in its sense of "to force roughly or hurriedly." With a verb like that you don't quite say he didn't leave voluntarily after all, but you don't not say it either.

Or take a standard *pars pro toto* of journalism: "Haiti votes." With a number of our most crucial allies, the name of the nation really stands but for a tiny group ("clique" if they weren't friends) in the capitals. But if we don't like a government, the distinction is surely and heavily made, and the media follow our Administrations obediently in those "mainland China-Republic of China" word games.

The power of such a semantic mobilization was shown in twenty years of United Nations debate that would quickly have run dry if the question had been phrased: "Should the seat of China in the U.N. be occupied by China or by the representatives of its former rulers now on Taiwan?" (Similarly, in a recent letter in this paper, the former U.S. Ambassador to Seoul blandly used the word "Korea" to mean "South Korea.")

Our people make speeches, no matter how boring, but a man like Castro speechifies; in Chile he was even *speechifying excessively*. You can taste his demagoguery in it without needing to read a word he said. Simple quotation marks are enough to turn black into white and vice versa: the President's famous winding down of the war is never in quotes; statements from Red sources are sprinkled with them.

US News and World Report has taken care of all antiwar sentiment with quotes: what we've had so far in this country were "peace" demonstrations and a "peace" movement. The "peace" movement has no aims, it has *avowed* aims. "To avow" is, "to declare frankly and openly," but here it means, to the contrary, that there's more there than meets the eye. Suppose you call the editor and protest. "Well, you're avowing that you aim for peace, don't you?" he answers.

A member of the "Vietnam Veterans Against the War" said to me the other day, "The Associated Press always refers to us as 'a group *calling itself* . . .' They never talk of the country as calling itself the United States." So-called and self-styled are other favorite stand-bys of loaded usage.

To cut through that word fog, just try transcribing one day's Indochina bulletins, accepting the facts as reported, but remembering that there's only one country Vietnam; that there are two opposed governments in Laos; that by all standards Cambodia has not a government but a regime; that there are pro-Hanoi Vietnamese in the South of that country; that the terrorists are the kind of men we call elsewhere resistance fighters or maquis heroes; and that the U.S. is not at war with anybody.

If you do that, you'll see "foes" and "enemies" disappear from the headlines, and our Government statements become what is called in logic: semantic paralogisms, or, if you will, nonsense. I think our news media should for once not trail the Government but declare their own peace of semantics there right now.

*The catch words and phrases of a
social group are the expression of its
values.*

The Semantics of the

Generation Gap

ROBERT A. HIPKISS

In an attempt to gain some insight into the differences
in values between the younger and older generations,
Hipkiss here analyzes how some terms invented by the
youth are understood by the middle class adult. The
differences in meaning for such terms as "trip," "acid,"
"way out," "now," "in," "happening," "to do your own
thing," and "tuning in" provide interesting insight into the
different values of the two generations and hence some
indication of at least some of the causes for the generation-
communication gap.

The catch words and phrases of a social group are the expression of its values. This is true of the youth of our society, and most adults have trouble translating the vocabulary of youth into their own terms. Occasionally, they do translate a term clearly, however, and this is because they share the same values as the young inventors of the term. They see and hear the word or phrase in a context they can appreciate. A father watching his young son work an algebra problem unsuccessfully for the fourth time and hearing him exclaim, "I'm hung up!" needs no course in New English to know what his son is talking about. Often, however, the translation is not so simple. The middle-class adult does not really understand the context in which a word is used, so if he uses it himself, it means something other than what his son means by it. Very often the term is simply untranslatable, because the parent has a normal "hang up" about using such words or because he really cannot understand them.

This situation suggests that if we take a random sample of terms recently invented by our youth and determine if and how they are understood by the middle-class adult, then we can gain some insight into just what the difference in values is between the younger and older generations. The initial selection of terms to be considered here was recalled at random from newspaper articles, periodical essays, and television commentary. Once a sufficient number of terms had been listed, they were grouped together in an order that seemed appropriate for reasonably coherent discussion.

One of the words used by the New Left and also by businessmen, labor leaders, Negro spokesmen, and educators, among others, is "dialog." All these people speak of the need to have direct communication between two people or parties, not merely conversation (which can be aimless) or discussion (which can include so many parties as to create more confusion than enlightenment). The word "dialog" also suggests the

From Robert A. Hipkiss, "The Semantics of the Generation Gap." Reprinted from Etc. 27 *(September 1970, pp. 327–338) by permission of the International Society for General Semantics.*

Platonic method of finding the truth through a trading of ideas from opposing points of view, with the parties eventually arriving at a mutually recognized truth or program of action. Further, there is the suggestion that in order to arrive at such a conclusion, the antagonists must be frank with one another, and frankness is best accomplished between two parties rather than three or more.

Why the emphasis on dialog on the part of so many disparate groups in our society? Perhaps it is simply because the sense of frustration at not being understood is common to so many people today in our highly interrelated and specialized society. There is everywhere a sense of isolation, alienation, an anxious need to break through the barriers created by class, occupation, religion, politics, and educational background. The emphasis on dialog is undoubtedly an expression of man's prime need to develop the human bond of sympathy and mutual understanding between people who find themselves, *de facto*, dependent upon one another for the satisfaction of their economic, emotional, and intellectual needs.

The sense of frustration at being unable to communicate to those who affect our lives is also endemic to the term "establishment," first used to refer to the controlling upper class in British society but now used by youth and adult alike to refer to any entrenched group in any organization. The establishment is impersonal, bureaucratic, conservative, frustratingly out of touch with contemporary social and individual needs, hidebound by antiquated regulations, unable to think in terms of new values or new requirements. It is not malicious in its operations, though, merely unprogressive, inertial.

The inability to conduct a meaningful dialog and the sense of being dictated to by the establishment have caused many of the younger generation to revolt. One form the revolt has taken is that of social protest. The sixties have been the years of the student "sit-in." The term connotes anarchy to the adult middle class, and when most middle-class adults use this term, it is in a voice of disapproval. To them, the establishment is a frustration, but in many ways they owe allegiance to it and its values. It is the conservator of tradition, property, stability, and order, all of which means little to the inexperienced and largely unpropertied youth but a great deal to the adults who have struggled to obtain the money and possessions they use to assure themselves of material comfort and personal well-being. So although they too will criticize the establishment, they are not about to revolt nor even to sympathize with that youthful manifestation of revolt, the sit in.

If the discontented young do not engage in social protest, they withdraw, making a kind of virtue of their alienation. They may take "acid" and go on a "trip," ending "way out" beyond the peripheries of normal day-to-day waking experience. "Trip" in the hippie sense of the word is not common parlance among the middle class. Trip implies total alienation and this is unacceptable to the sociable middle class. Also, "way out," as the middle class uses the term, means "crazy," out of touch with reality, whereas the "acid head" (user of LSD) uses the term to denote a heightened awareness that is superior to our usual reality. Here is a case, then, where the adult middle class uses the same term as the young, but because one is oriented toward an objective reality and a social existence and the other is looking inward to a supreme subjective truth, their meanings for the same term are opposites.

LSD is almost never referred to as "acid" by those not associated with acid heads. LSD is too potent, too terrible, too mysterious to be accorded a familiar nickname, except by those who know it fairly well. The contrary is true of marijuana. "Pot" is its nickname to hippies and squares alike. Pot comes in the acceptable social form of a cigarette, and it has been around longer. Its effects are not so unpredictable nor so terrible. To a middle class already tranquilizing its anxieties with alcohol, marijuana is not apt to seem so bad. Most people know that moderate use of marijuana increases rather than decreases one's social proclivities, just as alcohol does. So although relatively few people in the middle class smoke pot, many speak of it with a cautious curiosity that suggests that if it were not illegal and somewhat hard to obtain, they would probably try it.

The LSD trip is apt to end "way out," and this term has an interesting spatial connotation that goes back at least as far as the early 1960's. In 1961 and 1962, during the period of the early Mercury spacecraft flights, such terms as "all systems go," "blast off," and "in orbit" all became part of the common vocabulary. From the chant of "go, go, go" beard in the blockhouse during blast off came the appellation for the pulsating dancer of rock-'n-roll, the go-go dancer, one who puts herself and her empathizers into a self-imposed semitrance, not really out of touch with reality, not "way out" beyond the pull of gravity, but "in orbit." From orbit one can return to *terra firma*, but if one goes way out he may never return. Thus a middle-class drunk is apt to say he is in orbit, but he will seldom if ever say he is way out. The acid head is not so timid about his private journey, but he too has his fears about blasting off into inner space. He is afraid of "blowing his mind," of not being able to come back to reorient himself with his normal waking reality. His trips are interstellar, and he wants to be way out, but he is afraid that in order to get there he may overpropel himself and blast himself apart. He is, and he knows he is, at the extreme edges of human limitation, where he must be as careful as the leading driver at the Grand Prix.

Tired of the boredom and frustration of everyday existence, we all seek occasional holidays. The hippies say they "freak out." They may do it with drugs or not. What the term means is simply that by normal standards they are doing a freakish thing. There is a beneficent release in asserting one's independence from the standards of the squares, and no little sense of triumph in admitting one's desire to be different—to be a freak, in other words. Even squares seem to have occasional use for the term as they chafe against the conformity demanded of them by middle-class standards. They will apply it to such actions as leaving a party early, stopping their membership in a club, or to some other action that shows they are no longer identifying themselves with the goals and actions of a social group.

There is a difference in square and hippie usage of the term, how-ever. When a square freaks out, he is taking a temporary holiday from everyday life, but when a hippie freaks out, he is apt to be on a quest for something spiritual, for some kind of mystical intuition that will give him a sense of knowing life and himself and his own relation to the cosmos. His "trips" are quests of this kind. A trip is, after all, a trip somewhere, to some kind of place. For the square the old-fashioned word suggests a vacation, further suggesting the intention of the traveler com-ing back to resume where he left off, but to the hippie a trip is a matter of finding Nirvana and hoping that when he returns he will be able to begin anew, setting his life in new channels, taking a new direction, guiding himself by the enlightenment he has received. To attain this enlightenment, the hippie "tunes in," a term seldom heard among the squares. The hippie believes there is some kind of a spiritual wavelength that he can reach if he puts himself in the proper receptive mental state. The square is apt to be skeptical of such mysticism.

One of the popular means of protest today is, as already noted, the "sit in." Take this term in the sense of assembly for the purpose of deny-ing the rule and the values of the establishment and couple it with the concept of "tuning-in" and you have the "love in." The love in is often recognized as a protest against war. Actually, it is even more fundamen-tally a protest against certain hallowed values of middle-class society. It is a denunciation of middle-class proscriptions on natural displays of human affection. It is an expression of revolt against the middle-class idea that there is a human duty to work hard to accumulate material wealth. And it is an active declaration that human cooperation is more important than individual competition. It is, furthermore, a kind of revival-meeting attempt to create the right atmosphere for people to "tune in" *en masse* and be imbued with the overwhelming sense of love and peace that is the blessed state of the brotherhood of man as most of our religious literature describes it.

Our impatient young want fulfillment now. To the Negro militants, "now" means that they are no longer going to wait for the rights promised them with the Emancipation Proclamation of a century ago. They are going to assume and exercise their rights immediately, regardless of the social consequences. To the hippie, the only meaningful time is the immediate moment. At any moment one can change his direction, have a revelation, learn what he truly is. The past is unimportant, the future worthless, unless he prepares in the present. "Now" to both the black and to the hippie is opportunity; the present moment must be seized, lived, and known fully for existence to have meaning and for man to become at each successive moment more fully a man than he has been up to today.

The central difficulty with the idea of now, as used by the hippies, Negro militants, and the New Left, is that it not only invites people to create a new awareness and a new life, but it implies that the only way to do this is to shuck completely the experience of the past. There is implicit in the concept the idea that, because the past has failed to produce a satisfactory present, all the lessons of the past should be ignored. The Now Generation may be in danger of becoming so enamored with the dynamics of revolt that they become what Korzybski in *Manhood of Humanity* called "dynamic fools," or rebels, not without cause, but without a viable program.

In the rhetoric of the hippies, the New Left, and the Negro militants there is precious little recognition of the centuries-long struggle for a better-than-subsistence economy and for a democratic government. Among the New Leftists there is little talk about what actually happened to communism under what the liberals of the twenties called the Great Experiment, Marxism under Lenin and Stalin. Among the young engaged in the confrontations of the New Leftism and those who seek the mystic way through drugs and "dropping out" there is a fearful contempt for the historically documented, long, hard road to Utopia.

Yet it is no accident that the alienated try to wipe out history by concentrating on the present. In several important respects, history has been unsatisfactory. It has bred the values of the middle class, values the Negro and the young do not believe they can live by successfully. For the Negro to accept the black man's place in history as a guide to the future would be to accept the dominance of the white middle class and the oppression and discrimination that have been his lot since he first arrived in this country.. For the young to accept the historically developed values of their society as a guide to the future would mean accepting the traditional values of the middle class: accumulation of wealth, individual competition, patriotism, and sexual purity.

It is still not sufficiently recognized that America is passing beyond the stage when the mere accumulation of money and the material comforts it can buy is the primary goal of a citizen's labor. After one has accumulated a modicum of comforts, he looks for satisfactions of the mind and spirit. That this is true needs no more demonstration than the many surveys that are presently being conducted in colleges throughout the country, sampling occupational interest of the scions of our increasingly affluent middle class. There is an increasing interest in social service, teaching, and other humanistic pursuits, so much so that business is having a very difficult time recruiting the kind of men and women it needs to maintain and develop an enlightened and efficient management.

Competition, the shibboleth of the free-enterprise system, has become suspect. For every victor there are millions of losers in a society that permits free competition. The outraged losers in the system have made government spin a dense web of regulations, trust and labor laws, penalties, and subsidies in an effort to make competition sportsmanlike: so that bankruptcy is not permanent economic death, so that powerful victors like Standard Oil do not end competition completely, and so that the less powerful do have a chance to survive and even live decently. Competition, a password that opens the door to more frustration than reward for so many, is no longer regarded by our young people as the "open sesame" to the good life.

To the questioning young person, middle-class views of morality and patriotism seem perverted. A society that accepts racial discrimination and condemns homosexuality between consenting adults, a society that considers adultery at home a worse crime than killing the young men of their own and other nations in a war of doubtful purpose, a society that demands the censorship of art dealing frankly with sex but permits advertisers to lie and packages to cheat—such a society may seem indeed not to know what morality really is.

Many adults pay lip service to the ideals of their ancestors and yet go their own way in private. They shake their heads at a story of adultery because that is what they are supposed to do, and then discreetly have their own affairs. They know they are apt to be cheated in what they buy, and they are ready to drive as hard a bargain themselves as they can. All the while they tell their children to be honest, clean, and brave. They live by a double standard, one for outward show and one for their private underground life. Youth insists that men should not have to live underground, that they should be creatures of the sunshine and fresh air. They will not abide the double standard. They say that they want it "told like it is." They want man's beliefs to coincide with his understanding of the truth; they want what he does to be what he believes, and they want this revolution in thought now.

The middle-class adult also uses the term "now," but in a different sense. To him what is now is merely the latest in thrills, the latest thing that is new—in fashion, entertainment, or activity. To do what is now means doing what is socially "in." Just as the middle class never uses "now" in the same sense the hippie or New Left does, so the hippie never uses "in" in the sense that the middle class does. The hippie's ins are "love ins" and the New Left's are "sit ins," concepts unacceptable to the middle class. Where the young and the adult middle class differ in their nows and ins is simply in the orientation that each has to middle-class values. For the young, now is a revolt from the past; for Babbitt, now is apt to be a continuation of the past quest for status based on the old values of a predominantly commercial civilization. Thus a General Motors Fastback is a now car, and flying across the polar ice cap is a now thing to do. In both cases doing what is now is merely doing what the rich people do.

A term that is often connected with the concept of now is the "happening." This is a term the young use to suggest a significant event along the road to knowledge and self-realization. It may be a sit in, or it may be listening to a rock-and-roll group, or it may be an LSD trip. The happening can happen to an individual or to a group, but when it does, it grants the ones who experience it a new perspective on life, an insight into the why and how of things. The middle class has picked up the term and applied it to the advent of a new soft drink, to masquerade parties using psychedelic decorations, and in general to any new set of sights, sounds, tastes, or smells that constitute a boredom-breaker.

Nevertheless, youth share at least one traditional value of middle-class thought, and that is individualism. They believe that some things are just not a person's "bag" and that each one should be allowed "to do his own thing." For the hippie to find real meaning in his life, he must first discover what are his inmost desires and his most natural expressions of those desires, his bag. Then he must develop his own means of expressing his personality, doing his own thing. This credo strikes a resonant chord in the adult middle class, who have been raised on such tenets as "rugged individualism," or the "pioneer spirit," and "self-reliance." In fact, you can hear squares using the related hippie verbiage quite often today to indicate their own disaffection with pressures to conform and their own desires to realize themselves as individuals. The only difference in hippie and middle-class usage here is a central one that we find throughout the usages of common terms—namely that the hippie attaches a kind of mystical significance to them that the middle class does not. That is, for the hippie discovering your bag and doing your own thing are by implication related to tuning in, to the love in, the trip, and the happening.

What the various usages of these terms indicate is that, although the adult middle class shares youth's disaffection with the impersonal control of the establishment, it will not accept individualism to the point of violating the law or threatening the rights of property, nor to the point of complete individual withdrawal from society. It remains socially oriented, and though it chafes under the impracticability and hypocrisy of its professed beliefs, it is unwilling to reevaluate and begin anew. It rejects mysticism, and it usually rejects logic. It remains sentimentally attached to the old beliefs of the Puritan ethic and is content to relieve its frustrations with alcohol, games, and thrills.

Yet its resistance to the pressures of the young hippies, the New Left, and the rest of the young who have been influenced by them is not so great as it was to the "beats" of the fifties. In those years the middle class was quick to identify the beats as "beatniks," suggesting they were more Soviet than American in their way of life. They were "bums" and "the great unwashed." Today, however, there is no counter-term for "hippie," and the New Left, although often called radical, is not so often called communist, except by old-guard Republicans.

The beats had no philosophy, though it was their interest in Zen Buddhism and in the possibilities of drugs that, as much as anything, gave rise to the hippie movement. The hippies have developed a viewpoint on the world—not a complete one to be sure, but one with its own set of principles and its own terminology. The mere fact that some of their language has been made a part of the middle-class vocabulary is indicative of partial social acceptance. Even their flower symbol of love and peace was taken up recently by the middle-class campaigners for one of the candidates for the presidential nomination by the Democratic party.

The middle class, the mainstream of modern society, is always slow to change, but it will, if only because the youth of today are the middle class of tomorrow. Though most of the youth are not hippie or New Left, they have had close exposure to the ideas of these radical groups. They will at least understand the serious need for revaluation; they may even reduce the double standard to one-and-a-half; they will know the acid-head's meaning of "now" and "happening," and though they will have their doubts about "tuning in" and will still apply "way out" to those who seem crazy, they will know that cooperation is at least as important as competition and that man cannot live successfully by Ford alone.

The overall sound of rock music is pulsating and extremely loud. The shouting seems symbolic of a youthful desire to be heard, with the frustrating conviction that nobody is listening.

Rock-Tongue

MICHAEL L. HECHT

Of all the communications we receive perhaps none is as pervasive or as universally appealing as music. Although music is seldom approached from a language point of view, much, it seems, can be gained from such a perspective. Here Michael Hecht considers contemporary rock music as language and focuses on its meaning (semantic), structure (syntactic), and sound (phonological) dimensions. In this exploration Hecht offers some provocative hypotheses regarding rock's appeal and influence, its reflection of contemporary youth culture, and its possible implications for tomorrow.

H uman language can be analyzed on at least three levels. The semantic level deals with meanings, the syntactic level deals with forms and structures, and the phonological level deals with sounds. Contemporary music (and here I focus on rock music), and in fact all music, likewise has meanings, forms, and sounds. By looking at contemporary music on these three levels we may be able to gain insight not only into music, but into language as well. But, more importantly, by focusing our attention on contemporary music we gain a unique perspective on the attitudes and values of the present generation. Music seems to provide an amazingly accurate reflection of the thoughts and desires, the needs and interests, the loves and hates, the strengths and weaknesses of the present generation.

ROCK MEANING

A semantic analysis of human language would focus on the words or morphemes that the speakers use and understand. That is, semantics is concerned with those elements or units of language which communicate meaning. A semantic analysis of music would then focus on the lyrics and the meaning of rock as a musical form.

Rock, as a musical form, symbolizes revolt. The music is a rebellion against restraints, and liberation is expressed in the energy and power of electric instrumentation, high decibel levels, shrieking voice qualities lacking in formal refinement, a pulsating beat and the uninhibited presentation by the rock performer as well as the radical content of the lyrics. It is not surprising, therefore, to discover a deluge of rebellious young amateur performers participating in a musical form which strives to release them from restraints. With a driving swirl of energetic activity, rock music frees us from the humdrum and ideally liberates us to explore new forms of existence.

In its rebellion, rock music often rejects standard modes of expres-

Prepared especially for this volume by Michael L. Hecht and printed with the author's permission.

sion. This, it seems, occurs for a number of reasons. As a revolt, rock refuses to conform to standard word usage and word meanings. As a reflection of a particular generation, it uses the "in" talk of its members, the words the young use to proclaim their youth. It uses what Paul Goodman refers to as "sublanguage as social badge." Defying convention, rock music often deals with social deviance. But because disc jockeys, station managers, and program directors have generally proven to be conservative in what they will put on the air, many rock artists have chosen to place their message between the lines, disguised in an ambiguous phrase, vocally slurred over, or imbedded in slang forms. It is these slang forms which stand out in any review of rock lyrics.

Slang usage not only allows the artist to sneak meanings into his songs, but also helps establish a bond of identity between the artist and those in his audience who understand. Slang creates an "in group" and in doing so adds to the impact of the music on those who are "in." Slang and other camouflage create in listeners an orientation to seek deeper level analysis of the lyrics. Why else would people be predisposed to reading various meanings into the seemingly innocent simplicity of *Norwegian Wood* by Lennon and McCartney or *White Rabbit* by Grace Slick?

In *Norwegian Wood* John Lennon and Paul McCartney recall a simple encounter with a girl. The storyteller meets the girl, goes to her room, talks and drinks wine with her, falls asleep and awakens only to find the "bird" has left. A simple boy/girl tale? Why then does Richard Goldstein choose to entertain the suspicion that Norwegian Wood symbolizes marijuana usage?[1] *White Rabbit* by Grace Slick is a rock Alice in Wonderland, complete with rabbits, a smoking caterpillar, human chess, a White Knight, a Red Queen and a dormouse. Yet Richard Goldstein labels this song a "psychedelic anthem," a call to the audience to experience drugs.[2] In both these instances, it seems that we find the deeper meanings largely because we believe they are there and almost force ourselves to discover them.

On another level, slang closes off rock to people who might otherwise enjoy it. The use of geographically limited slang is one example of this. "Heat" is/was California slang for policeman and is used in *For What It's Worth* by Stephen Stills. How is an Easterner to decode the intended meaning? And what is to happen to the understanding of this expression even in California two or three years from now? Slang, in other words, also has a dysfunctional potential.

[1]Richard Goldstein, *The Poetry of Rock* (New York: Bantam Books, 1969), p. 10.
[2]Goldstein, p. 107.

The lyrics of rock music represent a contemporary commentary on language behavior. Rock reflects the language of those who create it as well as those to whom it is directed. From early rock with its emphasis on girls, adolescence and cars, to the present rock highlighted by drugs, protest and alienation, the music provides a rather clear mirror of the themes which its audience talks about every day. Robinson and Hirsch put it this way:

> Early rock'n'roll in the 1950s was essentially a lower class phenomenon, expressing attitudes, concerns and habits common to this stratum (boredom with school, drag-racing, dating). . . . The new rock, like its predecessor, reflects the concerns of its creators. Some songs express antiwar feeling (as in *Eve of Destruction* or *2 + 2*); a large number refer to drug usage (*Step Out of Your Mind, Strawberry Fields Forever*).[3]

On a second and deeper level, rock music comments on the way people communicate with each other. All revolt, and rock music is no exception, necessitates an object to revolt against. With rock music, this object is often the stagnating and dehumanizing experience of modern mechanistic society. From the neon symbolism of Paul Simon's *Sound of Silence* to the deaf ear image of the Who's *Tommy*, alienation and barriers to communication constitute recurring themes in the languages of rock music. These themes are equally apparent in the Beatle's *Eleanor Rigby*, and the Rolling Stones' *Mother's Little Helper*. It is possible to reassemble the letters of the first name of *Eleanor Rigby* and find "a loner." It is possible that Lennon and McCartney were commenting on a society in which people do not communicate and are thus alone. We cannot help but be frightened by the image of the housewife hiding from contact with other people behind her own drug screen in the Rolling Stones' *Mother's Little Helper*. It is perfectly natural for the language of revolt to comment (most often negatively) on the quality of the language behavior of a society it disparages. As a consequence, it probably influences considerably the language behavior of the generation(s) to which it communicates.

ROCK STRUCTURES

The syntactic level of language deals with structure, for example the different ways in which words may be combined to form sentences and

---

[3]John P. Robinson and Paul Hirsch, "Its the Sound," *Psychology Today*, 3 (October 1969), p. 42.

the rules by which various abstract linguistic structures may be transformed into sentences. With music we have structures for both the instrumental and lyrical dimensions.

Conventional poetry is linear in form. It is strung out for us, one word (one experience) at a time. It moves from one discrete unit (a word or a linked phrase) to the next, and the next, until the end. There are breaks between the words which are not part of the poetic experience, but exist because of the nature of language and words. That is, there is a space or a break between the words "that" and "is" which begin this sentence. Music, on the other hand, is generally a unified experience, with one sound flowing into the next. In a multi-instrumental situation there is an interaction between notes being played together, as well as a mixture of different patterns. There may be breath pauses, but they are generally filled with the sound of another instrument, or perhaps by holding the last note (this later technique is widely practiced by way of electrical amplification). For these reasons, any break in the rock performance is an integral part of the composition and presentation, as opposed to the poetic form which imposes discrete, noncontinuous units on its content. The sound of the lyric adds yet another dimension to the nonlinear form of music.

Thus, the poetry of the lyrics is linear, while musical form is a nonlinear experience. It is often difficult to reconcile this contrast, and in some of the poorer songs we sense that the words do not seem to belong to the musical form or that the music has been petrified by its association with the words. However, in the more effective compositions each dimension complements the other; the depth of the musical experience lends richness to the poetic experience and the poetry adds substance to the music.

Reconciling the linear form, poetry, with the nonlinearity of rock music is an extremely complex task. Many of the early rock artists chose to sublimate their lyrics rather than deal with this contradiction in form. They relied on the sound of the musical experience to give the substance to their work which was lacking in their poetry. Indeed, how many of the great jazz numbers were vocal? How many of the classics were known for both great music and great lyrics? And what can be said about the lyrics of most of the great operas other than they spotlight great voice performances? So it would be surprising to find great poetry evolving from a musical field.

Influenced by Woody Guthrie, Bob Dylan built the folk tradition of meaningful lyrics into a poetic rock form. Through the injection of rhythm into his poetry, in addition to frequent violations of poetic "rules," Dylan's lyrics become a nonlinear sound experience which highlights deeply involved symbolism. As Goldstein puts it, "He demolishes the narrow line and lean stanzas that once dominated pop, replacing them with a more flexible organic structure."[4] Retaining the sound quality of the early rock lyric, Dylan combined the meaningful orientation of the folk and protest forms with the rhythm and contagion of rock'n'roll and helped give birth to an era of meaningful contemporary rock poetry.

> Even Leonard Cohen, a recognized Canadian poet who has recently turned to song writing, says he prepared for his new role by listening to old Ray Charles records until they warped. It shows. Cohen's rock songs have the consistency of modern verse, but unlike linear poetry, they are wrapped tightly around a rhythmic spine.[5]

The lyrics or poems are written in free verse which complements and supplements the liberated and free-flowing feeling of the rock form. Even when the standard stanza form is utilized, conventional poetic structure is not closely adhered to.

The music takes two standard forms, strophic or verse/chorus. In the strophic form one piece of music is repeated numerous times. For example, there may be five different poetic verses to a song. In strophic form the music behind each of those verses will be identical. Strophic form is exemplified by the *House of the Rising Sun*.

Verse/chorus form is slightly different. In this form two different themes are alternately presented. Thus the verse is musically different from the chorus, yet all the verses are the same and all the choruses are also identical to one another. The lyrics of the poetic choruses would also be identical to one another. While the lyrics of the various verses would differ, the music behind them would remain the same from one poetic verse to the next. Thus the first poetic verse might be about frustration, the second about repression, and the third revolution, yet the music behind each of these verses would be the same. In between each verse would be a chorus. All the choruses have the same words and the same music. An example of this form is Bob Dylan's *Blowin' In the Wind*.

In both strophic and verse/chorus forms the music is not uniquely created to match the words and much repetition results. Although this structure lends unity to the piece, the music therefore cannot expressly match the desired meaning of a specific word or phrase, thus losing some of its expressive value.

Many of the verse/chorus songs have a musical interlude. Depending

[4]Goldstein, p. 6.
[5]Goldstein, p. 5.

upon the specific context this interlude may create tension or merely provide time to digest what has been presented or to anticipate what is to come. The musical breaks in *Rocky Raccoon* by Lennon and Mc-Cartney are effective examples of this technique.

ROCK SOUNDS

The phonological level is concerned with the sounds of the language and the rules for sound combinations. In human language individual sounds, apart from their occurrence in standard words, have little, if any, meaning except perhaps in exclamations and various interjections. And even here it can be argued that such exclamations and interjections are actually "words." In music, however, sounds have a more independent existence. In fact, there are many rock songs which are basically composed of sounds rather than words.

One finds this emphasis on various sounds from the very early days of rock in such songs as *Get a Job* (Sha da da . . . , Yip yip yip . . .) by the Silhouettes and *Who Put the Bomp* (Bomp ba-ba-bomp . . .) by Barry Mann and Gerry Goffin and the songs of Screamin' Jay Hawkins. Grace Slick, the Led Zeppelin and Janis Joplin all represent performers who have used a sound as opposed to a word technique. The sounds these performers use are an integral part of their message. William Hedgepeth contends that these sounds represent an area of consciousness which words are incapable of describing.

The sound of rock music can be approached from at least two perspectives. Robinson and Hirsch maintain that teen-age record purchasers are barely familiar with the themes of rock music.[6] What they are tuned into is the sound of the piece.

> . . . the primary purpose of a lyric in 1957 was to convey mood, not meaning. The ideal scat song had to be simple enough for any voice to maintain, but intriguing enough to survive incessant repetition. Though they looked absurd on paper . . . , it is impossible to even read these lyrics without becoming immersed in their rhythmic pulse. That involvement was the experience these songs intended to provide.[7]

The sounds of Janis Joplin and others go beyond simple enjoyment, moving into the realm of meaning. Artists such as Joplin refined the

[6]Robinson and Hirsch, p. 45.
[7]Goldstein, p. 4.

sound techniques of early rock so that the sounds they utter take on considerable meaning. While people danced and kept time to the "sound" of Elvis Presley's *Hound Dog* they probably derived little meaning. On the other hand, a Janis Joplin performance would probably lead listeners to obtain a moving and highly emotionally charged meaning. The sounds she created were expressive of deep personal involvement that traveled beyond the capability of words, delivered from the gut in wails, screams, and other nonword utterances. Joplin and other performers have used their sounds to transcend the pleasure aspect of the early sound techniques and convey deep personal feelings. Their success is dependent upon the establishment of strong bonds of empathy with the audience and the desire of that audience to experience with the performer the highly emotional aspects of the performance.

The overall sound of rock music is pulsating and extremely loud. The shouting seems symbolic of a youthful desire to be heard, with the frustrating conviction that nobody is listening. In fact, the music is so loud and overpowering that it almost seems a primal shout, a calling to be heard while in pain, a need to correct what seems to be obviously wrong, yet the feeling of powerlessness in this pursuit. Rock music seems to provide an outlet for these feelings and a means for the young to express what they know is wrong and wish to correct. They see the communication failures and breakdowns around them and wish to eliminate them. And yet, to choose a form so alien to those they must reach to accomplish this change may be self-defeating, and this may yet be another characteristic of the rock rebellion.

Language influences our perceptions, helping to determine what we see of the world as well as how we see it. The people who talk the rock language of revolt or listen to it, might well perceive the world differently from those who do not understand this language. If rock music is viewed as a language, then those who understand that language are rock-tongued. The behavior of these rock-tongues should reflect a radical departure from preceding generations if, indeed, language does influence perception, and if rock is a language which symbolizes revolt. As more of the rock generation moves into adult status, changes in our society should become clearer and more visible. Are the sexual swingers of the 1960s and 1970s the rock fans of the 1950s? It is the depth and permanence of behavioral changes such as this, which will be the measure of the effect of the rock language revolution.

*Our language, after all, is a thought
trap: when certain sorts of notions
don't fit into its framework they
remain unrecognized. It's a monstrous
handicap. We are so crippled we
haven't even the words to think about
all those thoughts that might-have-been.*

New Language

WILLIAM HEDGEPETH

Our language, Hedgepeth argues, forces on us certain
ways of thinking and prevents us from thinking certain
thoughts or in different ways. "What we need," says
Hedgepeth, "is a new basis for communication—a new
language and, along with it, a newly understood function
for language itself." This "new language," according to
Hedgepeth, should function "as a common ground for
interpersonal honesty" and for "a greater breadth of
nonverbal understanding." And, perhaps most importantly,
this new language "can mean a new freedom of thought."
These claims seem somewhat extravagant. Most language
scholars, I think, would dismiss these ideas on various
psychological, philosophical, and linguistic grounds. Yet, it
seems undeniable that this new language, the language of
Janis Joplin and so many rock artists, is in wide use and in
great demand. It would clearly not fall into the linguists'
definition of language, but as a form of communication it
can hardly be ignored.

Bands of light beam from the rear—flare, pale, flutter: blue, green, yellow, red; now it's red. Janis is red, writhing, wrenching words right out her pores. "Puh . . . Puhleeazze . . . " up straight from her toes, shot through cosmos, amplified 2,000 watts. Stompstompstompstomp. Oh, Momma! Janis Joplin! Room booms: thousands out there, in the dark, feel the vibes. Supercharged. Slow glow grows in eyes: Does she *mean* it? Does she *mean* it? "WAH!" Mike jammed to her teeth, kicking, stomping, keeping time. Crouch down, up slow, louder now—tell us, tell us— "Awww wah hoo heee." Cymbals: crash, crash. Drum thump. Silent. Now it's over. Stunned hush. Did she mean it? Did she? Wah? Yes! Yes! The hall explodes. Message gotten. Yes! Yes! And then—*wham*—out of the grayish-hazy auditorium air rolls a long, blurry clap-whistle-roar like a rattling of the world's largest sheet of tin. Janis drops the mike, shoulders suddenly limp, bleats a teeny "thankya" and turns away from the crowd to grope for a paper cup (Dixie Cup) of Southern Comfort sitting on the organ. Then back to the mike.

No pukey, careful-metered lines sung here. And who here can possibly disentangle more than a few bare words out of that jammed-together thunderation of wailed syllables? ("AhheeeWOG-Pleaghuhh woo," she erupts again.) Not me, anyway. But everybody gets the point. The point is how she feels, and they are eager to pick it up, share it, feel it with her. They are primed for this kind of thing. People don't speak this way to them anywhere else—even at home. No one lays it on the line; no one translates deep-felt feelings into language and says it like they sense it.

Probably because most often they can't. And because they can't say it, they can't imagine it being said. And because of that, if, somehow, they were able to, the chances are they wouldn't—at least not right off. So, as it turns out, there's a whole vast range not only of emotions but of newly grasped sensations that seems doomed to lie locked up, unwordable, in our heads. Our language, in its present shape, just can't handle

William Hedgepeth, "New Language," Look *(January 13, 1970), pp. 46–48. Copyright © Cowles Communications, Inc., 1969.*

it; and people—particularly young people—are slowly becoming aware of this flaw in their tongue.

They're becoming aware that—as a vehicle for conveying new sensibilities, perceptions of consciousness and the huge input of new ideas and information—straight English is inadequate. And because, at present, it's untrained to operate in this dimension, people are feeling around elsewhere for ways to express the new reality in words (or in wails, grunts, growls, shrieks or sounds no one's yet labeled). In parts of California, for example, young people are evolving a speech form some call "Sunbear." "It's based on how things sound and feel. It's street talk, family talk," says a turned-on girl in Palo Alto. "But our parents would never understand a word we're saying. Like, when we start rapping, we stop all the usual connections between thoughts."

"LAAww, ahh wahh . . . " (and louder) "OOOHHHh hooowooo Unngggghh" (like a stomp in the chest). Janis is looking out into the rotating, multicolored spots and undulating against them and against the sexual pulse-bump-mega-beat of the band. She humps and bumps, howling, and, for a moment, becomes an upright elastic gyration in the stuttering quick-flicker of the strobes. "Uhh uhhhh huh, awoooooo"— low, and with much anguish. Some near the front nod in sympathy. She is speaking now to them beyond words. Ahhhh.

Words develop from a mental tagging of experience. Today, though, the sudden gush of new sorts of experiences—in both inner and outer space—has not only outpaced the development of our language but also shown up the limitations of its structure. It's not that conventional language has become inadequate for communicating fresh concepts merely because of a lack of new words, it's because of the whole way of thinking that it forces us into.

Psychologists say all higher levels of thinking depend on language. But at the same time the structure of whatever language we use affects the way we see the world—influences, in fact, our attitudes and thought processes themselves. The difficulty today is that our brains have out-evolved our tongue. Every major language, says Dr. Mario Pei, started as a rough-hewn tool "fit only for material communication, and then proceeded to polish and refine itself to the point of becoming a vehicle for abstract, cultural thought."

Obviously, our language has done well in keeping its technological terminology polished up. But just where we need it most today, it lets us down. It's clear that there are important new realms of the mind, of interpersonal involvements and levels of perception that defy its ability to convey or communicate—or even to conceive. The whole business now-adays of people talking about ineffable vibrations they receive from this or that suggests the existence of dimensions of reality beyond the outer limits of our language's vocal range. Our language, after all, is a thought trap: when certain sorts of notions don't fit into its framework they remain unrecognized. It's a monstrous handicap. We are so crippled we haven't even the words to think about all those thoughts that might-have-been.

Then, too, there are concepts expressible in other tongues that simply don't translate into ours—except, perhaps, as vague approximations. The Hopi Indians, for example, can put forth ideas and feelings we can't even think about. The Hopi have a whole conception of time and space that's so far removed from *our* frame of reference it seems the work of Martians. What this means, in other words, is that there are other ways of regarding reality. "A change in language," wrote Benjamin Whorf, "can transform our appreciation of the Cosmos."

But today, our awareness of the Cosmos, our exploratory experiences (whether psychedelic or otherwise) into human consciousness, the whole content of our collective minds, in fact, have grown beyond the present capability *of any* conventional language to express. At the same time, the growing global nature of the human community is about to place enormous demands upon our capacity for interpersonal communication. "Our new environment compels commitment and participation. We have become irrevocably involved with, and responsible for, each other," says McLuhan. Our future, then, requires more than everyone becoming merely multilingual. What we need is a new basis for communication—a new language and, along with it, a newly understood function for language itself.

As it stands, we are harnessed to a tongue that's actually doing bad things to us. Much of our tradition-bound speech is structured in a way that creates a polarity between us and everyone (and everything) else. Our language forces us to conceive so much of life as an endless, goal-focused struggle, a war. And success, in even the most mild endeavors, is depicted in outright battlefield terminology: We grapple with, strive, clash, cross swords, lock horns, tussle, contend, engage, fight for or take the offensive to achieve (with flying colors) a triumph, victory, conquest, a win, a mastery, a put-down, a killing, etc. Roget's Thesaurus devotes 28 lines to "Peace" and 162 lines to "Warfare." Thus, at a time when we need to be dismantling barriers to human unity, we continue to generate tension as we talk—and our talk, in turn, influences our behavior. We tend, too, in this way, to use language not as a means of touching souls with others but as a defense, a barrier, with words deployed as little bricks to wall us in and hold other people off. Language tries to deal with reality by manipulating symbols of reality. It hinges on the mind's ability to link sounds with meanings and thereby transfer those meanings. Until we all become telepathic, we can't hope to grasp more than a hazy fraction of what's in another head; but meanwhile, we have to clear our existing channels of communication of all the subterfuge and conflict-laden verbosity that sand between us and what we could be.

Among young people, at least, a real frustration factor enters in here. For too long now, abstract feelings have largely been left in nonlinguistic limbo while our language has developed itself along more "practical" lines. To make things worse, so much irrational emotional baggage has been heaped on so many words that our ability to voice a gut-felt notion is stifled—unless we fall back on euphemisms that remove us even further from reality. If words are sounds that symbolize meanings, it's obviously the meanings not the sounds that are the things we try to get across. OK? Then why do you persist in the idea that "intercourse" or "lovemaking" is acceptable while — — — — is an unprintable moral affront? It's a perfect example of thinking backward, reacting to the symbol rather than the subject—a response so senseless that no one even knows why he does it. Somewhere along the line, things just got so turned around that now people are scared of their own words. We make ourselves feel guilty about our speech and sull up like treed possums when "unmoral" words are uttered—or perhaps it's just those word-sounds that touch a nerve or feeling or say a thing directly.

So, while the framework of our language hamstrings the brain's ability to think, we cramp our speech even further, just out of sheer perverseness. As a result, we go about transmitting at almost inaudibly low intensities with equipment that's inadequate to begin with.

If there is transfer of meaning, there is language. But this transfer doesn't have to be in sequential order nor in sentences nor even in words. Numbers or tones or computer beeps will do it. There are some American Indian tongues in which the verb can include the subject, object and all modifiers so that the entire sentence is a single word. The key element in this is a community of understanding, a willingness to comprehend each other's feelings, a group-consciousness—a quality of "usness." And it is precisely this aspect of speech—already a feature with many young people—that can spread worldwide.

Present national languages are a product of fragmentation. Today, though, due to global electronic communication, growing literacy, population density and travel, the drift is toward putting things back together. We're moving toward a world culture and ultimately universal consciousness. Eventually, an international language will supersede national languages—but hopefully sooner, for the lethal potential of this planet is already too great to tolerate continued mass misunderstanding, concealment of feeling and anything less than undistorted universal rapport.

Whatever it may be, our new language must serve this new function:

as a common ground for interpersonal honesty; and, by way of that honesty, a greater breadth of nonverbal understanding—i.e., "us-ness." New language, too, can mean a new freedom of thought. We will, at last, use words at peak capacity, and without guile, to make clear who we are and how we feel, to feel our own words and to level with each other by committing ourselves to what we say.

On a personal level, there'll be no need to cling to formal grammar to convey meaning. Speech doesn't have to be linear, it can come out as a compressed overlay of facts and sensations and moods and ideas and images. Words can serve as signals, and others will understand. The way a man feels can be unashamedly expressed in sheer sound, such as a low, glottal hum, like the purring of a cat, to indicate contentment. People need only enough openness about themselves not to feel silly about an honest sound. If it says it, say it. Feelings have meaning. Sounds have meaning. Open language can be a joy—a language we can grow with, growl with. Words can cramp your style.

Janis glares out across the darkened auditorium with a pained grimace and an "Ohhh ahh hoo hiweee" that tears at the very root of the heart. She leans back now and moos some sorrowful something into the mike—low, now high, shrill, other worldly, like a haunt, a siren, wraith, denizen of the darks, dawn goddess, knobby nymph, mooncalf, Ophelia: "UUnnh hoo youpleuzz Yeahhh." Lord, she can't live through this—being eaten inside out with pain. Run to her. Clasp her shoulders, cradle her tortured head. "PUHleazzee.' . . . " (Crowd: yeh, yeh, do it, do it.) "Yawhoo oo. . . " Up now, quick, before she dies, seize her. Cool her. Blow in her face. Marry her. Kiss her cheeks. Ply her limp lips with Southern Comfort. Anything, anything. Oh God . . . Janis, Janis, you've not said a word but I understand. We're in love. We don't need words, just meanings, just sounds of feeling, noises that say things. Oh, roar, hiss, bleat, bark, purr to me, snarl sweetly to me. Ahhhh . . . snaarrrll . . . ahhhhh, yes, I know, I know. . . .

*With words, therefore, we influence and
to an enormous extent* control future
events.

The Language of Social Control

S. I. HAYAKAWA

Language can be used to achieve numerous and diverse
ends. That of social control, however, is probably among
the most significant both from an individual and from a
societal point of view. Here S. I. Hayakawa provides a
rather unique perspective on the directive uses of language
—languages used to influence, direct, or control the
actions of other people. The nature of this type of
language, the promises, problems, and disappointments
created by it, and the societal functions it serves are here
analyzed with reference to advertising, political
speechmaking, propaganda, etc. Directive language
functions to hold society together and at the same time to
create distrust and disillusionment. Perhaps a more
thorough understanding of this type of language will help
to enhance the former and decrease the latter function.

*The effect of a parade of sonorous
phrases upon human conduct has
never been adequately studied.*
                —THURMAN W. ARNOLD

*Yet the layman errs in his belief that
this lack of precision and finality is to
be ascribed to the lawyers. The truth
of the matter is that the popular notion
of the possibilities of legal exactness is
based upon a misconception. The law
always has been, is now, and will ever
continue to be, largely vague and
variable. And how could this well be
otherwise? The law deals with human
relations in their most complicated
aspects. The whole confused, shifting
helter-skelter of life parades before it
—more confused than ever, in our
kaleidoscopic age.*
                —JEROME FRANK

MAKING THINGS HAPPEN

The most interesting and perhaps least understood relationship between words and the world is that between words and future events. When we say, for example, "Come here!" we are not describing the extensional world about us, nor are we merely expressing our feelings; we are trying to *make something happen*. What we call "commands," "pleas," "requests," and "orders" are the simplest ways we have of making things happen by means of words.

There are, however, more roundabout ways. When we say, for example, "Our candidate is a great American," we are of course making an enthusiastic purr about him, but we may also be influencing other people to vote for him. Again, when we say, "Our war against the enemy is God's war. God wills that we must triumph," we are saying something which, though unverifiable, may influence others to help in the prosecution of the war. Or if we merely state as a fact, "Milk contains vitamins," we may be influencing others to buy milk.

Consider, too, such a statement as "I'll meet you tomorrow at two o'clock in front of the Palace Theater." Such a statement about *future* events can only be made, it will be observed, in a system in which symbols are independent of things symbolized. The future, like the recorded past, is a specifically human dimension. To a dog, the expression "hamburger *tomorrow*" is meaningless—he will look at you expectantly, hoping for the extensional meaning of the word "hamburger" to be produced *now*. Squirrels, to be sure, store food for "next winter," but the fact that they store food regardless of whether or not their needs are adequately provided for demonstrates that such behavior (usually called "instinctive") is governed neither by symbols nor by other interpreted stimuli. Human beings are unique in their ability to react meaningfully to such expressions as "next Saturday," "on our next wedding anniversary," "twenty years after date I promise to pay," "some day, perhaps five hundred years from now." That is to say, maps can be made, even though the territories they stand for are not yet actualities. Guiding ourselves by means of such maps of territories-to-be, we can impose a certain predictability upon future events.

With words, therefore, we influence and to an enormous extent *control future events*. It is for this reason that writers write; preachers preach; employers, parents, and teachers scold; propagandists send out news releases; statesmen give addresses. All of them, for various reasons, are trying to influence our conduct—sometimes for our good, sometimes for their own. These attempts to control, direct, or influence the future actions of fellow human beings with words may be termed *directive uses of language*.

Now it is obvious that if directive language is going to direct, it cannot be dull or uninteresting. If it is to influence our conduct, it *must* make use of every affective element in language: dramatic variations in tone of voice, rhyme and rhythm, purring and snarling, words with strong affective connotations, endless repetition. If meaningless noises will move the audience, meaningless noises must be made; if facts move them, facts must be given; if noble ideals move them, we must make our proposals appear noble; if they will respond only to fear, we must scare them stiff.

The nature of the affective means used in directive language is limited, of course, by the nature of our aims. If we are trying to direct people to be more kindly toward each other, we obviously do not want to arouse feelings of cruelty or hate. If we are trying to direct people to think and act more intelligently, we obviously should not use subrational appeals. If we are trying to direct people to lead better lives, we use affective appeals that arouse their finest feelings. Included among directive utterances, therefore, are many of the greatest and most treasured works of literature: the Christian and Buddhist scriptures, the writings of Confucius, Milton's *Areopagitica*, and Lincoln's Gettysburg Address.

There are, however, occasions when it is felt that language is not sufficiently affective by itself to produce the results wanted. We supplement directive language, therefore, by *nonverbal affective appeals* of many kinds. We supplement the words "Come here" by gesturing with our hands. Advertisers are not content with saying in words how beautiful their products will make us; they supplement their words by the use of colored inks and by pictures. Newspapers are not content with saying that communism is a menace; they supply political cartoons depicting communists as criminally insane people placing sticks of dynamite under magnificent buildings labeled "American way of life." The affective appeal of sermons and religious exhortations may be supplemented by costumes, incense, processions, choir music, and church bells. A political candidate seeking office reinforces his speech-making with a considerable array of nonverbal affective appeals: brass bands, flags, parades, picnics, barbecues, and free cigars.[1] Often a candidate's smile or, as in

[1]The following are excerpts from reports of the Republican National Convention of 1948: "There on the stage a gigantic photograph of the candidate, tinted somewhat too vividly, gazed steadily out over the throngs. Around the balcony hung other photographs: the Dewey family playing with their Great Dane; the Deweys at the circus; Dewey on the farm. Dewey infantrymen passed out soft drinks and small favors to gawking visitors and gave every 200th visitor a door prize. William Horne, a Philadelphia bank employee, was clocked in as the 45,000th visitor and got a sterling silver carving aid." *Time* (July 5, 1948). "Over loudspeakers of the Bellevue-Stratford came a constant stream of official exhortations against undue crowding at the entrance to the Dewey headquarters. The warnings were part of the game, but they were also justified. Why wouldn't the Dewey headquarters be jammed when prizes—from chewing gum and pocket combs to silk lingerie and dresses—were being doled out with the largess of a radio quiz show? At one point the Dewey people even staged a fashion show, complete with eight bathing beauties. A bewildered foreign newspaperman asked a fellow-reporter, 'How can I explain to France what this has to do with electing a President?' . . . The Stassen managers appeared to be saving up their circus talent for Convention Hall, where it turned out to be considerable, ranging from an Indian chief in full regalia to a shapely girl in sailor pants who did a nautical rumba on the rostrum." *Nation* (July 3, 1948).

the case of President Kennedy, his wife's appearance and charm may be a powerful influence upon the voter.

Now, if we want people to do certain things, and if we are indifferent as to *why they do them*, then no affective appeals need be excluded. Some political candidates want us to vote for them regardless of our reasons for doing so. Therefore, if we hate the rich, they will snarl at the rich for us; if we dislike strikers, they will snarl at the strikers; if we like clambakes, they will throw clambakes; if the majority of us like hillbilly music, they may say nothing about the problems of government, but travel among their constituencies with hillbilly bands. Again, many business firms want us to buy their products regardless of our reasons for doing so; therefore, if delusions and fantasies will lead us to buy their products, they will seek to produce delusions and fantasies; if we want to be popular with the other sex, they will promise us popularity; if we like pretty girls in bathing suits, they will associate pretty girls in bathing suits with their products, whether they are selling shaving cream, automobiles, summer resorts, ice-cream cones, house paint, or hardware. Only the law keeps them from presenting pretty girls without bathing suits. The records of the Federal Trade Commission, as well as the advertising pages of many magazines, show that some advertisers will stop at practically nothing.

THE PROMISES OF DIRECTIVE LANGUAGE

Almost all directive utterances say something about the future. They are "maps," either explicitly or by implication, of *"territories" that are to be.* They direct us to do certain things with the stated or implied promise that if we do these things, certain consequences will follow: "If you adhere to the Bill of Rights, your civil rights too will be protected." "If you vote for me, I will have your taxes reduced." "Live according to these religious principles, and you will have peace in your soul." "Read this magazine, and you will keep up with important current events." "Take Lewis's Licorice Liver Pills and enjoy that glorious feeling that goes with regularity." Needless to say, some of these promises are kept, and some are not. Indeed, we encounter promises daily that are obviously incapable of being kept.

There is no sense in objecting as some people do to advertising and political propaganda—the only kind of directives they worry about—on the ground that they are based on "emotional appeals." Unless directive language has affective power of some kind, it is useless. We do not object to campaigns that tell us, "Give to the Community Chest and enable poor children to enjoy better care," although that is an "emotional appeal." Nor do we resent being reminded of our love of home, friends, and nation when people issue moral or patriotic directives at us. The important question to be asked of any directive utterance is, "Will things happen as promised if I do as I am directed to do? If I accept your philosophy, shall I achieve peace of mind? If I vote for you, will my taxes be reduced? If I use Lifeguard Soap, will my boy friend really come back to me?"

We rightly object to advertisers who make false or misleading claims and to politicians who ignore their promises, although it must be admitted that, in the case of politicians, they are sometimes compelled to make promises that later circumstances prevent them from keeping. Life being as uncertain and as unpredictable as it is, we are constantly trying to find out what is going to happen next, so that we may prepare ourselves. Directive utterances undertake to tell us how we can bring about certain desirable events and how we can avoid undesirable events. If we can rely upon what they tell us about the future, the uncertainties of life are reduced. When, however, directive utterances are of such a character that things do *not* happen as predicted—when, after we have done as we were told, the peace in the soul has not been found, the taxes have not been reduced, the boy friend has not returned, there is disappointment. Such disappointments may be trivial or grave; in any event, they are so common that we do not even bother to complain about some of them. They are, nevertheless, all serious in their implications. *Each of them serves, in greater or lesser degree, to break down the mutual trust that makes cooperation possible and knits people together into a society.*

Every one of us, therefore, who utters directive language, with its concomitant promises, stated or implied, is morally obliged to be as certain as he can, since there is no absolute certainty, that he is arousing no false expectations. Politicians promising the immediate abolition of poverty, national advertisers suggesting that tottering marriages can be restored to bliss by a change in the brand of laundry detergent used in the family, newspapers threatening the collapse of the nation if the party they favor is not elected—all such utterers of nonsense are, for the reasons stated, menaces to the social order. It does not matter much whether such misleading directives are uttered in ignorance and error or with conscious intent to deceive, because the disappointments they cause are all similarly destructive of mutual trust among human beings.

THE FOUNDATIONS OF SOCIETY

But propaganda, no matter how persuasive, does not create society. We can, if we wish, ignore its directives. We come now to *directive utter-*

ances that we cannot ignore if we wish to remain organized in our social groups.

What we call society is a vast network of mutual agreements. We agree to refrain from murdering our fellow citizens, and they in turn agree to refrain from murdering us; we agree to drive on the right-hand side of the road, and others agree to do the same; we agree to deliver specified goods, and others agree to pay us for them; we agree to observe the rules of an organization, and the organization agrees to let us enjoy its privileges. This complicated network of agreements, into which almost every detail of our lives is woven and upon which most of our expectations in life are based, consists essentially of *statements about future events which we are supposed, with our own efforts, to bring about.* Without such agreements, there would be no such thing as society. We would all be huddling in miserable and lonely caves, not daring to trust anyone. With such agreements, and a will on the part of the vast majority of people to live by them, behavior begins to fall into relatively predictable patterns; cooperation becomes possible; peace and freedom are established.

Therefore, in order that we shall continue to exist as human beings, we *must* impose patterns of behavior on each other. We must make citizens conform to social and civic customs; we must make husbands dutiful to their wives; we must make soldiers courageous, judges just, priests pious, and teachers solicitous for the welfare of their pupils. In early stages of culture the principal means of imposing patterns of behavior was, of course, physical coercion. But such control can also be exercised, as human beings must have discovered extremely early in history, by *words*—that is, by directive language. Therefore, directives about matters which society as a whole regards as essential to its own safety are made especially powerful, so that no individual in that society will fail to be impressed with a sense of his obligations. To make doubly sure, society further reinforces the directives by the assurance that punishment, possibly including imprisonment and death, may be visited upon those who fail to heed the words.

DIRECTIVES WITH COLLECTIVE SANCTION

These directive utterances with collective sanction, which try to impose patterns of behavior upon the individual in the interests of the whole group, are among the most interesting of linguistic events. Not only are they usually accompanied by ritual; they are usually the central purpose of ritual. There is probably no kind of utterance that we take more seriously, that affects our lives more deeply, that we quarrel about more bitterly. Constitutions of nations and of organizations, legal contracts, and oaths of office are utterances of this kind; in marriage vows, confirmation exercises, induction ceremonies, and initiations, they are the essential constituent. Those terrifying verbal jungles called *laws* are simply such directives, accumulated, codified, and systematized through the centuries. In its laws, society makes its mightiest collective effort to impose predictability upon human behavior.

Directive utterances made under collective sanction may exhibit any or all of the following features:

1. Such language is almost always phrased in *words that have affective connotations*, so that people will be appropriately impressed and awed. Archaic and obsolete vocabulary or stilted phraseology quite unlike the language of everyday life is employed. For example: "Wilt thou, John, take this woman for thy lawful wedded wife?" "This lease, made this tenth day of July, A.D. One Thousand Nine Hundred and Sixty-Three, between Samuel Smith, hereinafter called the Lessor, and Jeremiah Johnson, hereinafter called Lessee, WITNESSETH, that Lessor, in consideration of covenants and agreements hereinafter contained and made on the part of the Lessee, hereby leases to Lessee for a private dwelling, the premises known and described as follows, to wit. . . . "

2. Such directive utterances are often accompanied by *appeals to supernatural powers*, who are called upon to help us carry out the vows, or to punish us if we fail to carry them out. An oath, for example, ends with the words, "So help me God." Prayers, incantations, and invocations accompany the utterance of important vows in practically all cultures, from the most primitive to the most civilized. These further serve, of course, to impress our vows on our minds.

3. The *fear of direct punishment* is also invoked. If God does not punish us for failing to carry out our agreements, it is made clear either by statement or implication that our fellow men will. For example, we all realize that we can be imprisoned for desertion, nonsupport, or bigamy; sued for "breach of contract", "unfrocked" for activities contrary to priestly vows; "cashiered" for "conduct unbecoming an officer"; "impeached" for "betrayal of public trust"; hanged for "treason."

4. The formal and public utterance of the vows may be preceded by *preliminary disciplines* of various kinds: courses of training in the meaning of the vows one is undertaking; fasting and self-mortification, as before entering the priesthood; initiation ceremonies involving physical torture, as before induction into the warrior status among primitive peoples or membership in college fraternities.

5. The utterance of the directive language may be accompanied by other *activities or gestures calculated to impress the occasion on the mind.* For example, everybody in a courtroom stands up when a judge is about

to open a court; huge processions and extraordinary costumes accompany coronation ceremonies; academic gowns are worn for commencement exercises; for many weddings, an organist and a soprano are procured and special clothes are worn.

6. The uttering of the vows may be immediately followed by *feasts, dancing, and other joyous manifestations.* Again the purpose seems to be to reinforce still further the effect of the vows. For example, there are wedding parties and receptions, graduation dances, banquets for the induction of officers and, even in the most modest social circles, some form of "celebration" when a member of the family enters into a compact with society. In primitive cultures, initiation ceremonies for chieftains may be followed by feasting and dancing that last for several days or weeks.

7. In cases where the first utterance of the vows is not made a special ceremonial occasion, the effect on the memory is usually achieved by *frequent repetition.* The flag ritual ("I pledge allegiance to the flag of the United States of America . . . ") is repeated daily in most schools. Mottoes, which are briefly stated general directives, are repeated frequently; sometimes they are stamped on dishes, sometimes engraved on a warrior's sword, sometimes inscribed in prominent places such as on gates, walls, and doorways, where people can see them and be reminded of their duties.

The common feature of all these activities that accompany directive utterances, as well as of the affective elements in the language of directive utterances, is the deep effect they have on the memory. Every kind of sensory impression from the severe pain of initiation rites to the pleasures of banqueting, music, splendid clothing, and ornamental surroundings may be employed; every emotion from the fear of divine punishment to pride in being made the object of special public attention may be aroused. This is done in order that the individual who enters into his compact with society—that is, the individual who commits himself to the "map" of the not-yet-existent "territory"—shall never forget to try to bring that "territory" into existence.

For these reasons, such occasions as when a cadet receives his commission, when a Jewish boy has his *bar mitzvah,* when a priest takes his vows, when a policeman receives his badge, when a foreign-born citizen is sworn in as a citizen of the United States, or when a president takes his oath of office—these are events one never forgets. Even if, later on, a person realizes that he has not fulfilled his vows, he cannot shake off the feeling that he should have done so. All of us, of course, use and respond to these ritual directives. The phrases and speeches to which we respond reveal our deepest religious, patriotic, social, professional, and political allegiances more accurately than do the citizenship papers or membership cards that we may carry in our pockets or the badges that we may wear on our coats. A man who has changed his religion after reaching adulthood will, on hearing the ritual he was accustomed to hearing in childhood, often feel an urge to return to his earlier form of worship. In such ways, then, do human beings use words to reach out into the future and control each other's conduct.

It should be remarked that many of our social directives and many of the rituals with which they are accompanied are antiquated and somewhat insulting to adult minds. Rituals that originated in times when people had to be scared into good behavior are unnecessary to people who already have a sense of social responsibility. For example, a five-minute marriage ceremony performed at the city hall for a mature, responsible couple may "take" much better than a full-dress church ceremony performed for an infantile couple. In spite of the fact that the strength of social directives obviously lies in the willingness, the maturity, and the intelligence of the people to whom the directives are addressed, there is still a widespread tendency to rely upon the efficacy of ceremonies as such. This tendency is due, of course, to a lingering belief in word-magic, the notion that, by *saying* things repeatedly or in specified ceremonial ways, we can cast a spell over the future and force events to turn out the way we said they would. ("There'll always be an England!") An interesting manifestation of this superstitious attitude towards words and rituals is to be found among those members of patriotic societies who seem to believe that the way to educate school children in democracy is to stage bigger and better flag-saluting ceremonies and to treble the occasions for singing "God Bless America."

WHAT ARE "RIGHTS"?

What, extensionally, is the meaning of the word "my" in such expressions as "my real estate," "my book," "my automobile"? Certainly the word "my" describes no characteristics of the objects named. A check changes hands and "your" automobile becomes "mine" but no change results in the automobile. What has changed?

The change is, of course, in *our social agreements covering our behavior* toward the automobile. Formerly, when it was "yours," you felt free to use it as you liked, while I did not. Now that it is "mine," I use it freely and you may not. The meaning of "yours" and "mine" lies not in the external world, but in *how we intend to act*. And when society as a whole recognizes my "right of ownership" (by issuing me, for example, a certificate of title), it agrees to protect me in my intentions to use the automobile and to frustrate, by police action if necessary, the intentions of those who may wish to use it without my permission. Society makes this agreement with me in return for my obeying its laws and paying my share of the expenses of government.

Are not, then, all assertions of ownership and statements about "rights" directives? Cannot, "This is *mine,*" be translated, "I am going to use this object; you keep your hands' off"? Cannot, "Every child has a *right* to an education," be translated, "*Give* every child an education"? And is not the difference between "moral rights" and "legal rights" the difference between agreements which people believe *ought* to be made, and those which, through collective, legislative sanction, *have been* made?

DIRECTIVES AND DISILLUSIONMENT

A few cautions may be added before we leave the subject of directive language. First, it should be remembered that, since words cannot "say all" about anything, the promises implied in directive language are never more than "outline maps" of "territories-to-be." The future will fill in those outlines, often in unexpected ways. Sometimes the future will bear no relation to our "maps" at all, in spite of all our endeavors to bring about the promised events. We swear always to be good citizens, always to do our duty, and so on, but we never quite succeed in being good citizens *every day* of our lives or in performing *all* our duties. A realization that directives cannot *fully* impose any pattern on the future saves us from having impossible expectations and therefore from suffering needless disappointments.

Secondly, one should distinguish between directive and informative utterances, which often look alike. Such statements as "A boy scout is clean and chivalrous and brave" or "Policemen are defenders of the weak" *set up goals* and do not necessarily describe the present situation. This is extremely important, because all too often people understand such definitions as descriptive and are then shocked and disillusioned when they encounter a boy scout who is not chivalrous or a policeman who is a bully. They decide that they are "through with the boy scouts" or "disgusted with all policemen," which, of course, is nonsense. They have, in effect, inferred an informative statement from what is to be taken only as a very general directive.

A third source of disappointment and disillusionment arising from the improper understanding of directives results from reading into directives promises that they do not make. A common instance is provided by advertisements of the antiseptics and patent medicines which people buy under the impression that the cure or prevention of colds was promised. Because of the rulings of the Federal Trade Commission, the writers of these advertisements carefully avoid saying that their preparations will prevent or cure anything. Instead, they say that they "help reduce the severity of the infection," "help relieve the symptoms of a cold," or "help guard against sniffling and other discomforts." If after reading these advertisements you feel that prevention or cure of colds has been promised, you are exactly the kind of sucker they are looking for. (Of course, if you buy the product knowing clearly what was promised and what was not, that is a different matter.)

Another way of reading into directives things that were not said is by believing promises to be more specific and concrete than they really are. When, for example, a candidate for political office promises to "help the farmer," and you vote for him, and then you discover that he helps the *cotton* farmer without helping the *potato* farmer (and you grow potatoes)—you cannot exactly accuse him of having broken his promise. Or, if another candidate promises to "protect union labor," and you vote for him, and he helps to pass legislation that infuriates the officials of your union (he calls it "legislation to protect union members from their own racketeering leadership")—again you cannot exactly accuse him of having broken his promise, since his action may well have been sincerely in accord with his notion of "helping union labor." The ambiguities of campaign oratory are notorious.

Politicians are often accused of breaking their promises. No doubt many of them do. But it must be remarked that they often do not promise as much as their constituents think they do. The platforms of the major parties are almost always at high levels of abstraction ("they mean all things to all men," as the cynical say), but they are often understood by voters to be more specific and concrete (i.e., at lower levels of abstraction) than they are. If one is "disillusioned" by the acts of a politician, sometimes the politician is to blame, but sometimes the voter is to blame for having had the illusion to start with—or, as we shall say, for having *confused different levels of abstraction.*

Every word has its use and every word
has its history.

Rhetorical Qualities of Words

RICHARD E. HUGHES AND P. ALBERT DUHAMEL

In this article Richard E. Hughes and P. Albert
Duhamel focus on language in terms of words and
particularly the rhetorical or persuasive dimensions of
words. The authors analyze the nature of jargon,
euphemism, and metaphor and the ways in which words
may vary in terms of such scales as concrete-abstract,
popular-learned, and connotation-denotation. These
dimensions or qualities of words are of obvious importance
to the writer or speaker who attempts to make his message
effective and persuasive. Yet, they are perhaps even more
important to the student of language who wants to
understand some of the numerous resources of language
and the options which language allows for thinking and
expressing ideas.

A writer's choice of words can be the most important single factor in determining the effectiveness of his writing. Some critics have gone so far as to maintain that effective style is simply the right word in the right place, and they are supported by evidence found in the manuscripts of great writers. The manuscript of Keats' *Eve of St. Agnes* reveals how carefully he considered each word—writing first one, then another—before finally deciding which was the most likely to convey precisely the effect he intended. The style of some writers, such as Henry James, reflects in almost every sentence the search for the *mot juste*, that one word that can suggest a precise shade of meaning.

Another way of demonstrating the importance of words is to consider how much money is spent each year by all kinds of companies throughout the world to build up favorable associations between certain words and their products. At the annual convention of the Advertising Federation of America in St. Louis in 1964, it was reported that about one billion dollars had been spent to promote five words in one year: *white* as in "whiter than white"; *power* as in "cleaning power"; *mild* as in cigarettes; *refreshing* as in soaps and soft drinks; and *relief* as in "from tired blood" and/or "from headaches"!

Every word has its use, and every word has its history. Words can be studied from several points of view. We are concerned with two: first, how words have been selected and disposed by various writers to achieve their effects; second, how to apply the principles that have accounted for *their* success to our own writing.

The classifications according to which words will be studied may be considered as scales stretching between sets of extremes, such as abstract and concrete, denotative and connotative, popular and learned. Most words fall somewhere between the extremes; just where is not always easy to determine. Since the various scales are not mutually exclusive, the same word can be measured on several. The location of a particular word

Richard E. Hughes and P. Albert Duhamel, Principles of Rhetoric, © *1966, pp. 191–209. Reprinted by permission of Prentice-Hall, Inc., Englewood Cliffs, N.J.*

on a scale is also subject to change, according to its background or context. After studying a representative sample of a writer's style, it is possible to pick out any tendency he may have to use words which fall on a particular segment of these scales.

USAGE AND THE DICTIONARY

Grammar is concerned with clarity; rhetoric, with effectiveness. To be effective a word must be correct, but every correct word is not necessarily an effective word. To be aware of all the possibilities from which he can choose the most forceful word, or to understand why an author uses one word instead of another, the student of style must be a dedicated student of dictionaries. He must realize what dictionaries can*not* tell him as well as absorb what they can.

Dictionaries are not depositories of "true meanings." Words are arbitrary signs, and there is no necessary connection, except possibly in the case of onomatopoeic words, between the sound of a word and what that word signifies. What the word signifies depends on how it is used by educated speakers of the language.

Just as the stock-quotation pages of a newspaper list, but do not dictate, the values of stocks, so dictionaries list, but do not legislate, the meanings of words. The stock-pages can only summarize how a stock has behaved in the market in the past; they cannot predict what it will do in the future. The dictionary can only record how a word has been used in the past; it cannot predict its use in the future. Dictionaries like *Webster's New International* record all the most important meanings of the important words in the language. Other dictionaries, such as dictionaries of synonyms, slang, or American usage, are more specialized. The *Oxford English Dictionary* not only gives the definition of some 424,825 words but it also illustrates how the words were used at various stages in their history by quoting from contemporary documents. It is an essential reference work for anyone who wants to know just how effective a word was in a particular context and how its past meanings might give it a peculiar appropriateness in his own writing.

No writer could possibly expect to use, nor any reader to recognize, more than a fraction of the million or so words which are estimated to constitute the vocabulary of the English language. Among the major English writers, Robert Browning is frequently considered to have commanded the most extensive vocabulary—some 35,000 words in all. The average college student has been credited with the ability to use some 20,000 in his own writing. These figures indicate how small a part of the total English vocabulary even the average educated user of the language can bring into play.

Dictionaries strive to record all the words used by all speakers and writers, but the process of compiling a dictionary is so involved and requires so much care that a new edition cannot be published every year. Language, on the other hand, is a constantly changing, growing organism, always adding new words and altering the meanings of established words. Between the 1934 edition of *Webster's International Dictionary* and the 1961 edition, the English language was enriched by thousands of new words like *brainwash, countdown, lead-time, overkill.* Older words, like *rocket, jet*, and *computer* underwent extensive changes in denotation and connotation.

Constructing a definition for a word may be compared to searching for the least common denominator of a group of numbers. Some words, like *cirro-cumulus*, require only one definition, for all the citations recording their usage are reducible to one least common denominator of meaning. Other words, like *get*, may require dozens of definitions, for they are used in so many different ways that it is impossible to reduce all the citations to a few common denominators of meaning. The *Oxford English Dictionary* overcomes some of these limitations by illustrating the more generalized definitions of a word and by illustrating its actual use in the works of different writers. But to overcome the limitations of the dictionary, the student must train himself to observe how words are being used in current literature and speech.

The norm or standard used by sensitive speakers and writers is the usage of educated people on their best linguistic behavior. Standards of word usage can be compared to standards in social manners. Everyone may be said to have two sets of manners: informal and formal. The informal manners are called into play at home, among friends, in relaxed or familiar circumstances. More formal manners are reserved for those ceremonial occasions which require more rigorous standards of conduct. The writer should choose a standard in keeping with his purpose, his subject matter, and his expected readers.

The conservatives encourage the perpetuation of established usage by demanding near-formal behavior on all occasions. The liberals encourage growth and change by encouraging informal behavior on all but the most demanding of occasions. The only solution for the writer is to bear in mind that he is writing to be effective, not to make an issue of a particular word or expression. Whenever a writer uses an obscure word to impress or a vulgar word to shock, he is not furthering his purpose.

The problem of defining standards of usage is particularly important in English because the language is rich in synonyms for almost every word. Many of these synonyms are sufficiently similar that they might serve to convey the same idea with some clarity. For example, all the following words, as well as many others not cited here, could be used to convey the idea of a female person: *lady, madam, matron, mistress, dowager, girl, woman, wife, miss, mademoiselle, femme, frail, dame, skirt, sister, tomato, chick, squaw, goody, gammer, vixen.* Now no two of these words have exactly the same implications. A woman could not be both *miss* and *wife; girl* and *dowager* are far apart in age and behavior. But in some informal contexts the word *girl* could be applied to the same person, who would be called a dowager in a more formal context, to convey warmth of feeling, pathos, or heavy-handed irony. A standard dictionary would distinguish between *goody* and *gammer* but only the *Oxford English Dictionary* could give a writer a real feeling for the differences in their connotations. *Skirt, dame, chick, femme,* would all be labeled as colloquial or slang in the dictionary, but only current experience with the language would reveal which was still in use, which might be used to make a point in informal circumstances, and which was inadmissable even in an informal context.

PRECISE LANGUAGE AND MASS LANGUAGE

The words that make up the vocabulary of the English language can be used precisely or vaguely. A word is used precisely when it points specifically and uniquely to the thing for which it is a sign, so that the reader or hearer knows clearly and exactly the meaning the word is intended to convey. A word is used precisely when it has one and only one *referent*, object to which it refers. A word is used vaguely when it either has more than one referent or points to the general area of the referent instead of directly at it.

Let us consider two adjectives, *wonderful* and *awful*, both of which can be used precisely. *Wonderful* is used precisely when it refers to something which can create wonder, which can stimulate in the beholder a feeling of astonishment at something unusual or marvelous. *Wonderful* is vaguely used when it refers to objects or experiences that cannot be said to occasion astonishment in the hearer or beholder. A commonplace hat, car, even if it is new, can not be properly called "wonderful." *Awful* is frequently used in a vague sense, as when it suggests an undefined foreboding or disappointment ("The exam will be awful"; "I saw an awful movie last night"). *Awful* is precisely used in the lines from Shakespeare's *Richard II*: "How dare thy joints forget/To pay their awful duty to our presence?" (III, iii). *Awful* here means precisely "full of awe"—the king's subjects should be kneeling in awe before him.

The precise use of words, and its corollary—the use of precise words—impose continuing obligations upon a speaker or writer. He must constantly search for the word that refers exactly to the referent he has in mind, and he must constantly assess the extent to which his words have a clear signification. This constant self-examination results in the realization of the need for an ever-expanding vocabulary to provide the words necessary to communicate an ever-growing experience. There is always a tendency to avoid meeting these obligations, which leads to satisfaction with a word that is only vaguely right and only generally satisfactory. Thus the words *wonderful* and *awful* are not reserved to signify the kinds of unusual experiences to which they might be properly applied but are applied to a wide spectrum of experience, some of which may be only mildly pleasing or notable. Anything not *un*pleasant is frequently labeled "great"—whether a soul-moving encounter with a classic or a walk across campus.

The frequent use of words imprecisely or vaguely can lead to enslavement to what might be called "mass language." Mass language is made up of words which, although they have a precise referent, are used to refer to a vague, general area of experience which might merely *include* the word's specific referent. For example, when one uses the word *wonderful* to refer to a casual meeting with an acquaintance, he is not using it to signify what it precisely intends, but he is referring to a general idea of pleasing experience that might include the experience of wonder.

Mass language suggests rather than pinpoints the effect it hopes to achieve. When a student describes a lecture as "terrific," he is not pointing precisely to the reaction occasioned by the lecture, but is suggesting the area of the general kind of experience occasioned by the lecture. Instead of using the word to point to a specific kind of experience, or of searching for the precise word that would describe the experience of the lecture, the student is pointing to experience in the mass. Every use of mass language is a compromise with precision and accuracy. It is a compromise that must be resisted, because it endangers effectiveness by substituting vague for precise communication.

Mass communication has perhaps contributed to a more widespread use of imprecise language today that at any other time in the history of language. Examples are as close as the editorial page of any newspaper. A single editorial yielded the following examples of a passion for clichés: "heap of trouble," "drown in red ink," "jobs for the many," "tolerable proportions," "irresistible demands," "modestly called," "occasion no astonishment," "pervades our existence," "conjure up bugaboos," "ingenious way," "make life easier," "normally perceptive." To make sure that the first newspaper examined was not an unusual example, another paper of the same date supplied the following on its editorial page: "ill service," "candid realization," "not too much hope," "inevitable delay," "permanent fixture," "manifest an interest," "adopt sanctions," "childish petulance," "brought dangerously close," "engage in activities," "call for a new look," and, appropriately, "outworn stereo-types."

The use of mass language in daily speech is not as severe a detriment to clarity or effectiveness as it is in writing; in speaking, gestures, intonations, pauses, and other circumstances can combine to make some of the vague, overworked words more effective. But a writer who uses a mass word instead of a precise word invites his audience to bend that word to fit into its own categories and preconceptions, to force his ideas into old patterns of thought. The writer who is determined to be effective must use every opportunity, every word, to influence and direct his audience.

Mass language also has an effect on the writer himself, for it serves to block the development of original thought or style. Effective writing must not only be clear writing, it must also have color and emphasis. The overworked cliché is neither colorful nor emphatic.

Mass language has many symptoms: clichés, jargon, pretentious phrases, euphemisms, and worn-out metaphors. All of these vices of language share a common quality: imprecision. They are all approximations, compromises, or substitutions for more precise terms. A more responsible use of language—a use which continually strives for effectiveness —requires greater reflection, greater care, and greater precision.

Jargon

Jargon, in its strict sense, is the technical language of a trade or profession. A lawyer frequently uses sentences with many conjunctions such as "nevertheless," "whereas," and "therefore," for he must try to incorporate into his contracts provisions for as many contingencies as he can foresee. A scientist who is not yet certain of the range of significance of his present findings may use expressions such as: "it would seem possible," "it is not unreasonable to suppose," or "it might be considered feasible." Jargon in this sense is not a vice but a dialect of the language necessary for communication to members of a profession.

Jargon, however, can become a vice when it is adopted by speakers or writers who cannot justify its use. Consider the following sentence, which was written for a general audience. In it the writer has adopted a pseudo-scientific pose.

> It would seem that it is nothing more nor less than a comparative social condition depending on a relative control over economic goods, the standard of comparison being a group possessing a maximum of such control, called the rich or wealthy.

Although it may be difficult to perceive at first, all that is concealed behind this pretentious phrasing, the conditional mood, the gratuitous "more or less," is a definition of poverty. The cautious, circumscribed expressions of a social scientist or economist, which constitute the legitimate jargon of their professions, have been misappropriated by a writer addressing himself to a general audience; here this jargon serves to obscure the thought and to hinder the effective achievement of the writer's purpose.

Not every use of jargon is an improper use. Occasionally, the jargon term is the only available precise word. If a writer tries to avoid it, he may find himself involved with a far less accurate circumlocution. "Standing head," "headline," and "by-line" are part of the jargon of the newspaper composing room. Anyone attempting to discuss the makeup of the front page without using these terms is making a lot of unnecessary work for himself. Any writer who uses these terms, once he has defined them, is using jargon justifiably and is fulfilling his responsibilities to precise use of language.

When a writer borrows words or phrasing from a profession, not to make his writing more precise, but to make his writing sound like the writing of a profession currently in high regard, he is using jargon unjustifiably. Such a writer may even mistake bad professional writing—for example, poor writing on economics or social science—for effective professional writing. Misconceptions about what constitutes good writing, whether for a professional audience or for the general public, can lead a writer to use phrases such as "in the matter of" when he means "about," "a long period of time" when he means "a long time," "in the capacity of" when he means "as," "resembling in nature" when he means "like," and "in some instances" when he means "sometimes." He may believe that the longer phrases are characteristic of good writing in the science or philosophy he admires. To this first mistake, he adds a second when he imports these expressions into his own writing because he thinks they will give it greater authority.

The misuse of jargon is frequently characterized by a passion for the polysyllable. "Activate," a common word in military correspondence, has proven irresistible to writers who would be better served by such simpler words as "form" or "establish." Sonority seems preferable to clarity, so the misuse of jargon is frequently marked by references to "areas of study," "problems in terms of which," "variant factors," "in this regard," "in countless cases," which may be supposed to give the reader the impression that the subject must be more complex than he has thus far noticed. The jargonist is self-defeating. He confuses where he should be trying to clarify; he calls attention to his language instead of to the ideas he should be trying to communicate; and, finally, he creates the suspicion in the minds of alert readers that a better writer would be using language more economically, more unobtrusively, and more precisely.

One of the by-products of the misuse of jargon is the development of a style with a high proportion of structural words (prepositions, conjunctions, articles, and auxiliary verbs) to content words (nouns, adjectives, verbs, and adverbs). The misuse of jargon, or the imitation of poor professional writing, usually involves a lot of unnecessary maneuvering to work such words into one's writing. The antidote is a passion for honesty and precision.

Euphemism

Another failure to use words effectively is known as euphemism—the substitution of a word with pleasant implications for a word with unpleasant suggestions. The obvious euphemisms of the Victorian period, *limb* for *leg*, and a *love child* for *bastard*, have become very rare. However *passed away* is still used as an euphemism for *die*, and the newspapers prefer *criminal assault* to *rape*. Euphemisms are commonly used to make jobs seem more important or socially more acceptable. *Bill collectors* are now known as *adjusters*, *janitors* as *sanitary engineers*, and *undertakers* as *morticians*. Students graduating from college are never looking for *jobs*; they are all looking for *positions*.

Euphemisms are logically indefensible, but socially unavoidable. They are illogical because, as Juliet says, "a rose by any other name would smell as sweet." It is the thing which is good or bad, not its name. What is unpleasant to contemplate is not the word *die*, but the fact of death. Changing the word but keeping the message intact is like using a code, but who is being taken in? *Love child* or *illegitimate child* carry the same social stigma as *bastard*. It is the idea of illegitimacy which society has found censurable, not the sound used to express it.

But euphemisms are a form of taboo, and like the taboos of any society, they form part of the social code. In some societies these take the form of dietary restrictions; in others they may be forbidden places, persons, or names. Contemporary society insists upon the observation of fewer taboos than primitive societies, and today's writer need not use as many euphemisms as the Victorian. Knowing what euphemisms form an active and integral part of the social manners of a society is an aspect of that general sensitivity to language usage which must be part of the equipment of every effective writer.

A subtle form of euphemism is known as "elegant variation." According to the rules of elegant variation a paper on Shakespeare, for instance, may name its subject only once. After that, he must be referred to as "Ben Jonson's contemporary," "the Bard of Avon," "the author of *Romeo and Juliet*," and "the creator of Hamlet." Although monotonous repetition is to be avoided, its distracting or obscure alternatives may defeat their purpose.

Worn-out Metaphor

One final source of imprecision worth mentioning is the worn-out metaphor. Among the more common are: "ring the changes on," "take up the cudgels for," "toe the line," "run roughshod over," "stand shoulder to shoulder," "play into the hands of," "no axe to grind," "grist for the mill," and "fishing in troubled waters." If figurative language is to be used, it must be original.

In a brilliant essay on "Politics and the English Language," George Orwell suggested six rules which would help a writer achieve an expressive style:

1. Never use a metaphor, simile, or other figure which you are used to seeing in print.

2. Never use a long word where a short one will do.

3. If it is possible to cut a word out, always cut it out.

4. Never use a passive phrase where you can use an active.

5. Never use a foreign phrase, a scientific word, or a jargon word if you can think of an everyday English equivalent.

6. Break any of these rules sooner than say anything outright barbarous.[1]

These are sound rules, not only for effective writing, but also for effective thinking. Ineffective use of language is too widely and firmly entrenched to be exiled overnight. But a start can be made by avoiding the tendency to think in terms of ready-made phrases, pretentious sounding words, clichés, worn-out metaphors or euphemisms. Part of the revision of any piece of writing is the removal of every obstacle to effectiveness.

CONCRETE AND ABSTRACT WORDS

Concrete words refer to specific things which can be pointed to or experienced or felt. Abstract words are signs or symbols for relations,

[1]From *Shooting an Elephant and Other Essays* (New York: Harcourt, Brace, and World, Inc., 1960; London: Brandt & Brandt).

ideas, and concepts which are not directly sensible. The word *abstract* comes from the combination of the Latin *trahere*, meaning to *draw*, and the preposition *abs*, meaning *out of*. An abstract word is, therefore, a label used to identify certain general qualities which have been drawn out of several particulars. Everyday language is a mixture of the abstract and the concrete: "our car," "our home," "our books," "our neighbors," "right," "truth," "democracy," and "fair play."

Although both types of words are essential to communication, the abstract can pose more problems than the concrete. Disagreements over concrete words can be resolved by referring them to the objects themselves. Even the most unusual concrete word, from *adytum* to *zymogen*, can be so clarified. The word *fair*, as it is commonly applied to denote a just or unbiased act, is a much more common word and yet much harder to define because it stands for an abstraction. Although there is usually a core of established meaning in every abstract word, there is also usually an indefinable periphery of implication.

Semanticists discourage the use of abstract words. Consider the following sentence from the *National Review*.

> The stark political realities of Western retreat are the direct product of decades of cultivation of characterological weakness on the bases of a sedulous propagation of the philosophical error which goes under the name of relativism: the doctrine that no truth in reality exists; that whatever a culture believes is as good as what any other culture believes (cannibalism or human sacrifice are not wrong, only "culturally relative" modes of human action); that therefore the West has nothing of which to be proud, nothing for which to fight, nothing worth dying for.

The reader encountering such a sentence has to supply some kind of concrete meaning for "political realities," and "Western retreat." Then he must decide just what is meant by "direct product" and "characterological weakness." "Decades of cultivation" is also puzzling because it is not clear just what and how many decades are intended, or what is meant by "cultivation" in this abstracted sense. By the time the reader arrives at "relativism," he is grateful for the definition the writer provides; but whatever the sentence gains in clarity from that point on by a greater use of more concrete words, it loses through the use of interrupting clauses.

It is always a good idea to define any abstract word which is going to be crucial to any discussion and to illustrate it as clearly as possible. The following sentence actually contains a larger percentage of abstract words than the preceding one, but it is not as difficult to understand. John Locke demonstrates that it is possible to use abstract words without forcing the reader to supply his own clarification. He sometimes uses words and clauses in pairs, one throwing light on the other. Thus "choose" helps clarify the abstract use of "authorize"; and the clause "to destroy that which everyone designs to secure by entering into society" helps define the succeeding clause, "that for which people submitted themselves to legislators of their own making." Also Locke sometimes adds a few words of clarification, as in the phrase, "as guards and fences to the properties of all members of society."

> The reason why men enter into society, is the preservation of their property; and the end why they choose and authorize a legislative, is, that there may be laws made, and rules set, as guards and fences to the properties of all the members of the society: to limit the power, and moderate the dominion, of every part and member of the society: for since it can never be supposed to be the will of the society, that the legislative should have a power to destroy that which every one designs to secure by entering into society, that for which the people submitted themselves to legislators of their own making; whenever the legislative endeavor to take away and destroy the property of the people, or to reduce them to slavery under arbitrary power, they put themselves into a state of war with the people, who are thereupon absolved from any further obedience, and are left to the common refuge, which God hath provided for all men, against force and violence. Whensoever therefore the legislative shall transgress this fundamental rule of society; and either by ambition, fear, folly or corruption, endeavor to grasp themselves, or put into the hands of any other, an absolute power over the lives, liberties, and estates of the people, by this breach of trust they forfeit the power the people had put into their hands for quite contrary ends, and it devolves to the people, who have a right to resume their original liberty, and, by the establishment of a new legislative (such as they shall think fit), provide for their own safety and security, which is the end for which they are in society.[2]

If the writer's purpose requires the discussion of an abstract subject he must use the necessary terms; but since it is also part of his purpose to persuade his readers to his point of view, he must do what he can to make that point clear and easily understood. Contemporary readers expect much less demanding fare than unrelieved abstract discussions. In 1946 Dr. Rudolf Flesch published a book entitled *The Art of Plain Talk* which contained a Readability Formula. According to this formula the greater the number of short sentences, concrete words, and personal references, the easier a book is to read and the more likely it is to be

---

[2] John Locke, *Treatise on Civil Government.*

read. Devotees of this formula can go to extremes, writing everything in a style usually associated with a first-grade reader. Ease of reading is not synonymous with quality of expression, but the writer who is working with abstractions can increase his chances of reaching a wider audience by illustrating some of the abstractions with concrete applications and supplying synonyms or parallel expressions. If some of his sentences tend to be long, he should be sure to make the interrelations of the parts particularly clear.

POPULAR AND LEARNED WORDS

Frequently confused with the scale which distinguishes between concrete and abstract words is the scale which distinguishes between popular and learned words. The English language has a large number of pairs of synonyms, one of which is popular and frequently heard in daily speech; the other, referred to as the "learned word," is only occasionally heard but more frequently read. In *Words and Their Ways in English Speech*, Greenough and Kittredge named some pairs:

> The same, identical; speech, oration; fire, conflagration; choose, select; brave, valorous; swallowing, deglutition; striking, percussion; building, edifice; shady, umbrageous; puckery, astringent; learned, erudite; secret, cryptic; destroy, annihilate; stiff, rigid; flabby, flaccid; queer, eccentric; behead, decapitate; round, circular; thin, emaciated; fat, corpulent; truthful, veracious; try, endeavor bit, modicum; piece, fragment; sharp, acute; crazy, maniacal; king, sovereign; book, volume; lying, mendacious; beggar, mendicant; teacher, instructor; play, drama; air, atmosphere; paint, pigment.[3]

The popular word in each pair tends to be monosyllabic and direct (round, thin, fat, and bit). The corresponding learned word tends to be polysyllabic and more vague in its implications (circular, emaciated, corpulent, modicum). Actually, of the 34 popular words, 19 are monosyllabic, 14 dissyllabic, and only one polysyllabic. The popular word is usually of Anglo-Saxon origin (king, book), whereas the learned word is frequently a borrowing either directly from Latin or through the French (sovereign, volume, deglutition). A style based mainly upon popular words tends to be more direct and straight-forward; one which contains a high percentage of learned words tends to be more sonorous, involved, and demanding of the reader.

[3] J. B. Greenough and G. L. Kittredge, *Words and Their Ways in English Speech* (New York: The Macmillan Company, 1920), p. 20.

There is always a tendency to equate popular words with concrete words and learned words with abstract words, but the two scales involved are based on completely different criteria. The concrete-abstract scale is based on the referents of words; the popular-learned scale is based on the level of usage. The same word can be both concrete and popular, as *behead*; or concrete and learned, as *decapitate* or *deglutition*. The same word can be popular and abstract, as *brave, fair, just*; learned and abstract, as *valorous* and *veracious*.

The older borrowings from Latin, French, and Italian retain little of their original color. More recent borrowings from Arabic, Russian, Hindu, or the South Seas languages—words like *harem, intelligentsia, pariah, taboo*—still retain some of the flavor of their original contexts. The writer who is aware of these overtones of meaning can use the evocative power of these words very effectively, not only to add color in narration and description, but to lend vigor to any passage.

The writer who finds himself with a choice between words in a learned-popular pair must be guided first by a desire to be clear and precise in his communication. Then he can take into consideration the tone he wants to give to his composition as a whole and the circumstances of his writing—his audience or the occasion. Although these word-pairs are synonyms, there are shades of difference between them; *annihilate*, to take but one example, does not mean exactly the same as *destroy*. Then there are some words in these pairs which are obviously pedantic: *deglutition, conflagration, mendicant,* or *umbrageous* should not be used in place of *swallowing, fire, beggar,* or *shady*. An audience would rightly suspect that they had been used for the impression they might make. A notorious government directive once instructed office workers to "terminate the illumination" when what was intended, of course, was "put out the lights." Painfully unusual words call attention to themselves when their proper purpose should be to call attention to the idea. The reader who is driven to a dictionary to discover the precise meaning of a learned word which is out of place in the midst of an otherwise undistinguished piece of informal prose will not return to his reading impressed with the writer's erudition. He will return irritated, impatient with the pretenses of the writer, and oblivious to the trend of the argument.

There are times when there is no proper substitute for words like *antinomies, recidivist, irredentist, analeptic, ambages, cerements, passementeric, supererogation, cramoisy,* and *autochthonous*. At such times, the writer should not hesitate to use them, provided he is sure of their exact meaning and their appropriateness both to context and to audience. As the use of learned words in proper context does not constitute jargon, so the use of popular words in proper context is not to be confused with vulgate. Vulgate is the substandard dialect of English, with a very limited vocabulary, which is used by uneducated people. It disregards rules of syntax, links singular nouns with plural verbs and pronouns to incorrect antecedents, and almost completely reverses the rules governing the copula. Vulgate can be readily detected by its use of expressions like *O.K., jerk, ain't, guy, caf, dope,* and *fink.* Vulgate is admissible in narrative writing only to characterize persons who would normally speak that way, but it must otherwise be avoided.

CONNOTATION AND DENOTATION

Words can also be ranged on a scale which distinguishes denotation from connotation (see also Chapter 4). Except for such structural words as articles, conjunctions, prepositions, and verbal auxiliaries, all words have a connotation as well as a denotation. English is remarkably rich in groups of words all having similar denotations but very different connotations.

The denotation of a word, it will be recalled, is what the word specifically points to, its core of meaning. The connotation of a word is what the word suggests, a less easily definable aura which can expand and contract with time and the experience of its readers.

The chemists use formulae like H_2O; mathematicians, symbols like π; botanists, terms like *Acer Rubrum*; and zoologists, labels like *Felis Leo*; all of which are intended to point clearly, simply, and directly to specific things and to be as free as possible from overtones and suggestions. Next in line on the denotative-connotative scale, moving from the pole of pure denotation toward pure connotation, are everyday words for everyday things. Words like *chair, water, house, car, book,* and *desk* also point to very specific things and are without much connotation for most people. Indeed, the more specific the referent of a word, the more likely the word will be more denotative; the vaguer the referent, the more likely the word to tend toward the connotative end of the scale. Adjectives like *archaic* and *venerable* have a core of meaning, *aged* or *antique,* but they also have suggestive power. Words like these occupy almost the very center of the scale, and the context in which they are used may tip them in one direction or the other. Next, there is a group of words which, though not without specific referents, seem to be used more for their flavor than for what they expressly point to. Words like *troika, samovar, hansom, crenellated, hashish* can evoke more than they state. Finally we come to words which have been created for their connotative powers, words like *scrumptious* or *feathery,* which have been used so frequently in advertising contexts that their residual function is almost purely connotative.

In any group of synonyms, some of the words will be more connotative than others. All the following words have a core meaning which means approximately to *criticize—admonish, chide, scold, rebuke, reprimand*—and yet their connotations are very different. *Rebuke* is almost all denotation; it means to criticize sharply. *Chide* is perhaps at the other end of the scale for it suggests light and almost indulgent correction. *Scold* and *admonish* are somewhere near the middle of the scale for both indicate criticism, but the first implies irritation and the second exhortation. *Accuse, charge, incriminate*, and *indict* all denote the same idea of calling someone guilty of an action, but all imply different degrees of severity and modes of procedure. *Hesitate, falter, procrastinate*, and *dawdle* are another group of words with a common meaning but different overtones.

Words acquire their connotations from social and personal sources. For the boy who grew up on a Midwestern farm, a *plug* may be an old faithful farm horse; for the city-bred, it may be a broken-down old horse; for the race track tout, it may be any poor bet. The first time we hear or read a word, the connotation is slight. The oftener a word is used, the greater the number of connotations it acquires. Words heard in a favorable context acquire favorable connotations; those associated with unfavorable contexts become themselves unfavorable. The word *communism* and *facism*, when used today, always elicit an unfavorable connotation among hearers who would be hard-pressed to distinguish between them. When these two terms first came into general use in the early years of this century they were learned terms, with precise denotations. Creators of propaganda succeeded in giving them unfavorable connotations by repeated use in association with unfavorable ideas. The word *propaganda* was itself once a neutral word meaning the dissemination of ideas and information. It still means the same today but it connotes dissemination of information with biased intent.

The difference in effect of styles which use mainly connotative words can be illustrated by comparing two poems on the same general subject. The first group of lines is taken from Robert Herrick's seventeenth-century poem entitled "The Hock Cart." (Hockcart was the last cart-load of the harvest to be taken to the barn.) Herrick's poem describes the harvest in terms which are specific, mainly denotative, frequently concrete, and popular.

> Some bless the cart; some kiss the sheaves;
> Some prank them up with oaken leaves:
> Some cross the fill-horse, some with great
> Devotion, stroke the home-borne wheat:

While other rustics, less attent
To prayers, than merriment,
Run after with their breeches rent.
Well on, brave boys, to your Lord's hearth,
Glitt'ring with fire; where, for your mirth,
Ye shall see first the large and chief
Foundation of your feast, fat beef:
With upper stories, mutton, veal
And bacon (which makes full the meal)
With sev'ral dishes standing by,
As here a custard, there a pie,
And here all tempting frumenty.

John Keats' "To Autumn" also celebrates the joys of harvest, but in an almost unrelieved series of connotative terms. Every line suggests rather than specifies a picture.

Season of mists and mellow fruitfulness,
   Close bosom-friend of the maturing sun;
Conspiring with him how to load and bless
   With fruit the vines that round the thatch-eves run;
To bend with apples the moss'd cottage-trees,
   And fill all fruit with ripeness to the core;
      To swell the gourd, and plump the hazel shells
   With a sweet kernel; to set budding more,
And still more, later flowers for the bees,
Until they think warm days will never cease,
For summer has o'er brimm'd their clammy cells.

To say that one poem uses more connotative words or fewer than another is to say that one poem is better or worse. Different kinds of words have a decided effect upon the kind of poem and reflect a difference in the poet's intentions.

This difference of effect resulting from word choice can also be illustrated in two prose passages which do occur not very far apart in Edmund Burke's *Conciliation Speech*. In both instances Burke was defending the same proposition: that Parliament should conciliate the colonies. In the first passage, his reason was the growing importance of colonial trade. Here he felt sure of his facts and addressed himself to his readers in denotative terms. He lets the statistics speak for themselves; the speech is direct, the words without emotional implications.

Excuse me, Sir, if turning from such thoughts I resume this comparative view once more. You have seen it on a large scale; look at it on a small one. I will point out to your attention a particular instance of it in the single province of Pennsylvania. In the year 1704, that province called for £11,459 in value of your commodities, native and foreign. This was the whole. What did it demand in 1772? Why nearly fifty times as much; for in that year the export to Pennsylvania was £507,909, nearly equal to the export to all the colonies together in the first period.

In the following passage Burke's reason for demanding a conciliatory attitude toward the colonies is their growing resourcefulness in extending their fishing industry. Here Burke does not rely on statistics or the denotative words, though these were available. Instead he addresses himself to his readers' imaginations and emotions with stirring, connotative evocations of the adventuresomeness of the Americans.

As to the wealth which the colonies have drawn from the sea by their fisheries, you had all that matter fully opened at your bar. You surely thought these acquisitions of value, for they seemed to excite your envy; and yet the spirit by which that enterprising employment has been exercised, ought rather, in my opinion to have raised your esteem and admiration. And pray, Sir, what in the world is equal to it? Pass by the other parts, and look at the manner in which the people of New England have of late carried on the whale fishery. Whilst we follow them among the tumbling mountains of ice, and behold them penetrating into the deepest frozen recesses of Hudson's Bay and Davis's Straits, whilst we are looking for them beneath the arctic circle, we hear that they have pierced into the opposite region of polar cold, that they are at the antipodes, and engaged under the frozen serpent of the south. Falkland Island, which seemed too remote and romantic an object for the grasp of national ambition, is but a stage and resting-place in the progress of their victorious industry. Nor is the equinoctial heat more discouraging to them, than the accumulated winter of both the poles. We know that whilst some of them draw the line and strike and harpoon on the coast of Africa, others run the longitude, and pursue their gigantic game along the coast of Brazil. No sea but what is vexed by their fisheries. No climate that is not witness to their toils. Neither the perseverance of Holland, nor the activity of France, nor the dexterous and firm sagacity of English enterprise, ever carried this most perilous mode of hard industry to the extent to which it has been pushed by this recent people; a people who are still, as it were, but in the gristle, and not yet hardened into the bone of manhood.

*We spend the major part of our
waking time making such observations
and inferences, and it may well be
that our way of formulating them
symbolically—of reporting them to
ourselves, as it were—serves as a mold
for the observations and inferences, so
that our verbal reports both reflect and
shape our view of the way things are.*

Statements

LOUIS B. SALOMON

Philosophers, semanticists, linguists, psychologists, and others have devoted considerable time and energy to the analysis of statements. These analyses, however, have yielded insight not only into the structure and function of statements but also into such issues as truth, ambiguity, persuasion, verification, and prediction. Although these concepts are by no means limited to language, a language analysis provides a most interesting perspective for their study. Here Salomon analyzes the nature of statements in relation to these and various other issues.

THE REPORTING OF EXPERIENCE

It would be an invidious and profitless task to try to choose which one of the five language-uses in discourse is the most important—indeed, it is difficult to imagine ourselves functioning as social beings were we denied any of them—but in view of the purpose and tenor of this book it seems reasonable to give first priority in discussion to the informative function: that is, the reporting of observation or inference, whether about the extensional world (including language itself) or about the speaker's own state of mind. We spend the major part of our waking time making such observations and inferences, and it may well be that our way of formulating them symbolically—or reporting them to ourselves, as it were—serves as a mold for the observations and inferences, so that our verbal reports both reflect and shape our view of the way things are.

Just as with the arbitrarily imputed relation between a single verbal symbol and its referent(s), however, it behooves us to distinguish between the information conveyed by a complex utterance and the particular verbal pattern used to convey it. The former, the molecular item of observed fact or inference, we shall refer to as the statement or the proposition (using the two terms interchangeably); the latter, the linguistic unit for reporting a state of affairs, we shall call the sentence. The proposition might be thought of as the referent of the sentence. Any given proposition can be communicated via a variety of sentences: "It's a hot day," "The day is hot," even "What a hot day!" or "Isn't it a hot day?" all convey the same proposition, as, for that matter, would any number of sentences in French, Russian, Urdu, or Swahili. Conversely, a given sentence may convey various propositions depending on context and what we choose as meaning for one or more of the verbal symbols in the sentence. The usual vehicle for propositions is a declarative sentence, but

From Semantics and Common Sense *by Louis B. Salomon, pp. 69–85. Copyright © 1966 by Holt, Rinehart and Winston, Inc. Reprinted by permission of Holt, Rinehart and Winston, Inc.*

this is not the only possible vehicle, nor, as we have seen, are all declarative sentences primarily informative in their meaning.

LANGUAGE AS A MOLD
FOR REALITY

The grammar of any given language, however, does impose certain limits on the ways in which a proposition can be verbalized, and hence on the way the users of that language conceive propositions—in other words, on what they mean by "a fact." "It is the 'plainest' English," said B. L. Whorf, "which contains the greatest number of unconscious assumptions about nature."

Just as there may be a tendency to equate our convention of word separation with a notion of experience as divided into neat little separate packages, there may also be a chicken-and-egg relationship between the subject-predicate form of the declarative sentence in most modern languages and our habit of thinking of propositions themselves in terms of "objects" on the one hand and "attributes" or "predications" on the other. We look at a certain animal; we recollect seeing and hearing a summer shower—and we state the propositions: "That horse [object] is brown [attribute]"; "Rain [object] fell [predication] on the roof [further predication, involving another object]." This structure does not necessarily correspond to the structure of the experiences, which consist of total interaction between the mind and the nervous system of the observer: that is, we do not, in daylight with normal vision, perceive the horse apart from its color, or the rain and the roof and the downward motion as separate entities. Even the assumption that something (for example, a horse) outside of both the mind and the nervous system of the observer is triggering the interaction remains a not altogether indispensable assumption, though it is firmly built into, and consequently buttressed by, our linguistic conventions. P. W. Bridgman, while not etherealizing the horse, commented on a discrepancy in the way we report our reason for believing in the animal's existence: "To say 'I see a horse' gets recognizably closer to the direct experience than to say 'There is a horse.' "

It is at least possible to conceive of a language in which the form of our declarative sentence would be unknown, in which there were only nouns, or only verbs, or only adjectives; the users of this language might view reality very differently from the way we do, perhaps as a chain of mystic insights into the workings of a cosmic mind, or as a never-ending struggle between wills, in which the place is always here and the time is always now. It would be extremely difficult for them not merely to communicate, but even to conceive of, what we have called propositions or statements, those "items of observed fact or inference" which to some extent reflect the grammar (that is, the sum total of the linguistic conventions) of the language in which we formulate our observations.

SIGNIFICANCE AND TRUTH

It takes more than conformity to the rules of syntax, of course, to make a sentence significant, to make it symbolize a conceivable state of affairs. The grammar of a language includes its lexicon, the generally accepted meanings of its words; thus, "A three-sided hexagon thinks long thoughts" qualifies as a sentence according to the English sentence-pattern of adjective-substantive-verb-adjective-substantive, and each of its terms is a standard English word, but because our lexical rules disqualify hexagons from either having three sides or thinking, it is nevertheless not significant, has no conceivable state of affairs as a referent, hence makes no cognitive statement.[1] It is possible, as we shall see, to construct sentences that are neither so obviously insignificant as this one nor so unmistakably significant as "The cat is licking its fur."

Note that in calling this last sentence significant we do not commit ourselves to the proposition that the cat actually is licking its fur. But one important quality of significant sentences used cognitively is that the statements they embody have a truth value; that is to say, they are true, or they are false, or they may be assigned some sort of value on a scale of which truth is one polar extreme and falsity the other. The stumbling block here for us, as for Pontius Pilate, lies in the question "What is truth?" The answer is: truth is (that is, we use the word *truth* to mean) several very different qualities, and until we have determined which of its senses is applicable to a given statement we may not even know what kind of statement we are dealing wtih.

TAUTOLOGY

First, there is the "necessary" truth of logic: a quality of statements which, within the framework of a strictly schematized branch of discourse, like arithmetic or Euclidean geometry—or even the grammar of a language, in so far as it is presented as a logical structure—cannot be

[1]Emotively, of course, it may convey a great deal of nonpropositional meaning.

denied without producing contradiction within that closed system. Logic is a game, in the sense that it is based upon rules, which may have more or less applicability to the ordinary business of life but must be adhered to without any exception as long as the game—be it logic, chess, golf, or football—is being played. If the teams representing State College and Eastern U. on Saturday afternoon consisted of any number of men, armed with whatever weapons they chose, and with no restrictions on when they started or ended hostilities or on the tactics they might use to put the ball across the line, the result could be a fascinating rumble but it would not be regulation football. Why not? Simply because we have agreed to define the game, football, in an extremely explicit way: the complete definition for any given year, in fact, is the current rule book. A visitor from Mars might measure the distance between goal posts and report that they are always a hundred yards apart, or he might report that the players never use brass knuckles; but in the rule book these "truths" are set forth not as observed facts but simply as defining qualities of the game itself.

In some of the less athletic disciplines these statements are called axioms, which is another way of saying not that they are observed facts of nature but that they are among the agreed-upon rules of that branch of discourse: for example, the Euclidean statements that a straight line is the shortest path between two points or that parallel lines in the same plane can never meet, even the arithmetical statement so often cited as an example of fundamental or "absolute" truth, two and two are four. There are lots of other games—mathematical systems, for instance, in which a straight line is not the shortest path between two points, in which parallel lines in the same plane do meet—but if you want to play the Euclidean game you must not vary one jot from its rules. Still another way of putting it is that these axioms, even though they sometimes sound like statements of observed fact, are really definitions of terms as used within that particular scheme of logical discourse. Suppose, for example, you measure a line that looks to you like the straightest possible line between points A and B; then someone draws another line which, on measurement, proves to be shorter. Will you say, "Well, I guess that proves a straight line is not the shortest path between two points after all"? Certainly not. You will say—if you want to stay within the rules of the Euclidean game—"This proves that the first line was not really straight." Why? Because one of the rules defines *straight line* as "the shortest path between two points," and a logical definition is like an equation (which, by another rule of the game, is reversible: if $A = B$, then $B = A$).

This, then, is what we mean when we say that a statement tantamount to an equation is necessarily true. It does not consist of an observation or an inference from an observation but merely stipulates an equivalence of terms, with *is* or *are* usually replacing the equal sign in nonmathematical, workaday discourse. Such a statement is called analytic or tautological, whereas a statement of observation or inference from observation (for example, "Your coat is on fire," "You have been smoking too much") is called synthetic. Synthetic statements are not, in any sense of the word, necessarily true.

THE AMBIGUITY OF "TO BE"

The copulative verb obviously carries in itself the seeds of a bumper crop of ambiguities, since a sentence of the form "*A* is *B*" may be either reporting an observation or merely stating a tautology. The former is arguable, the latter is not. The sentence "War is a state of armed conflict between nations," for example, conveys the same proposition as "A state of armed conflict between nations is war," the proposition being merely that wherever we use the term war we could just as well substitute the phrase *a state of armed conflict between nations*, and vice versa. A sentence may be tautological, however, even if the subject and predicate are not interchangeable, provided it states merely that category *A* is a part of category *B* by stipulation. Thus "War is a state of armed conflict" is analytic since it states one of the defining qualities of *war*: a rule of linguistic usage, not an observation about experience.

In certain circumstances, of course, even the utterance "War is a state of armed conflict between nations" may be a report of observation about language usage, tantamount to "The overwhelming majority of English-speaking people today use the term *war* in the sense 'a state of armed conflict between nations.'" If, and only if, this is the prime intention (as in dictionary definitions), then the statement is synthetic. The statements represented by such sentences as "Religion is the quest for the highest truth," "Selling military information to a potential enemy is treason," "Communism is the system of social organization prevailing in Russia today" must either: (a) set up unarguable equations for an algebra of communication, translatable into the form "If you want to understand my meaning in the following discussion you must remember that I use the term *communism* interchangeably with *the system of social organization prevailing in Russia today*"; or (b) convey reports on word usage, synthetic statements translatable as "Most English-speaking people today use the term *communism* in the sense . . . and so forth" which could be verified as pragmatically as the great-circle distance between Washington and Moscow.

PERSUASIVE DEFINITION

Although neither of these alternatives would seem to furnish much ground for polemics, yet observation shows that an overheated, often explosive tone characterizes debates over questions like "What is religion?"; "What is communism?"; and "What is democracy?" To give rise to this intensity of disagreement, a third force must somehow have become interjected into such exchanges.

The third force, presumably, is the strong emotive charge of favor or disfavor carried by words like *religion, democracy, progress, selfishness, traitor, tyrant.* In our society, for example—indeed, in most modern societies—the word *democracy* or its equivalent carries such a charge of warmth, good feeling, and reverential intonation that no one wants to admit even to himself, much less publicly, that he could be against it by any reasonable-sounding definition whatsoever. A sentence of the form "Democracy is . . . " or "*Democracy* means . . . ," therefore, unless offered as a frankly stipulative definition, is usually intended at least as a persuasion or warning, a purpose the speaker often betrays by prefacing his verbal definition with *true* or *real*—thus distinguishing it from the various "wrong" or "perverse" definitions circulated by individuals or groups attempting to undermine the roots of morality or national character. No one ever bothers to speak of the "true" meaning of *hydrogen* or *cytoplasm,* because such a definition does not prod you into doing something about hydrogen or cytoplasm; but when the emotive connotation of *true* or *real* (which are "purr-words," with the force of ethical terms) is coupled with a definition of another emotively charged word, the resulting utterance operates neither as a tautology nor as a lexical report but as a directive: "This is not only my political philosophy but that of all right-thinking men and women. If you don't agree, you must be some kind of nut, or worse. Therefore, do thus and so." Since these words, however, would sound overdogmatic (and *dogmatic* is usually a "snarl-word" in our society), most people prefer to do their political and moral finger-shaking in the form of a persuasive definition of the strongly loaded word.

Thus an American might say, "The only true democracy is a government elected at frequent intervals by popular vote so as to reflect at all times the will of the majority of its adult citizens"; whereas a totalitarian zealot from one of today's "people's democracies" might say, "The only true democracy is a government that has the power and the stability to devote its energies entirely to promoting the welfare of its people, without the distraction of partisan politics and the need to curry popular favor." And both of them might say, "The real meaning of *treason* is not overt acts of violence against the government or selling military secrets to foreign powers but subtly demoralizing the people by circulating false notions about what democracy really consists of."

The argumentative "truth" of this variety of definition, needless to say, differs from the necessary truth of genuine analytic statements or tautologies, which constitute the preliminary agreements for a vocabulary. Unless we accept these preliminary agreements we simply cannot use that vocabulary to communicate our observations or inferences about the world of experience—that is, to formulate synthetic statements.

FORM AND FUNCTION IN INDICATIVE SENTENCES

While it may be the protean *is* and *are* that give persuasive definitions the illusory air of conveying analytic statements—just as in the seemingly airtight tautology of the "Business is business" formula, where the "same" word is used in two different senses—the absence of any form of the verb *to be* does not necessarily signal a synthetic statement. Sentences like "A gentleman always gives up his seat to a lady" or "A neurotic feels no confidence in his ability to cope with the world," delivered in a properly impressive tone of voice, often sound like sage observations, but they generally function as elliptical definitions, or statements of equivalence of terms: "A gentleman [is a man who] always gives up his seat to a lady"; "A neurotic [is a person who] feels no confidence in his ability to cope with the world." Conversely, a form of *to be* is often the only verb in a sentence conveying a synthetic statement. When we say, "John is an engineer," we are reporting that among John's traits we find those that we have posited as defining qualities of a certain category of human beings, just as when we say, "John is a great fellow," or even, with a bit of rhetorical acrobatics, "A great fellow is John," we are reporting our judgment about John, not stating that we use the terms *John* and *a great fellow* interchangeably. Such reports have a truth value: the degree of their congruence or incongruence with the way things really are.

VERIFIABILITY

This brings us back to the basic epistemological dilemma mentioned in an earlier chapter. *If* there is an absolute reality independent of any possible observing consciousness, then any proposition either coincides with the real state of affairs, and hence is true, or does not coincide with it, and hence is false. Unfortunately, but just as inexorably, since no two observations can be made from the same points of reference in space, time, and consciousness, we can never know whether this correspondence exists or not; hence the paradox that the common sense attitude of most people toward the world, the attitude which philosophers sometimes call "naïve realism," has only the evidence of the senses to support the conviction that there is something in the world beside sense data. Yet without such a conviction the words *true* and *false* as applied to synthetic statements can have at most a polarity of meaning and thus might be applied interchangeably to the same statement.

Such a predicament may not turn out to be any more intolerable than the one that permits us to accept "War is peace" or "Freedom is slavery," but it does suggest a clear need to make distinctions as to kinds of statement meaning. Just as in the case of word meaning, it may be found useful to distinguish along operational lines. A statement such as that there is an absolute reality independent of any possible observing consciousness is, by its own terms, incapable of either proof or disproof by any conceivable act of observation or reasoning based on observation; therefore, it has no *operational* meaning. We are not concerned here with mere technological inadequacy, as in the statement that the moon is made of green cheese (which, at least at the time of writing, had not been put to the most reliable test of all); by "absolute . . . independent of any possible observing consciousness" it rules out the pertinence of any evidence gathered into human consciousness by any conceivable means at any time. This is not to say that it has no meaning of any kind —it undoubtedly expresses a deeply felt inner conviction which affects much of our behavior—but only that, being unverifiable in *principle*, it is a statement of a very different order from "There goes Charley" or even "The farthest known galaxy is a billion light years away." A statement that is unverifiable in principle may be called metaphysical; some semanticists call it a nonsense statement, to indicate that the terms of the statement itself bar the applicability of any possible sense data as criteria of its truth or falsity. This does call attention very pointedly to a useful distinction, but to avoid the pejorative associations of the word *nonsense* we shall use the hyphenated form *non-sense*.

It is a moot question whether reports of an individual's emotions or value judgments ("I hate you"; "Tennyson is a great poet") should be classified as non-sense or not. The individual himself surely knows whether his statement about his intensional state is true or not, and may even conceivably have sense impressions by which to verify it—impressions that translate hate into seeing red, fear into going weak in the knees, and so forth. As for value judgment, Emily Dickinson said that when she read what she judged to be great poetry she felt as if the top of her head had been blown off; A. E. Housman reported that if he read great poetry while shaving, his whiskers bristled so that the razor would hardly cut them. All we can say is that, just as the Housman test was unavailable to Miss Dickinson,[2] so any report of emotion or value judgment is incapable in principle of being verified by anyone other than the reporter. Here the speaker not only determines what is said by the words in which he verbalizes his report but, unless emotions are defined in behavioral terms, he has sole access to the evidence by which to verify the statement.

What is usually meant in saying of a statement that it is verifiable in principle is that we can specify conditions under which *anyone* might gather sense data, either directly or with the aid of instruments, demonstrating its truth or falsity, regardless of whether we can now produce those conditions or not. In principle it is possible to set up publicly usable operational criteria of meaning for value terms—for example, to be "beautiful" a painting might have to contain specified colors, or show workers struggling, or adhere to a certain formula of perspective drawing; to be "wise" a man might have to predict accurately the outcome of three successive elections, or score at least 95 percent on a certain "intelligence test," and so forth. But in general the way we recognize a value term (in ethics, esthetics, or whatever) is by observing that its use in a declarative sentence causes that sentence to function as either a directive or a report of the speaker's intensional state. If this be accepted as an operational definition of *value term*, then it is merely tautological to say that a statement of value judgment like "Wallace Stevens was a great poet" (unless intended as an equivalent to "Ninety-eight percent of the English teachers queried said that Wallace Stevens was a great poet") does not present a verifiable report about the world outside the observer's consciousness.

Some semanticists take the position that the entire meaning of any informative statement is simply the operation or set of operations necessary to verify it. "This golf ball is a sphere" thus would mean that if it is true you will see or feel a certain shape sensation if you look at it or cup it in your hand. The test condition (hence the meaning) for "The earth is a sphere," however, is—or was until the onset of the astronaut age—that if you kept traveling in the same direction on the earth's surface you would return to your starting point; since this was found to

[2] An outsider, say, a barber, could have verified the refractoriness of Housman's beard at any given moment, but could he have proved that exposure to what Housman considered great poetry was the only stimulus that produced this toughness?

occur, you inferred that *if* you could back far enough away, or *if* you had big enough hands, you would experience the shape sensations you associate with sphericity.

The meaning of "The students are passing through the gateway" is that if properly placed you could observe some physical bodies in rectilinear motion within a specified area; the meaning of "The sun is passing through the windowpane" is that you can see the sun just about as well with the glass interposed between it and your eyes as without the glass. What you actually mean by *passing through* in each of the sentences is defined by the operation that determines whether the statement is true or false, and inferences drawn from mere similarity in linguistic structure are apt to be highly misleading.

Zeno's famous paradoxes, such as that Achilles can never overtake a tortoise with a head start or that an arrow can never reach its mark, either are synthetic statements about moving bodies whose falsity is easily demonstrable or, if they are true in any sense, must have a totally different criterion of truth (for example, the necessary truth of a logical game, with a nonoperational definition of *overtake* and *reach* as one of the game's rules) and hence a totally different meaning.

In interpreting reports on inner psychological and emotional states of anyone than the speaker—and perhaps even the speaker's own—it is particularly helpful to sort them out according to criteria of verification, since their meanings may range all the way from reports on behavioral symptoms through disguised directives to metaphysical or non-sense statements. "Johnny is below average in intelligence," for example, as uttered by an educational psychologist, very likely means that on certain tests Johnny made more pencil marks on the machine-scoring sheet in places the compilers of the test had agreed to call wrong than did fifty percent of the other children who took the same tests, most of them at other times and places. Without this or *some other operational criterion of verification*, it is hard to read any meaning into it except as a behest (for example, "Don't bother trying to make a Ph.D. out of Johnny"), to which truth value is inapplicable, or as a purely individual value judgment which, as explained above, is verifiable only by the speaker himself. The statement conveyed by "The witness lied in his answer to such-and-such a question," even if it is operationally verifiable, may depend for its testability on such very different kinds of observation as that one or more other witnesses gave testimony conflicting with his, or that when he gave the same answer elsewhere an instrument recorded certain changes in his pulse rate or blood pressure or respiration rate as compared with the readings when he answered an assortment of routine questions.

CONCLUSIVE VERIFICATION
VERSUS PROBABILITY

But in what way does any operation actually prove the truth or falsity of a proposition, even the simplest statement of observation? Take the statement conveyed by "That wall is yellow"; we verify it by looking at it carefully in good daylight, or better yet by having a number of people look at it and report. If say, a thousand observers all agree that it is yellow, we call the statement true; if 999 report that it is yellow and one denies it, we still say the statement is true and attribute the dissenting voice to color blindness, insanity, perverseness, misuse of terms, or whatnot. Even if we ourselves look at it a thousand times, seeing yellow 999 times and a very different color more or less midway in the series, we ascribe the variant observation to some abnormal condition of ourselves or the lighting, or to a prankster's having somehow temporarily tinted the wall, and we confidently call the statement true. But what if the observation results divide 950:50, 872:128, 500:500? If we insist that a proposition (other than a logical one) must be called either true or false, we must arbitrarily choose some point at which to mark the total shift in truth value. On the other hand, we can avoid this dilemma by applying a truth meter which operates less like an on-or-off electric switch than like a rheostat, which can give us innumerable gradations of current in between. The operational meaning of *true* and *false*, then, would become synonymous with a statistical report on the observations actually made.

For that matter, even though a thousand observations, or ten thousand, or a million, all agree, we have no certainty but only probability that the next one, made under as nearly the same conditions as possible, will not begin an equally long series of contradictory results. The meaning of "That wall is yellow," therefore, includes, if only by implication, a time designation, the time during which the evidence is gathered, so that the truth value of the statement will not be altered by the fact that the painter may show up five minutes later to change the décor or that over the years the color may fade to grayish-white. By the same token the statement embodied in "It is 5:30 P.M., April 15, 1965," includes an implied place designation, the place where the remark is made. Carried to the logical extreme, this means that every statement can be at most true or false only for the particular recording consciousness at that point in time and space, and, since by definition these conditions cannot be duplicated, no conclusive verification is possible. But logic, as we have said, is a game, and for practical purposes we do accept, obviously must accept, the weight of an overwhelming preponderance of evidence as a sign of a statement's truth or falsity. Pragmatically, it is this statistical preponderance (together with the implied time or place designation) and this only, that the statement means.

Some people find this ultrapragmatic view repellent, since it seems to rule out the possibility of (or at least to eliminate the usefulness of the phrase) "self-evident truth." It is presented here not as the only valid approach but as one that enables us to make some useful differentiations among *kinds* of meaning in significant cognitive sentences: for example, statements of direct observation, statements of inference from direct observation, statements of inference from other inferences, statements that report only the speaker's inner feelings and are therefore unverifiable, except in strictly behaviorist terms, by anyone else's direct observation. All of these statements have meaning, all of them may be true by one standard or another, but their meanings are of different orders and it is fruitless to debate their truth unless we know upon what criteria their truth or falsity depends.

PREDICTIONS

A rather special case is presented by predictions, that is, statements about the future. A prediction of a single event ("It will rain here tomorrow"; "In five seconds you will hear thunder") can in principle be proved to be either true or false. But there is another kind of prediction that comes disguised in the form of statements of general inductive inference in which *all* or *always* or *everywhere* (or, conversely, *no* or *never* or *nowhere*) is either expressed or implied ("All men are mortal"; "Lightning is always followed by thunder"; "Small, hard, green apples are sour"; "The volume of a gas varies directly with temperature and inversely with pressure"). Such statements, particularly if formulated in scientific terminology, are often popularly called "laws of nature," and since the statutory meaning of *law* is usually learned before the scientific application there is a common tendency, despite the high mortality rate of "laws" in the history of science, to think of a "scientific law" as a statement that has been conclusively proved true. Yet it is a characteristic of such formulations that, while a single valid exception can prove them false, they can never be finally proved true, since there is always the possibility that the next observation will run counter to all the previous ones. They function, then, less as statements of facts already observed than as forecasts: "Whenever you bite into a small, hard, green apple you will find it sour"; "Every time you see lightning you will, unless it is too far away, hear thunder soon after." Since truth, for such predictions, is a concept that has no operational meaning, a more appropriate value scale to apply to them would be that of usefulness, in gamblers' terms: that is, judged according to statistical probability. Thus a prediction that a given pair of dice will always roll seven will be proved false if it ever turns up another number, but if the prediction is accurate 999 times out of a thousand the dice roller can well afford—and his faders can ill afford not—to treat its meaning as a virtually sure thing. The probability ratio for the most useful scientific laws runs far higher, perhaps millions of millions to one, but their meanings still partake of the uncertainty of experience rather than the necessary truth of analytic statements.

EQUIVOCAL SENTENCES

Synthetic propositions, then, are indeterminate for much the same reason that symbolic categories are inexorably vague in outline. Sentences, furthermore, often have equivocal truth values because of the potential ambiguity of the words that compose them. Even after we have decided that a given sentence functions as the vehicle for a statement rather than imperatively, expressively, or evocatively, we sometimes find that, depending on the interpretation of one or more of its words, it may convey either a synthetic or an analytic statement; thus it may not only have different meanings but be subject to very different standards of truth value. Take, for example, "Good citizens never falsify their income tax returns." If you mean by it that you would never apply the term *good citizen* to anyone who falsified an income tax return, regardless of his other qualifications, then you are simply stating one of the defining qualities of the term as you use it; this makes the statement analytic, therefore unarguable, though of course the associations of *good* actually place it more in the category of persuasive definition. If, on the other hand, you have established another set of defining qualities for *good citizen* (for example, voting in all primaries and elections, having no record of traffic violations or arrests, contributing regularly to charity), you may be using the sentence to convey either of two synthetic statements: (a) the operationally verifiable one that no member of that class has ever falsified—or anyway, been caught falsifying—a tax return; (b) a prediction that no member of that class ever will falsify a return—a prediction to which, as we have just said, the standard of usefulness is more applicable than that of truth or falsity.

These discriminations are not merely academic exercises; moral and social attitudes sometimes hinge upon an uncritical acceptance of a sentence's meaning. Consider the various implications of that cliché of modern psychology: "People do what they really want to do." If the definition of *want* points to observable behavior antecedent to the desired act (for instance, what people *say* they want to do, or their bodily response to anticipation of the act), then this is a synthetic proposition subject to testing for statistical probability. If *want* is regarded as an operationally undefinable term (and the presence of *really* lends support to this hypothesis), we have a non-sense statement, perhaps fraught with emotive overtones and directive force but not reporting anything verifiable. Finally, a no less plausible interpretation is that we have a tautology: a stipulation that the only defining quality of the class of what people want to do is what they actually do. Another sentence, varying interpretations of which have left a tremendous imprint on human history, is "The king can do no wrong." The meaning depends on whether you define *king* solely as "reigning monarch," and thus make a more or less useful prediction about the behavior of crowned rulers, or whether you add "infallible moral arbiter" as a defining quality, and thus merely state a necessary tautological truth.

In cases of this kind ambiguity is not necessarily being exploited for ulterior motives. Such exploitation, however, is an ever-present possibility, and we should not close our discussion of the cognitive use of language without taking note of sentences that may be interpreted, by selective reference to a dictionary of the language, as conveying two or more different verifiable statements, at least one of which is true and at least one of which is false. This furnishes an almost unlimited field for evasion, equivocation, and a kind of linguistic slapstick comedy such as that of Shakespeare's clowns who willfully interpret statements or questions in a way the speaker might have intended but almost certainly did not. What standard of truth are we to apply, for example, to my declaration, "I keep your picture in my bedroom," if in fact I keep your picture face down under the bedroom rug along with floor sweepings and old newspapers? Perhaps we should distinguish between what we might call functional truth and selective dictionary truth—that is, a standard applicable to the statement I intend my sentence to suggest to my hearer and a standard applicable to the statement(s) I can fall back on if I have to defend myself against a charge of perjury.

The value of dictionary truth is well illustrated by the anecdote of a New England horse-trader who sold a farmer a nag under the guarantee that she was "sound of wind and limb, and without fault." When, on the way home, the farmer's new purchase walked bang into a stone wall, he turned back and remonstrated furiously that the horse, despite the warranty, was blind. "Ah, sir," replied the dealer, "blindness is not her fault; it's her misfortune."

Perhaps it was this same merchant who once observed, "I don't know why people tell lies when the truth can be just as misleading."

*It must be realized that our lives are
lived on the silent, objective levels, that
whatever we "think," "feel," and "do"
happens as such silently, and that only
as a secondary matter does talk come
in. Actual living happens silently and
is first in importance before speech.*

When to 'Keep Still'

IRVING J. LEE

It may seem strange to conclude a book on language
with an article on silence. Yet, if language is to be
understood in terms of what it can and cannot do, the
role of silence is crucial for we live our lives and experience
our experiences on the silent level. Our talk about the
experience, therefore, is only an abstraction of the
experience; words are not things. This, of course, is
obvious. Yet, as Lee so clearly demonstrates we often fail
to make the distinction between words and things and
often give primary importance to what is said rather than
to what is experienced. In reading this article be sure to
experience what Lee asks you to experience; otherwise,
you will gain little from this most perceptive analysis of
silence.

ON SILENCE

If the reader will do what he is told here, he will gain immeasurably the sense of what this chapter is about. What is asked may seem pointless, but the experience of many students of language in its relation to life facts indicates that the procedure is effective. This is a plea for participation.

Pinch your finger. Say no words. Notice the experience. Do it again. Notice that something happened on the silent level. You had a direct experience which may be described verbally in many ways. But whatever might be said in words would not be what you felt by the pressure of the pinch. You should continue to remain silent so that you may become more aware of what goes on inside-your-skin. The nature of that inside feeling, of whatever happens, of whatever comes to awareness is not an affair of language, but is in its entirety an un-speakable matter. This may seem obvious, but unless it is sharply realized that what was felt belongs to the realm of silence, that it is quite different from what may be said in the realm of discourse, we shall miss a most important factor in the process of proper evaluation.

Pick up an object, a pencil or a book. Turn it over in your hands. Handle it. Drop it to the floor. Say nothing as you go through these operations. Look at the object. Now say the word "book." Notice that what you said was not the object itself. What you handled is not words. You might write with the pencil, but you could not write with the word "pencil." You could drop the book to the floor, but you could not drop the word "book" unless the word was objectified by being written on paper. You must see that you are dealing with two distinct levels, one verbal, one silent.

From "When to Keep Still" (pp. 211–222) from Language Habits in Human Affairs *by Irving J. Lee. Copyright 1941 by Harper & Row, Publishers, Inc.; renewed 1959 by Laura Louise Lee. By permission of Harper & Row, Publishers, Inc.*

Stand up and walk the length of your room. Notice the movements of your feet. Say nothing about what you are doing. Don't even talk to yourself "inside." Merely realize that you are engaging in a form of physical action. After walking, sit down. The action is now ended. Is it clear that the walking took place on a level that was non-verbal, that you merely did something? Now you might try to describe the process of walking, the way your legs move, the shifting positions of your body, the character of the action as you felt it. Regardless of the clarity or complexity of what you have just said, that description will not be on the silent level of the actual walking. No matter how you walked, that action will not be on the level of what you said. Whatever you may say about your behavior, the behavior itself will be different.

In short, the "feeling" of the pinch, the objective pencil or book, the action of walking and sitting belong to a *silent* universe, while anything said belongs to a *verbal* universe. It must be clearly understood that what was called "a pinch," "a pencil," and "walking" are matters which exist on un-speakable levels, very much different from whatever exists on speech levels. Students who are in any doubt about this point should reread the preceding paragraphs and follow the directions before going on.

What is the importance of this emphasis on the difference between the silent and the verbal?

In the first place, it must be realized that our lives are lived on the silent, objective levels, that whatever we "think," "feel," and "do" happens as such silently, and that only as a secondary matter does talk come in. Actual living happens silently and is first in importance before speech. When you sit down to dinner hungry, you are primarily interested in the silent food before you. The digestive system, blood stream, etc., could not be nourished by words, but only by life facts capable of being digested. As Emerson says in "New England Reformers,"

> The sight of a planet through a telescope is worth all the course
> in astronomy; the shock of the electric spark in the elbow outvalues
> all the theories; the taste of the nitrous oxide, the firing of an arti-
> ficial volcano are better than volumes of chemistry.

Language enters to serve auxiliary functions as a convenience at a different level of life. Whatever use that language serves will be a use quite different from the use to which the food is put in the stomach. Experiences of anything are primary in human living. And whatever may be said of them does not appear as a part of that silent living.

Secondly, objective levels, objects, feelings, happenings, actions, etc., are infinitely diverse and complex in their characteristics. So full of particulars are they that their fullness can never be reached by words. The classic example of the inadequate coverage of speech appears in the futile attempt to describe the taste or color of something to one who has never had a similar direct experience. To know a taste or color it is necessary to go beyond the words to the experience itself. Though the tasting or the seeing may be immediate and seemingly simple, the full perception is so inconceivably complex that one cannot get to it by words alone. It can be reached only as a first-order direct effect of the experience. The same may be said of objects. One may pick up an object and say "This is a book" without recognizing the false-to-fact character of what was said. The object appears as an absolute individual full of countless characteristics and it is not words and never can be; to speak as if they are "identical" may be described as delusion. Further, to say that it is a "book" is to say something that does not correspond to the totality of the object. Whatever is said is not "all" that can be said. The manifold uses, interpretations, characteristics of the silent objects and first-order experiences with which we become acquainted are ever so infinitely complex and diverse that talk cannot exhaust them. A feeling of this may be at the bottom of Maeterlinck's view in *Treasure of the Humble*:

> It is idle to think that by means of words, any real communication can ever pass from one man to another. From the moment we have something to say to each other, we are compelled to hold our peace.

And in the Book of Job (ii:13):

> So they sat down with him upon the ground seven days and seven nights and none spoke a word unto him: for they saw that his grief was very great.

For us, even more important is this: an understanding of this silent universe will help dissolve the false-to-fact character of our limited, too-often dogmatic talk.

In the third place, when you realize the complexity of un-speakable levels, you may not be so eager to "burst into speech." It is easy to say something about anything. It is not so easy to be conscious of the limited, partial character of what is said. Verbal levels represent abstractions of some details from the fullness of the silent objects, actions, and experiences. This *consciousness of abstracting* whenever one talks will be more readily acquired when one stops to notice the silent levels. The acquisition of this habit is most difficult. Existing educational procedures somehow generate habits of speaking as the primary human function, so that students too readily speak without awareness that the first-order experiences about which they speak are unreachable by words. To train students to be silent, to know they live on a level comparable to the level of "things" goes contrary to conventional training. And yet training in silence seems to be the most practical means by which to become aware that there are un-speakable realms in actual living. One must learn to be silent outwardly as well as inwardly. Students should learn to look at objects and actions while closing their lips with one hand. To see what is going on and to evaluate it properly without identification *we must be silent*. There must come a consciousness that as soon as we speak we shall be leaving out differences and emphasizing similarities. Learning to point with a finger will keep the silence. Looking and pointing are silent means of expression, analogues of the silent world. *Silence on the objective levels* may well be the first step to the achievement of a consciousness of abstracting and of the realization that there is much more in our world than we normally take cognizance of.

In the fourth place, one of the more immediate beneficial results of acquiring the habit of silence is the development of an awareness that study and analysis are on-going, never finished. When once this is understood, the student develops a *creative* outlook; more and more of the limitless content of the world about him comes into view. Silence gives opportunity for observation. There is time to see what there is to be seen. Arguments, debates, conflicts are quickly generated when the objects, situations, people are known only in part but thought and talked about otherwise. The habit of silence gives one time to look first before speaking. And that looking is, after all, the creative source of what we know as science, art, technology, etc.

The experience of those who have learned silence on the objective level reveals a heightened development of critical attitude. Constant and continuing use of silence when writing or speaking may develop sharply the memory of characteristics left out, no matter what the subject under consideration. Statements are not the un-speakable world; the demarcation of the two levels automatically suggests that statements will leave some things unsaid, some characteristics omitted. Inquiry, investigation, further searching—these are the hallmarks of useful criticism. Students will learn, once silence is fundamental in their reactions, to ask questions: "What do you mean?" "Does that statement cover all?" "Where was the abstracting?" Questions inevitably lead to further search and more talk and an understanding of the limited reasons for whatever conflicts arise.

Our eagerness to make statements on matters which may be foreign to our experience or knowledge may well be a major source of the superficiality of so much speech-making and writing. Students too readily take what they hear and see as the full expression and the complete experience, instead of sharply realizing that too often those statements are merely introductory to the matter in question. As Lippmann has said, "For the most part we do not first see, and then define, *we define first and then see.*"[1] The achievement of silence should reverse this unnatural pattern. Looking at the silent world, we must first be silent. For unless we have learned to observe the vast panorama, "the great blooming buzzing confusion of the outer world," we shall pass over too much that we might know about.

It is important to point out that "we *do not* repress or suppress . . . the bursting into speech; a gesture of the hand to the labels reminds us that words are *not* objects, or actions, or happenings, or feelings."[2] Lapsing into silence will have a jarring effect, which is not to repress but to make for the realization of an important evaluation mechanism in which we must be trained, if we would avoid the harmful effects of speech which becomes false-to-fact when too little is considered.[3]

PHATIC COMMUNION

Silence must be regarded as a methodological device of first importance when it functions to induce delay, to aid the inspection of life facts, and to achieve a non-allness orientation. But there are, as Jespersen says, occasions when we do not wish to keep still, when we talk for the sheer joy of talking.

> There are people everywhere who are equally capable of being intoxicated with their language and revelling in the enjoyment of their own voices, or who at any rate do not wait to open their lips till they have something to say which is worth hearing. In what I have written about the language of children, I have pointed out that children would never learn to talk at all if they were surrounded exclusively by thinkers who only used language as a means of . . . [describing and inferring]. Luckily for them in their earliest years they have the chance of hearing those about them, especially mother

[1]Walter Lippmann, *Public Opinion.* New York: Harcourt, Brace & Co., 1922, 81.

[2]Alfred Korzybski, *Science and Sanity, an Introduction to New Aristotelian Systems and General Semantics.* Lancaster, Pa.: The Science Press Printing Co., 1933, 481.

[3]For the substance of the material on "silence," see *ibid.*, 34–55, 399–400, 416–417, 476–477, 481–485.

and nurse and other women, talk on end with everlasting repetitions even when they are absolutely certain that the dear baby does not understand a syllable of what they say. Notice again how people who are fond of animals will talk at length to their dog or cat or horse. We shall have a later opportunity of drawing attention to all that meaningless jingle which in more or less metrical form makes up a great deal of what men say or sing. We must then never forget that the organs of speech besides serving for . . . [description and inference], and before they begin to be used for that purpose, are one of mankind's most treasured toys, and that not only children but also grown people, in civilized as well as in savage communities, find amusement in letting their vocal chords and tongue and lips play all sorts of games.[4]

There are, in addition, situations when silence takes on asocial characteristics. The necessity of working with and meeting people in the affairs of the day amidst the folkways of group life often have the effect of suggesting, as Malinowski has said, that "another man's silence is not a reassuring factor, but, on the contrary, something alarming and dangerous"; and furthermore, "taciturnity means not only unfriendliness but directly a bad character."[5] To preserve silence and not to engage in talk with others carries the marks of ill will. Conversation ceases when friendliness is no more.

We should see that our key word here represents at least two different states of affairs.

Silence$_1$ should be taken as a mode of delay preliminary to talk. Refraining from impulsive commenting, even momentarily, provides occasion for further observation and the recognition that abstracting goes on. This kind of silence does not do away with speech, it merely paves the way for speech that is a better representation of the life facts.

Silence$_2$, on the other hand, is the sort to which Malinowski seems to refer. It has to do with the failure or refusal or unwillingness to speak. The purpose of this silence may be variously described, but it will most likely not suggest that the individual is preparing for talk to come later. This non-communicative state will have in it the suggestion of strangeness and uncertainty, especially where others expect talk to flow freely. Silence$_2$ goes counter to fellowship and acquaintance. It makes for

[4]Otto Jespersen, *Mankind, Nation and Individual from a Linguistic Point of View.* Oslo: H. Aschehoug & Co., 1925, 8. Reprinted by permission of the President and Fellows of Harvard College.

[5]Bronislaw Malinowski, "The Problem of Meaning in Primitive Languages," Supplement I in *The Meaning of Meaning* by C. K. Ogden and I. A. Richards. New York: Harcourt, Brace & Co., 1930, 314.

"strange and unpleasant tension" whenever people face each other. In short, there are social situations when silence$_1$ might breed intelligence, whereas silence$_2$ might breed unpleasantness.

The affairs of the day are not all serious. There are occasions when we don't have to "think," when productive work can be set aside, when problems of adjustment are not involved. Such occasions are not dependent upon solving problems, but they do have purposes. They provide a means of relaxation, ways of reducing tension. Such restful functions may even take place in the course of practical work. The work songs, the gossip around work tables, the verbal play of road gangs and loggers, the pleasantries that accompany group efforts are to be understood as the use of speech which may not only ease the effort but also establish rapport between individuals. Free, easy, aimless give-and-take between men makes for co-operation in their communal undertakings.

The list of occasions in our society in which talk seems to have primarily social purposes is by no means a small one. Consider only the teas, smokers, dinners, dances, club meetings, dates, reunions, celebrations, commemorative gatherings, etc.

Such conversation as is here referred to exists in general for the mutual exchange of non-practical talk. In its simplest stage we know it as "weather talk," where there is a sharing of views and attitudes in which none of the parties expects "real information." Small talk and polite give-and-take provide a form of social communication which breaks down the barriers of strangeness and establishes the participants on a plane of more intimate relationships. What is said is by no means as important as the fact that the talk establishes friendly feelings. Stereotyped comments on the state of the weather, pleasant inquiries about the health of the one spoken to, generalized references to affairs of the moment act as lubricants to the establishment of mutuality between people. The complex routines and specialized activities which prevent individuals from speaking the language of others seem to make necessary the existence of methods of approach which will break through the barriers. These simple exchanges serve to set up avenues for further communication.

Common sentiments, an atmosphere of sociability, the production of companionship—these may be the concomitants of "the breaking of silence, the communion of words" which establishes those links of fellowship, "which is consummated only by the breaking of bread and the communion of food."[6] Our alumni gatherings, women's clubs, business men's luncheons, lodge meetings, etc., are some of the situations in which there exists that "type of speech in which ties of union are created by a

[6]Bronislaw Malinowski, "The Problem of Meaning," 314.

mere exchange of words,"⁷ called by Malinowski *phatic communion.*

One frequently hears cynical comments about the "low state of intelligence" exhibited when people get together for an evening. One may also hear derisive references to the need which people seem to have for card games, bridge clubs, and visits to the movies so that they will not have to endure the rigors of thinking and talking. Such comments are relevant only if the social nature of our non-reflective group life is disregarded. Talk built around polite nothings breaks the tensions of existence, and it may not be designed to be reflective and intelligent. The achievement of this relaxation and bonds of friendship between people need not necessarily occur as a by-product of talk; they may arise just as well as a by-product of group action, i.e., games, visits to see things, etc. The important point to be grasped is this: The manifestations of good will do have a role in our society, and the purpose of social speech must not be confused with the purposes of an anthropologist on a field trip or a chemist making observations in his laboratory or a man trying to decide where to go on a vacation. The use of language which results from these latter activities has an important place in the efficient functioning of our lives, but it must be seen that they are not the purposes of that social intercourse called *phatic communion.* The aims of a hostess at dinner should not be confused with the aims of a chairman of a group deliberating the problems of national defense.

We shall be properly evaluating speech situations when we distinguish between talk supposed to do work and talk supposed to bring release from work. Confusion arises and analysis often goes askew because these two forms are identified rather than differentiated.

Recognition of abstracting may help avoid the identification. People who talk about trivial matters and subjects which provoke no antipathy but which do make for pleasant interchange are simply abstracting those particular features from the complex of possible relationships while neglecting others. The scientist, on the other hand, might proceed to abstract a set of particulars in his own work, which features are relevant because of the peculiar context in which he operates. The selective character of the interests which motivate non-practical talk has been well described by Znaniecki.

> The first requirement of the art of "polite" conversation is that subjects be chosen and treated in such a way as to make the process of social communication easy and interesting, without ever stimulating active tendencies or suggesting the possibility of any practical use for the data communicated. Everything told should be sufficiently new to be a real addition to the realm of experiences already

⁷*Ibid.,* 315.

shared by the talker and the listener; and yet not too new, for the listener must share without difficulty the experience of the talker. The subjects should be many and varied, particularly in general conversation, so that the common field will extend rapidly in several directions; and yet not too many or varied, lest the extension be superficial, and no single experience truly shared. Every subject ought to be sufficiently interesting in itself to stimulate a desire to share it, and yet none so interesting as to absorb attention and distract it from the conversation as a social activity and the conversing people themselves. Vital subjects are not altogether avoided, as in periods of spontaneous relaxation on lower stages, but must be handled lightly and carefully, viewed in their nonexciting aspects: this is where the "leader in conversation" needs the most consummate refinement. In short, the art of polite conversation imposes actions dominated by the specifically social tendency to share experiences rather than data as a duty on every participant, and demands that this duty be performed in spite of all temptations to subordinate the conversation to any utilitarian tendencies.[8]

One point of view taken toward idle conversation says that merely to talk for talk's sake is to talk "nonsense." Even though a certain innocent pleasure results, nevertheless the "nonsensical" character of the speech act is what is ridiculed. The defenders of this view might admit the impossibility of eliminating such talk because it is so often satisfying They would, however, insist upon putting such talk in its unintelligent place.

If nonsense$_1$ be taken to represent "foolishness" and nonsense$_2$ be taken to represent "absence of purpose," then it must be argued here that *phatic communion* is neither (though it might be either in individual cases), for it may be not foolish but pleasant, and not "meaningless" but designed for relaxation. Nonsense$_3$ may be taken to represent talk which is supposed to correspond to life facts but does not. One may find few productive, demonstrable results from sessions of *phatic communion*, if "results" are measured in terms of new findings and the charting of new relationships. That there are observable effects of social talk must be admitted. We get mired in new confusions if the subtle variants of "nonsense" are unrealized. There is danger in the wholesale ascription of the term "nonsense" to everything that is not scientifically descriptive and verifiable. It is far better in terms of proper evaluation if we are conscious that the peculiar manifestations of *phatic communion* are something different from the abstracting procedures of those bent on charting

[8]Florian Znaniecki, *Social Actions*. New York: Farrar & Rinehart, Inc., 1936, 527–528. Reprinted by permission.

the universe, and if we refuse to permit one to happen as if it were the other.

IN SHORT

Silence on the objective levels is paralleled by silence in human responses. To get to silent levels, we must keep still. Silence$_1$ makes possible consciousness of many details and the abstracting therefrom, gives time for more looking, develops a more critical attitude, and helps to induce delay-of-reaction. Silence$_2$ in the play of social situations may breed antagonism and ill will, for the conventions of group life encourage idle conversation and *phatic communion*.

New habit to be acquired: Get to silent levels by learning silence.

FOR FURTHER READING

For Further Reading

The following bibliography should provide you with some guidelines for further reading. I have attempted to include here works which span the broad area of language study rather than limit the works to any one approach, for example, linguistic, semantic, psycholinguistic, speech-communication, etc. With the few exceptions noted these works are all introductory in the sense that no prior background in language study is required for their understanding.

Those marked with an asterisk (*) are currently available in paperback.

*Alexander, Hubert G. *Language and Thinking: A Philosophical Introduction.* Princeton, New Jersey: D. Van Nostrand, 1967. 350pp.
A basic text for philosophy and logic this work has much of interest for the study of language. Particularly valuable is the first part, "Symbols: Intellectual Coins."

*Allen, Harold B., ed. *Readings in Applied English Linguistics*, 2nd ed. New York: Appleton-Century-Crofts, 1964. 535pp.
Contains 62 articles on language covering such areas as English Linguistics Today, Linguistics and Usage, and Linguistics and the Study of Literature.

*Alston, William P. *Philosophy of Language.* Englewood Cliffs, New Jersey: Prentice-Hall, 1964. 113pp.
Discusses theories of meaning, meaning and the use of language, criteria of meaningfulness, and dimensions of meaning. This is an excellent introduction to language as viewed by the philosopher.

*Barker, Larry L., and Robert J. Kibler, eds. *Speech Communication Behavior: Perspectives and Principles.* Englewood Cliffs, New Jersey: Prentice-Hall, 1971. 382pp.
Seven essays reviewing various aspects of speech communication behavior, e.g., acquisition and performance of communication behaviors, human information processes and diffusion, and persuasion and attitude change, are each followed by several reprinted articles relevant to the topics of the essays.

*Boulton, Marjorie. *The Anatomy of Language: Saying What We Mean.* London: Routledge & Kegan Paul, 1959. 170pp.
Brief essays on "Understanding and Misunderstanding," "The Misuse of Language," and "Literary Semantics." The purpose of this book is "to stimulate a thoughtful, critical, and socially useful interest in the meaning of words."

*Brown, Roger. *Words and Things.* New York: Free Press, 1958. 398pp.
A valuable introduction to the psychology of language covering such areas as the analysis of speech, metaphor, meaning, language in animals, lan-

guage development, linguistic relativity, persuasion and propaganda, and language pathologies. More recent works by Brown which cover some of the same topics include *Social Psychology* (Free Press, 1965) and *Psycholinguistics* (Free Press, 1970).

*Burke, Kenneth. *Language as Symbolic Action: Essays on Life, Literature, and Method.* Berkeley: University of California Press, 1966. 514pp.
Contains 24 essays "explicitly concerned with the attempt to define and track down the implications of the term 'symbolic action,' and to show how the marvels of literature and language look when considered from that point of view." Particularly relevant are "Definition of Man," "Terministic Screens," and "A Dramatistic View of the Origins of Language."

*Carpenter, Edmund S., and Marshall McLuhan, eds. *Explorations in Communication.* Boston: Beacon Press, 1960. 210pp.
Contains 24 articles on various approaches to communication and language. Particularly interesting are Dorothy Lee's "Linguistic Reflection of Wintu Thought" and "Lineal and Nonlineal Codifications of Reality," Northrop Frye's "The Language of Poetry," and McLuhan's "Classroom Without Walls" and "Media Log."

*Carroll, John B., ed. *Language, Thought and Reality: Selected Writings of Benjamin Lee Whorf.* Cambridge, Mass.: M.I.T. Press, 1956. 278pp.
Contains 18 articles by Whorf on language and its relationship to thought, culture, and behavior. A forward by Stuart Chase and an introduction by John Carroll place the work of Whorf in historical perspective. Also included is a thorough bibliography of Whorf's published and unpublished writings and of books and articles relating to Whorf's writings.

*Chomsky, Noam. *Language and Mind,* Enlarged Edition. New York: Harcourt, Brace Jovanovich, 1972. 194pp.
In the first three chapters Chomsky evaluates past attempts to study language and the mind, discusses contemporary issues in linguistics relevant to the study of mind, and speculates on the directions that the study of language and mind might take in the future. The three essays following these explain many of the assumptions and implications of recent work in generative grammar.

Clark, Margaret L., Ella A. Erway, and Lee Beltzer. *The Learning Encounter: The Classroom as a Communications Workshop.* New York: Random House, 1971. 210pp.
The authors offer "a set of parameters for viewing student/teacher relationships and for teaching interpersonal communication with the hope of opening up new vistas and stimulating student and teacher to extend their thinking, to probe their potential for cooperative creativity." Considerable attention is given to language, dialects, and language experiences.

DeCecco, John P., ed. *The Psychology of Language, Thought, and Instruction: Readings*. New York: Holt, Rinehart and Winston, 1967. 446pp.
Contains 43 articles dealing with various aspects of language, e.g., language and social class, language and meaning, reading instruction, the development of language and thought, and instruction in language and thought.

DeVito, Joseph A. *The Psychology of Speech and Language: An Introduction to Psycholinguistics*. New York: Random House, 1970. 308pp.
An introduction to some of the psychological dimensions of language and speech, covering theoretical foundations (linguistic, learning, and communication theories) and speech and language acquisition, breakdown, differences, and effects.

Gordon, George N. *The Languages of Communication: A Logical and Psychological Examination*. New York: Hastings House, 1969. 334pp.
After providing an orientation to the logics and psychologics of communication, Gordon considers symbols, mediums, qualities, and instruments of communication. In a final section Gordon speculates on the future of communications.

*Hayakawa, S. I., ed. *The Use and Misuse of Language*. Greenwich, Conn.: Fawcett, 1962. 240pp.
Contains 19 articles originally published in *Etc.* on semantics and general semantics grouped under "The Art of Communication," "Semantics Around Us," and "Human Insight." The articles are entertaining yet insightful of many problems caused by the misuse of language.

Hill, Archibald, ed. *Linguistics Today*. New York: Basic Books, 1969. 291pp.
Contains 25 original articles reporting on recent developments in different areas of linguistics, e.g., phonology, morphology and syntax, semantics; the relationship of language study to anthropology, psychology, literature; different approaches to language study, e.g., the Prague School, Glossematics, and Generative Grammar.

*Jennings, Gary. *Personalities of Language*. New York: Thomas Y. Crowell, 1965. 282pp.
After providing some background on the development of speech and writing and of different languages, Jennings deals with dialects, slang, taboo, names, and the specialized uses and abuses of languages. This is a highly entertaining yet informative introduction to language.

*Jespersen, Otto. *Mankind, Nation and Individual: From a Linguistic Point of View*. Bloomington: Indiana University Press, 1964. 198pp.
In this work (originally published in 1946) Jespersen treats the influence of the individual upon language, the relationship between standard language and dialects, as well as such issues as taboo, poetry, slang, and mysticism in language.

*Lee, Irving J., ed. *The Language of Wisdom and Folly: Background Readings in Semantics*. San Francisco, California: International Society for General Semantics, 1967. 361pp.
Contains 72 articles covering such areas as "The Functions and Purposes of Language in Use," "Questions and Answers," "The Structural Patterns and Implications of a Language," and "Escape from Verbalism." Represented here are some of the leading language theorists.

*Lenneberg, Eric H., ed. *New Directions in the Study of Language*. Cambridge, Mass.: M.I.T. Press, 1964. 194pp.
Contains seven papers on language acquisition and development, anthropological aspects of language, and language and psychology.

*Lyons, John, ed. *New Horizons in Linguistics*. Baltimore, Maryland: Penguin, 1970. 367pp.
Contains 17 original articles on various aspects of language study, e.g., speech reception and perception, phonology, generative syntax, semantics, stylistic analysis, biology of communication, language acquisition, and sociolinguistics. A useful glossary of technical terms follows the articles.

*Oldfield, R. C., and J. C. Marshall, eds. *Language: Selected Readings*. Baltimore, Maryland: Penguin, 1968. 392pp.
Contains 25 articles on language organized into five sections: acquisition and development, perception and production, psychological aspects, quantitative and mathematical aspects, and pathology and brain function. Represented here are many of the leading language researchers, e.g., Roger Brown, George Miller, C. E. Shannon, E. H. Lenneberg, and A. R. Luria.

*Postman, Neil, Charles Weingartner, and Terence P. Moran, eds. *Language in America*. New York: Pegasus, 1969. 240pp.
The authors of these articles address themselves to the question: "To what extent is the language of (politics/advertising/psychotherapy/education bureaucracy/etc.) facilitating or impeding our chances of survival?" The volume contains 21 major articles along with a number of brief pieces.

*Salomon, Louis B. *Semantics and Common Sense*. New York: Holt, Rinehart and Winston, 1966. 180pp.
A brief introduction to semantics dealing with such issues as taboo, definition, classification, ambiguity, and translation. An excellent section, "Topics for Investigation and Discussion," provides the reader with numerous opportunities for applying the principles discussed in the text.

*Smith, Arthur L., ed. *Language, Communication, and Rhetoric in Black America*. New York: Harper, 1972. 388pp.
Contains 29 articles dealing with Black Language, Language and Ethnicity, Rhetorical Case Studies, Criticism and Social Change, and Social and Historical Dimensions.

*Stevenson, Charles L. *Ethics and Language.* New Haven: Yale University Press, 1944. 338pp.

An analysis of meaning in language, the meaning of ethical judgments, and the methods for supporting ethical judgments.

*Ullmann, Stephen. *Words and Their Use.* New York: Hawthorn, 1966. 125pp. A brief introduction to semantics, covering language and meaning, meaning and ambiguity, the vocabulary in motion, and words and things. More advanced treatments of these and related topics may be found in Ullmann's *Semantics* (Barnes and Noble, 1962) and *The Principles of Semantics* (Barnes and Noble, 1957).

*Wagner, Geoffrey. *On the Wisdom of Words.* Princeton, New Jersey: D. Van Nostrand, 1968. 345pp.

Wagner argues that "the recognition and awareness of word-wisdom today becomes a biological necessity. Semantics can be no less than a technique for survival." Advertising, television, politics, psychology, and more here come under attack.

*Wilson, Grahman, ed. *A Linguistics Reader.* New York: Harper and Row, 1967. 341pp.

Contains 36 articles on such topics as correctness, linguists and their critics, and grammar. Particularly valuable is the section on "The Science of Language" which contains articles by Noam Chomsky, George Miller, and others. The Foreward by Paul Roberts is an especially good introduction to linguistics.

Winterowd, W. Ross. *Rhetoric: A Synthesis.* New York: Holt, Rinehart and Winston, 1968. 228pp.

Winterowd, attempting "to bring together in coherence the various fragments of a new rhetoric," ranges from Aristotle through Campbell and Blair to Burke, Chomsky, and the psycholinguists. Particularly valuable are the lengthy discussions of style and form.

Index

to Concepts

and Processes

A

Abstract words, 256–59
Acquisition of knowledge, 96
Acquisition of language, 34–36, 102–3, 110–20
  Humboldt's view, 98
"Aggressiveness," 149–50
Ambiguity of "to be," 270
Analytic statements, 272
Animal communication, 24–38
Anti-logos, 205–6
Arbitrariness, 28
Argot, 48, 54
"Atavism," 155–56

B

Badge language, 48
Basic English, 132
Benevolence, language of, 158–59
Black English, 50
Blending, 34
"Blood and consanguinity," 154
Broadcast transmission and directional reception, 27

C

Child language, 110–20
Chordates, classification of, 32
Class languages, 46–55
Cliché talk, 204–5
Commercial speech, 204

Communication:

Communication:
  language and, 196–290
  mass, 69–84, 252–53
  purposes of language, 41–42
  systems, 33
Comparative method, 24–38
Concern, language of, 159–60
Conclusive verification, 276–77
Concrete words, 256–59
Connotation, 164–70, 261–64
Consciousness of abstracting, 283
Contract group, 197–208
  defined, 198n
Control, language of social, 235–46
Coordination, 22–23
Counter cultures, 212–20
Creativity of language, 12–13, 22, 29, 34, 97
Creoles, 51

D

Date, as extensional device, 141–44
Deep structure, 20–23, 101 passim
Definition, persuasive, 271–72
Delayed responses, 41, 141–44, 286
Democratizing English, 167
Denotation, 261–64
Design features of language, 24–38
Developmental psycholinguistics, 110–20
Dialects, 51
Dialogue, 202–4, 214
Dictionary, usage and the, 249–51
Directed response, language of, 162–63

Directional reception, 27
Directive language, 235–46
  with collective sanction, 241–44
  and disillusionment, 245–46
  features of, 242–43
  promises of, 239–40
Discreteness, 28
Disillusionment, directives and,
  245–46
Displacement, 28–29, 35–36
Distances in social relations, 62–63
Distinctive features, 18
Drugs, language of, 214–16
Duality of patterning, 29, 36–37

E

Education, language and, 46–55,
  164–70
Embedded sentences, 22–23
Empiricist view of knowledge, 96
Encounter groups, 197–208
Equivocal sentences, 278–79
Etc., as extensional device, 141–44
Ethics, 85–92
Euphemism, 255–56
Experience, language and, 17–19
Expression, as purpose of language,
  41–42

F

Feedback, 27

G

Games, 203–4
General Semantics, 133–44, 235–46
Generation gap, semantics of, 212–20
Generative grammar, 14–23, 95–109
Genkind, 171–82
Germanic languages, origin of modern,
  30–31
Group communication, language in,
  197–208

H

"Heredity," 153–54
Hippie language, 212–20
Human communication:
  defined, 9
  and language, 7–23
Human language:
  definition in terms of design features,
    24–38
"Human nature," 148

I

Imperatives, 40–41
Index, as extensional device, 141–44
Indicative sentences, 272
Innate properties of language, 96–109
"Instinct," 148–49
Interchangeability, 27
Interjections, 40–41
Interpersonal communication,
  language in, 197–208
Intimate distance, 62

J

Jargon, 253–55

K

Kinesics, 11–12, 56–68

L

Language:
  consequences of, 3–6
  creativity of 12–13, 22, 29, 34, 97
  of drugs, 214–16
  and education, 164–70
  evolution of, 32
  forms and functions of, 1–92
  of generation gap, 212–20
  hippie, 212–20

Language: (cont.)
  in interpersonal communication,
    197–208
  kinds of, 202–6
  limitations of, 133–44
  and logic, 121–32
  and the mind, 95–109
  of music, 221–28, 229–34
  origin of, 24–38
  potentials of, 201–2
  precise, 251–53
  and prejudice, 157–63, 164–70,
    171–82
  problems of, 44–45, 198–201
  productivity of, 12–13, 22, 29, 34, 97
  of racism, 164–70
  of responsibility, 85–92
  of self-deception, 145–56
  of self-disparagement, 160–61
  of self-reproach, 161–62
  of sexism, 171–82
  in small group communication,
    197–208
  and social class, 46–55
  of social control, 235–46
  and sound, 15–17
  "square," 212–20
  and structure, 14–23 passim
  and the study of human
    communication, 7–23
  and syntax, 19–21
  and thought, 43, 93–194
  and truth, 268
  uniqueness of, 12–14
  universals of, 24–38, 108
  uses of, 39–45, 236–46
  vague, 91, 251–53
  versatility of, 9–10
"Law of the jungle, the," 151
Learned words, 259–61
Learning, 97–99
  the language, 110–20
  model for, 99
Limitations of language, 133–44
Linguistic relativity, 121–32, 267–68
Listening, 89–90
Logic, languages and, 121–32

Logos, 197–208
" 'Lower' animals, the," 151–52

M

Mass communication, 69–84, 252–53
Mass language, 251–53
Mass media, language of, 69–84
Meaning in rock music, 222–24
Medium of transmission, 9
  sound as, 9
Memory, 106–7
Metaphor, 256
"Miscegenation," 154–55
Morpheme, 19–21, 29, 104
Music:
  design features of, 33
  language of, 221–28, 229–34

N

Negation, 119
New language, 229–34
New languages, 69–84
Newspeak, 183–93
Nonverbal communication, 10–12,
  56–68

O

Operational meaning, 273
Origin of language, 24–38
Origin of speech, 24–38

P

Paralinguistic phenomena, 33
Paraphrase, 101
Pathos, 200–201, 205
Perception, 97
  model for, 97
Personal distance, 62
Persuasive definition, 271–72
Phatic communion, 139–40, 285–90
Phoneme, 15–17, 104

Phonemic symbols, 16
Phonetics, 18
Phonological rules, 15–17
Popular words, 259–61
Potentials of language, 201–2
Precise language, 251–53
Predictions, 277–78
Prejudice, 157–63, 164–70, 171–82
Principles of Newspeak, 183–93
Problems of language, 44–45, 198–201
Productivity of language, 12–13, 22, 29, 34, 97
Proxemics, 56–68
Psycholinguistics, 96–109
  developmental, 110–20
Psychophysical conditioners, words as, 145–56
Public distance, 62
Purposes of language, 41–42

R

Racism, 164–70
Rapid fading, 27
Rationalist view of knowledge, 96–97
Recursion, 22
Reporting of experience, 266–67
Responsibility, language of, 85–92
Rhetorical qualities of words, 247–64
Rock music, 221–28, 229–34
Rock-tongue, 221–28
Rules:
  in child language, 119–20
  phonological, 15–17

S

Self-deception, language of, 145–56
Self-disparagement, language of, 160–61
Self-reproach, language of, 161–62
Semantic devices, 141–44
Semanticity, 28
Semantics:
  defined, 18

of generation gap, 212–20
of war, 209–11
Sensitivity group, 197–208
Sexism, 171–82
Sexist language, 171–82
  defined, 174
Signal reaction, 140–41
Significance of statements, 268
Silence, 88, 280–90
  sounds of, 56–68
Slang, 54–55
Social class languages, 46–55
Social control, language of, 235–46
Social distance, 62
Social talk, 140
Sociolinguistics, 46–55
Sound:
  and language, 15–17
  as medium of transmission, 9
  in rock music, 227–28, 229–34
Specialization, 27–28
Spectogram, 37
Speech perception, 97
"Square" language, 212–20
Standards of usage, 250–51
Statements, 265–79
Structure:
  of language, 14–23 passim
  in rock music, 224–27
Subhuman primate calls, 37
Sublanguages, 46–55
Subordination, 22–23
Subverbal responses, 140
Subvocal speech, 166–67
Surface structure, 20–23, 101 passim
Symbol reaction, 141
Syntax, language and, 19–21
Synthetic statements, 269–70, 273

T

Taboo, 255
Tag questions, 117–19
Tautology, 268–70
Thought, language and, 43, 93–194
To-me-ness, 137–38

Total feedback, 27
Traditional transmission, 29
Transformational grammar, 14–23,
    95–109
Transformations, 20–23, 104–5
Truth of statements, 268

U

Understanding, 85–92
Universals of human language, 24–38,
    108
Usage, 249–51
  and the dictionary, 249–51
  hippie, 212–20
  "square," 212–20
  standards of, 250–51
Uses of language, 39–45, 236–46

V

Vague language, 91, 251–53
Verifiability, 272–75
Verification:
  conclusive, 276–77
  versus probability, 276–77
Vocal-auditory channel, 27
Vulgate, 260–61

W

War, semantics of, 209–11
Women's liberation, 171–82
Words, rhetorical qualities of, 247–64
Worn-out metaphor, 256

Index
of Names

B

Bellugi, Ursula, 110–20
Bernstein, Basil, 51–53
Birdwhistell, Ray L., 66

C

Carpenter, Edmund, 69–84
Chomsky, Noam, 50, 95–109

D

Darwin, Charles, 150–51
Davis, Ossie, 164–70
Duhamel, P. Albert, 247–64

E

Egan, Gerard, 197–208
Eliot, T. S., 75, 78–79

G

Girsdansky, Michael, 3–6
Goffman, Erving, 68, 205
Goodman, Paul, 46–55, 223

H

Hall, Edward, 56–68
Hall, Mildred, 56–68
Hayakawa, S. I., 235–46

H

Hecht, Michael, L., 221–28
Hedgepeth, William, 229–34
Hess, Eckhard, 59–60
Hipkiss, Robert A., 212–20
Hockett, Charles F., 24–38
Hughes, Richard E., 247–64
Humboldt, Wilhelm von, 97, 98, 107

J

Jespersen, Otto, 48, 285–86
Johnson, Wendell, 85–92

K

Koning, Hans, 209–11
Korzybski, Alfred, 135, 140, 141–42,
    217, 285

L

Lee, Irving, J., 134, 280–90

M

McLuhan, Marshall, 83–84, 204, 232
Malinowski, Bronislaw, 139, 286–88
Miller, Casey, 171–82
Montagu, Ashley, 145–56
Moulton, William G., 7–23

O

Orwell, George, 183–93, 256

R

Russell, Bertrand, 39–45

S

Salomon, Louis B., 265–79

Seamans, Eldon L., 157–63
Swift, Kate, 171–82

W

Weinberg, Harry L., 133–44
Whorf, Benjamin Lee, 121–32, 267